PEOPLE'S MOVEMENT FOR HIMALAYAN REJUVENATION

Concept's Discovering Himalayan Series (CDHS)

1. People Participation in Himalayan Eco-System Development : A Plan for Action / M.L. Dewan.
2. Nut Fruits for the Himalayas / M.L. Dewan, M.C. Nautiyal and V.K. Shah.
3. Vedic Philosophy for Himalayan Eco-system Development / M.L. Dewan and B.D. Joshi.

About the Authors

Madan Lal Dewan (Ph.D., Cornell), a Soil Scientist, started work on soil conservation in the Damodar Valley Corporation during 1949-52. He had a distinguished career as an international Civil Servant with the Food and Agriculture Organization for over three decades (1953-83). He worked as Chief of the FAO Regional Bureau for Asia and the Pacific and in this capacity had the privilege to serve Asian countries, including India. He had FAO assignments in Iran and Bulgaria and was at FAO Headquarters in Rome for 14 years.

Dr. Dewan's association with the conservation of the Himalayas actively started in 1975 as Chief of the FAO Regional Bureau for Asia and the Pacific in Rome. His extensive travels and intimate work with the local groups in different parts of the Himalayas made him believe that the Himalayas were bleeding and crumbling, and needed a much closer look. So, over the past 25 years and particularly for the past sixteen years after his retirement, he has travelled widely and written extensively about the Himalayas. He was a member of the National Land Use and Conservation Board of Government of India during 1984-87. He has also been Chairman, Vice-Chairman and Member of several Non-Government Organisations working in the Himalayas. He is founder Chairman and Trustee of HIMCON (Himalaya Consortium for Himalaya Conservation) and has established a Centre "HIMALAYA SANRAKSHAN ASHRAM" at Ranichauri, District Tehri Garhwal, UP. HIMCON is executing several projects for Himalayan conservation, watershed management, tree plantation, medicinal and ayurvedic plants.

Soil of Iran, Soil Conservation in Iran and Agriculture and Rural Development in India, People's Participation and Rejuvenation of Himalayan Environment and seven other books are amongst his published works in addition to more than 100 papers on various aspects of soils, soil conservation, land and water development and technical cooperation between developing countries in Asia. His special interest lies in the Himalayan eco-system and he has also prepared special reports on the subject. He has brought out three booklet entitled Themes of Development I, II and III, besides another publication, Man in Pursuit of Happiness.

Piyoosh Rautela hails from Almora in the Kumaun Himalayas and is an Earth Scientist by profession. After post graduation in Applied Geology from University of Allahabad he started his research career at the Wadia Inotiute of Himalayan Geology, Deharadun and obtained his D. Phil degree from Garhwal University. He has a P.G. Diploma in Operations Management from Indira Gandhi Open University and is well versed with Geographical Information System and Remote sensing techniques which he has applied extensively for landslide hazard zonation and risk assessment.

The Post-doctoral research work of Dr. Piyoosh has been supported by the Department of Science and Technology (Government of India). Dr. Piyoosh has been associated with many Non Govt Organisations of the region and has contributed his energies for the welfare of the masses. He has been closely associated with the grass-root level activities of Himalaya Consortium for Himalaya Conservation and has gained experience of the ground realities that the masses of the region face.

Concept's Discovering Himalayas Series No. 4

PEOPLE'S MOVEMENT FOR HIMALAYAN REJUVENATION

Second Revised and Enlarged Edition

M.L. Dewan

Piyoosh Rautela

Foreword by
DR. KARAN SINGH

CONCEPT PUBLISHING COMPANY, NEW DELHI - 110059

ISBN-81-7022-815-8

First Published 1990

Second Revised and Enlarged Edition 2001

Published and Printed by

Ashok Kumar Mittal
Concept Publishing Company
A/15-16, Commercial Block, Mohan Garden
NEW DELHI-110 059

Phones : 5648039, 5649024
Fax : 091-11-5648053
Email : publising@conceptpub.com

Dr. Karan Singh
Member of Parliament
(Rajya Sabha)

सत्यमेव जयते

15 Institutional Area
Lodhi Road
New Delhi - 110 003
Tel. : 461 6067
Fax : 462 7102

World Environment Day
5 June 1999

Foreword

"The Himalayas are not merely a geographical feature, a mere chain of mountain ranges. They epitomise a people's civilisation that goes back to the dawn of history. If these majestic mountains were not there, the rain clouds sweeping up from the Indian Ocean would have passed over our sub-continent into Central Asia leaving it a burning desert. The Himalayas have nurtured this land with life-sustaining water and enabled a civilisation to blossom. Archaeological evidence reveals that urban civilisation first emerged in the river valleys coursing down from these mountains. When man elsewhere was cautiously emerging from his cave shelters, spectacular cities flourished at *Mohen-jo-daro* and *Harappa* in the Indus valley. *Vedic* hymns, some of the oldest spiritual texts in the world, were composed in the richly wooded valleys of these mountains which resonated with their chanting by our forebears. The *Upanishads* were written here more than three thousand years ago. The great poet, Kalidasa, in his epic poem, *Kumara Sambhava* invested these mountain ranges with divinity. Divine they indeed are because from the dawn of human history the Himalayas have influenced our way of life and thought. Ours is an *aranyaka* civilisation, a sylvan civilisation born in the verdant lap of these mountains. The mighty and sacred rivers, on whose banks our ancient civilisation took root, survived and flourished, have their birth in their snowy Vastness.

But today the entire Himalayan range, with its rich and unique biological diversity, is facing a deep crisis and is in danger of being destroyed. It is being relentlessly denuded of its rich forest cover. Man, in his cupidity and hubris, is posing a threat to our ancient civilisation by destroying the ecological base that sustains it. The forests are being ruthlessly exploited for their timber without realising that trees are only secondarily producers of timber. Their primary function is to promote rain, absorb moisture and recharge ground water. As a part of our culture, we worship trees because of this vital nexus between them and the life-giving waters. Our *Vedic* prayers are centred around the environment. The 63 verses of the *Bhumi Suktam* in the *Atharva Veda* express a worldview which highlights the spirituality inherent in nature and stresses a holistic and harmonious relationship between it and man. Through the long passage of time, this magnificent vision has eroded and we seem to have entered a dark age, which is witness to the malign impact of massive human intervention in natural processes.

These mountains must be protected from further damage from human greed and degradation. They have to be rejuvenated so that their past wounds are healed. It is a gigantic task. Clearly, government as a lone instrument is incapable of achieving this. The people who live in the shadow of these mighty mountains must also be involved in the task. While it is facile to say that "people's participation is essential for sustainable development", many questions remain. But how does one motivate a poverty stricken and ill-informed individual to protect the natural resources for his long-term benefit? How does one convince him that we have not inherited this Earth and its resources for our immediate consumption but hold it in trust for the generations yet unborn? How does one make him feel that it belongs to him and is to be used sustainably so that his children and their children are not deprived of their sustenance? It is not enough to preach to him the benefits of environmental sustainability of development. He must be made to feel that he is also a stakeholder and his resource base belongs to him and not to a distant government.

The 73rd and 74th Amendments to our Constitution have brought democracy to the grassroots, where the mass of people live. It decentralises power and vests it in *gram panchayats*. These *panchayats* are the instrumentality of people's participation. They can be made more effective if the control of their natural resource base is transferred to them and they are made accountable for its sustainable use. The participatory process has also to be further strengthened. The level of people's preparedness for participation in rejuvenating the Himalayas has to be enhanced. If the people participating in the consultative process are not equipped with adequate information, they will not have the capacity to properly guide the collective decision-making process. The building of people's capacity for informed decision making is an essential component of people's participation. Environmental education and awareness are significant inputs in this capacity building process.

Dr. Karan Singh

Foreword to the First Edition

Dr. M.L. Dewan has devoted his life to the cause of promoting ecologically sustainable economic development. After a long and distinguished career in the FAO, he is now devoting his time and talent to heal the wounds inflicted on the Himalayas through thoughtless human activities. These wounds, which unfortunately are being inflicted even today, owe their origin either to commercial greed or careless technology (e.g. road construction, fruit packaging, etc.) or the genuine needs of the poor for water, food, fodder, fuel, fibre and fertilizer. Such damage has undermined not ony the prospects for a sustainable livelihood security of the people living in the Himalayas but is threatening both the food security of the nation and the livelihood security of the inhabitants of the Indo-Gangetic Plain. Thus, damage upstream has serious consequences in downstream areas as is evident from the frequent flash floods and soil problems such as salinity and alkalinity in the plains.

In this comprehensive monograph Dr. Dewan provides a malady-remedy analysis of the problems and possible solutions. His plan of action emphasizes the need for achieving a blend of political will, professional skill and people's action. Without such a blend, it may not be possible to convert the growing agony into an enduring ecstacy.

The Himalayas are rich in biological diversity. Many parts of western and central Himalayas as well as the eastern hill States are veritable mines of valuable genes. The economic value of the rich genetic estate provided by the Himalayas has been greatly enhanced by the opportunities now available for moving genes across sexual barriers through genetic engineering. We need a grid of biosphere reserves, national parks and sanctuaries along the Himalayas. The Himalayas also afford on opportunity for establishing a low-cost *in situ* Genetic Resources Conservation Centre under perma-frost conditions.

How are we going to safeguard the rich cultural, spiritual and genetic heritage which the Himalayas has blessed us with? Dr. Dewan has provided valuable suggestions which should be implemented at the catchment, block, district and State levels. Throughout he has emphasized that ultimately it is the "people's power" alone that can save the Himalayas for the generations yet to be born.

If human action has been part of the ecological tragedy of this unique mountain eco-system, it is also human action which can restore the damage already done and which can help us to *take the mountains* once again to their pristine glory. The power of the people's action is clear from the impact of the *Chipko* movement, *Sukhomajri* watershed management strategy and several other unique examples. The challenge now is the conversion of such *unique success into a universal movement* for the sustainable management of the hill eco-system. Fortunately, the Himalayas are studded with universities and research institutions. The faculty and students of the educational institutions all along the Himalayas can take the lead in implementing a *Charter for Nature* in their respective areas.

I hope this book will stimulate positive thinking and action. We have recently witnessed the hold of the Ganges on the Indian mind. The millions of pilgrims, who had their holy dip at the Prayag in Allahabad during February 1989, believe that God manifesting as Gangadhar held the might of the torrential Ganges in the locks of his hair. In a way this myth symbolizes the control of the gushing streams by the dense forests of Tehri Garhwal. Unfortunately, today the forests are disappearing and the gushing streams flow down unchecked, causing siltation of rivers and frequent floods. When forests disappear, the associated fauna, flora and microbial population also vanish. Loss of biological diversity enhances our vulnerability to biotic and abiotic stresses. Thus, the "future" of our national food security system depends to a great extent on the ecological security of the Himalayas.

Dr. Dewan has shown how the ecological security of the Himalayas can be safeguarded. He has outlined a seven-pronged strategy for the conservation of the Himalayas and has pleaded for vocationalization of Environmental Careers for technical support of conservation programmes by the people, voluntary agencies and the Government. He has also proposed ways and methodology for moving towards self-reliant Himalayan communities and suggests institution of a "Himalayan Conservation Fund". Let us heed his advice and act now.

M.S. Swaminathan
President, National Academy of Sciences
of India and of International Union for
Conservation of Nature and Natural Resources

New Delhi
1990

Acknowledgements

The First Edition of this Book was commissioned by the National Land Use and Conservation Board. This work and the second edition also owes much to the help, cooperation and inspiration received from a large number of people. It would be a Himalayan task to acknowledge their contribution individually. However, we are indebted to the following.

1. Dr. Karan Singh who as a Resident of the Himalayas has inspired considerable work on Himalayan Rejuvenation. He has kindly written the Foreword to the Second Edition.
2. Dr. M.S. Swaminathan, who as Chairman of the Himalayan Task Force was responsible for bringing out the Report of the Task Force for the study of Eco-Development in the Himalayan Region (Planning Commission, March 1982).
3. Vice Chancellor of H.N. Bahuguna Garhwal University, Srinagar, Garhwal, Prof. P.S. Saklani, Prof. A.N. Purohit, Director of the High Altitude Plant Physiology Research Centre, Garhwal University, and Principal P.S. Rawat of Garhwal Campus. Special thanks are due to dear M.C. Nautiyal, of Pant Nagar Agriculture University, Hill Campus, Ranichauri and colleagues and friends Dr. M.C. Tripathy, Dr. Vir Singh and Dr. V.K. Kadiyal of the Hill Campus and specially of the Krishi Vigyan Kendra.
4. The National Land Use and Conservation Board (NLUCB) Government of India which stimulated the publication of the First Edition.
5. The Centre for Policy Research, its Director, Dr. Pai Panandikar and Members, under whose aegis, The First Report under this series was brought out in 1985.
6. The Collaborators For People's Participation and Rejuvenation of Himalayan Environment who are detailed in the Chapter 18 where A Centre for Himalayan Rejuvenation is proposed. Special Acknowledgement is due to the inspiration direct and/ or indirect specially of Late Shri Darbari Seth of Tata's,

Shri Sunderlal Bahuguna and Shri Chandi Prasad Bhatt, Founders and Promoters of CHIPKO Movement, Prof. P.S. Ramakrishnan, Prof. A.N. Purohit and Dr. L.M.S. Palni, successive directors of GB Pant Institute of Himalayan Environment and Development, Kosi, Almora.

7. Many colleagues and associates of various Non-Government and Government bodies especially, Shri Kanai Lal, Chairman CHIRAG, (Central Himalayan Rural Action Group), Dr. B.D. Joshi, of Gurukul Kangri, Dr. R. Sreedhar, of Academy of Mountain Environics, Dr. Anil Joshi, HESCO, Dehradun and many other collaborators of NGOs in Tehri Garhwal District specially Shri Visheshwar Datt Saklani, Vriksha Mitra Award Winner.
8. Dr. P.L. Gautam, Formerly Jt. Director, then Dean Forest of UHF Solan and the Director, National Bureau of Plant Genetic Resources, GOI, New Delhi—special word of thanks always goes for warm collaboration of Trees for Life (TFL) Founder Balbir Mathur.
9. Manoj Pande, Trustee HIMCON and all members of HIMCON and sister NGOs in the Himalayas who are devoting their life to the betterment of the Himalayan watersheds.
10. Last but not the best to my wife Smt. Sudershna Dewan, who bears with me for all the travels and works in the Himalaya Region on which this book is based. Thanks are also due to Dr. Indu Patnaik of Planning Commission for helping in the editing of this book.

Madan Lal Dewan
Piyoosh Rautela

CONTENTS

List of Figures

List of Plates

1
Introduction

The Himalayas have been revered from times immemorial. They are the source of mythological rivers that shaped the cultural values of Hinduism. Adorned with immense natural beauty and devotional sites they have been the centre of attraction for pilgrims and explorers. Many unsung Pundits devoted their lives in unfolding the mysteries of this land. If Tibet was a great mystery, the mesmerism of *Nanda Devi* was no less. Countless explorers contributed to our present day understanding of the land. This divine land (*devabhumi*), is gifted with diverse flora, fauna and minerals. *Sanjivani*, was over and again requisitioned from this land for diverse purposes. Human greed has however subdued natural regenerative processes and many of the species are threatened and many more are extinct or are on the verge of extinction.

It is generally accepted that the natural environment of the Himalayas is deteriorating. Several theories have been put forth to explain the causes. Ironically, several of the widely accepted assumptions for the deterioration are either without factual support, or were demonstrably unsupportable (Ives & Messerli 1989). A synthesis of literature indicates some common points of different theories:

- Unprecedented population growth followed the introduction of modern health care systems after 1950.
- Immigration from the plains is adding to the growing population of the hills.
- Increased population in the hills has led to:
  - — Reducing amount of land per family
  - — Deepening poverty
  - — Massive deforestation

The impact of these factors has been described as the vicious circle, in that the needs of the burgeoning subsistence population are exerting increasing pressure on the forest cover leading to massive deforestation which is the cause of accelerating rates of mass wastage.

The deforestation, that includes cutting of agricultural terraces on steeper and more marginal mountain slopes, has led to a catastrophic increase in soil erosion, and loss of productive land through accelerated landslide incidence, and to the disruption of the normal hydrological cycle. This situation, has in turn, led to increased runoff during the summer monsoon accompanied by disastrous flooding and massive siltation in the plains, and lower water levels and the drying up of springs and wells during the dry season. Related ills are: rapid siltation of reservoirs; abrupt changes in the courses of rivers; spread of barren sand and gravel across rich agricultural land on the plains; and increased incidence of diseases in the downstream areas. Deforestation is also perceived as the main cause for reduced rainfall.

The continued loss of agricultural lands in the mountains due to the anthropologically induced processes triggers another round of deforestation to enable the construction of more terraces on which to grow subsistence crops. Yet, as the labour of walking greater distances from the village to fuelwood supplies increases with receding forest perimeter, a critical threshold is reached whereby the available human energy (principally female) becomes progressively overtaxed and an increasing quantity of animal dung is used for fuel.

Consequently, another vicious circle is linked to the first one: terraced soils are deprived of natural fertilizer— the animal dung now being used for fuel, thus depriving the agricultural terraces, in many instances, of their only source of fertilizer. This lowers crop yields. Also, the ensuing weakened soil structure further augments the incidence of landslides. Even more trees are cut on more marginal and steeper slopes to make room for more agricultural terraces to feed the ever-growing subsistence population.

To worsen the situation further there has been commercial cutting of the forest to meet the timber demands of the lowland population centres. Due to strategic importance, roads are being constructed in remote areas. These enhance the incidence of landslides, commercial exploitation of the resources and the movement of the population. Moreover the women become progressively overworked and undernourished and thus the next generation of children begins life more deficient in essential nutrients, so that the situation worsens further.

The entire Himalayan terrain is at present facing an acute resource management crisis. The age old traditional system of resource management has been disrupted while the alternatives put forth have proved to be far from satisfactory. People's participation that was central to the traditional system has been pushed to the corner and the little communities of the region have no option, but to be helpless spectators to the deteriorating scenario.

Despite wide variation in cultural, social and ethnological identity of the people of the Himalayan region, under-development is the common factor bringing them together. Barring a few localised centres density of population in the region is low. This together with topographical features has hindered development of the region.

Due to the lack of industrial growth the Himalayan region is faced with out-migration of able-bodied workforce. This causes depletion of working hands and thereby traditional industries and handicrafts of the region are dying out fast. This also adds to the drudgery of the females in the hills.

In order to improve the quality of life of the people of the region a suitable system of development involving the local populations needs to be evolved. Small scale industries, and entrepreneurship need promotion through soft loans and other incentives. At the same time marketing links need to be strengthened to ensure adequate remuneration to the artisans and entrepreneurs.

A welfare state should have been alarmed at the utter socio-economic backwardness and inequalities of the people of the Himalayan region. The entire area is ecologically sensitive and therefore warrants better consideration than it has so far received. Facilities and infrastructure have no doubt developed in the post-independence era and this is often dubbed as being development. Length of roads, number of schools, colleges, PHCs, veterinary centres, and educated unemployed, are however no yardsticks for adjudging development. If at all development has to be scaled it has to be done with regard to the improvement in the quality of life of the poorest of the poor in the region. Has infrastructural growth really added to the quality of life of the poor? Impact has however been made upon the social, cultural, and economic life of the people, be it for good or worse. Many of the gains of development have however been eroded by faulty planning, environmental degradation, deforestation, overgrazing, reckless road construction and other heavy engineering activities on the fragile Himalayan slopes.

People's participation in various developmental schemes in the region has been minimal and the masses are ignorant about the large number of welfare schemes launched by both central and state governments. The officials need to promote this vital connection so essential for the development of the region. Recognising the lacuna in the policies the government is poised to change its attitude and is involving Panchayats and various voluntary organisations in the developmental work being undertaken by it. The watershed has long been recognised as the unit of development and the message of integrated watershed management is being propagated aggressively by the authors through the years. The efforts seem to be bearing fruit and many developmental plans and endeavours are being undertaken with watershed development strategy. Voluntary agencies working in the region are busy building the confidence of the masses and it is with them that hope lies. The authors therefore Dedicate this Volume to the Numerous Unsung Heroes Devoting their Energies Selflessly for the Cause of the Welfare of the People of the Himalayas. It is their undaunted devotion towards the majestic mountains that has inspired and built a dedicated cadre of young professionals in the voluntary sector who are busy recasting a greener, healthier, and, prosperous Himalayan region.

Though pertinent to the entire Himalayan terrain this book focuses specific attention upon Uttarakhand (the hills of Uttar Pradesh) extending between rivers Kali and Tons. Though tough, an attempt has been made by the authors to bring forth a happy blend of theory and practice. A large number of case studies have therefore been incorporated in the presentation. These cover a variety of different issues and would provide an insight into the ground realities in the Himalayas.

M.L. DEWAN
PIYOOSH RAUTELA

2

People's Participation : Principles and Practices

Development including ecological development presents unusual challenges to both activists and researchers in the field of development. Development connotes different meanings to different persons; to most it is however the improved infrastructure that reflects development. It is due to this faulty and biased definition of the word that the lot of the masses still remains pitiable. Going by this definition the region has witnessed manifold development in the post-independence era. Development however implies improvement in the quality of life of the people rather than mere growth of infrastructure. Development should be people oriented and the voice of the people should be reflected in the theme of development. This is the fundamental premise on which ends and means must stand totally reconciled. Indeed the dependence of development either on resources or on technologies is decreasing; attention is focussed increasingly on people and institutions which can mobilize and manage resources and extend and adapt technologies for the common good.

The essence of development is to raise productivity through an integrated approach to land, labour, know-how and capital and is defined as economic development. What the economist calls labour, the social scientist and development practitioner call people. Technologies, resources and people's institutions, each contribute in different but complementary ways to raise productivity.

Strategies and concerted action have the best results if the people who participate in such implementation understand and see their own interests, both short and long term, in such development. The masses should identify themselves with the developmental works and should consider these to be their own. The focus should thus be upon strengthening local capacities for planning and implementing developmental activities.

The programme framework should clearly define the following dimensions of participation and collective action: *Who* participates *Why* in *What* kind of programme and *How* the programme is to be implemented—voluntary, coercive, participatory, and on continuous or *ad hoc* basis.

The dimensions can be described as ranging from highly selfish to highly altruistic, from highly individualistic to highly cooperative. These dimensions define a space within which people's values can be located. The concept of *social energy* to account for the dynamism is observed in certain grassroots projects. The work carried out by Trees for Life (TFL)/Himalaya Consortium for Himalaya Development (HIMCON) in the remote villages of Tehri Garhwal district clearly shows this. The people of these villages identify themselves with the activities of HIMCON and the extension workers of HIMCON have carved out a distinct place in the hearts of the people through their selfless work for the cause of the masses. During the process of implementation of the programmes the opinion of the masses is fully respected and every effort is made to bring about unanimity. While constructing the spring water rejuvenation tank at Lawadhar the opinion of the experts of HIMCON conflicted with that of the people of the village on the choice of the appropriate depth of the structure. In order to convince the masses the experts had to visit the village more than four times. Ultimately through practical demonstrations in the field the people were convinced and unanimity of opinion was brought about. In the construction of the structure the entire village contributed material and labour support; for it was to be their own structure and was being erected with their consent. This greatly reduced the cost of the structure. The erected structure, its wide use and adequate maintenance by the masses reflect the consequence of honouring their opinion. Similarly, going beyond the project framework extension work was carried out outside the demarcated boundaries of the watershed in Paturi village in order to win the confidence of the people. A concept like energization although neither quantifiable nor predictable can still have real and significant consequences. When the results are achieved, they are remarkably cost effective.

The possibility of *free riding* will inhibit collective action in general and individual acts of *piracy* will inhibit regimes of natural resources management such as soil and water conservation in the Himalayas. There are plenty of examples of political interference for free riding at the local level in and outside the Himalayas.

The *tragedy of the commons* is created by persons who overuse a common property resource to their advantage, even to the point of destroying the resource. This is what is happening in most parts of the Himalayas. The Government has failed to manage common resources without full participation of the local institutions, mainly because of its bureaucratic approach, distance from the site as well as inadequate interest. Development of organisational capacity for farmers to participate in the management of common resources should ensure for them a continuous role in the planning, operation and maintenance of the common system so that it does not revert to its unproductive condition.

Development of Local Institutions

The creation of local institutional capacity to manage natural and other resources through collective action, not dependent entirely on the structures and authority of the state, offers an important alternative to the bureaucratic approach, if such capacity can become viable. One of the reasons for ambiguity and confusion in much of the thinking about local institutions is that it has both a social and geographic meaning and neither may match the administrative definition given to the term.

It is useful to recognise that there are at least ten levels of decision making and activity that range from the international (supernational) down to the level of individual decision makers. Of these, levels six to eight come within the ambit of what is usually meant by local.

1. International level
2. National level
3. Regional level
4. District level
5. Sub-district level
6. Panchayat level
7. Community level
8. Group level
9. Household level
10. Individual level

The first two levels are far removed from local conditions and activities. The next three are closer to but still not local in any sociological sense, being essentially administrative entities. There is no basis or capacity at these levels for organising activity to promote development, except through formal political channels or through diffused market relationship.

Only when we get to a set of communities which have some established patterns of communication, economic exchange and social cooperation, usually corresponding to what is often called a market town or development block, do we approach a potential for collective action—which could be enlisted to carry out some of the responsibilities and burdens otherwise handled by the government.

People within a locality have some acquaintance with each other directly or indirectly, through inter-marriage, trade, religious festivals or participation in local activities. This establishes some common identity that makes collective effort possible.

Need for Bureaucratic Reorientation

In the search for more effective approaches towards involving the people, especially the rural people in their own development or in that of their environment (eco-development), attention has been focused almost exclusively on the intended beneficiaries/participants. There is a familiar tendency to blame the intended beneficiary. Failure to establish or maintain local institutions and to get individual cooperation is usually attributed to the people—their attitudes, their poverty, their culture, their illiteracy and to low levels of awareness. But too often overlooked is the reality that the response of the poor to government programmes is shaped by the way the services are administered. The level of participation is decided by:

- How accommodating or inflexible are the services ?
- How satisfying or humiliating is the treatment ?
- How readily do the poor get access to services, or how much more readily can the more resourceful utilise the same?
- Whether the government staff adopt a problem solving

stance or a conventionally bureaucratic one?

- How attuned is the staff to actual conditions and needs of the people ?
- Whether the staff deals with the poor as responsible adults or as basically ignorant and irresponsible people ?

It is quite unrealistic to expect the poor man's participation when the style of programme administration curbs their initiative, problem solving behaviour and development of increased capacity for rural resource mobilisation and management at the local level—all essential elements for an authentic development process. Where programmes are viewed by the professional as solutions to presumed beneficiary problems, any effort on the part of the beneficiaries to engage in independent problem solving may even be construed as uncooperative or obstructionist. Seemingly omnipotent programme formulators are often not conversant with the local ground realities and formulate policies and programmes that are not acceptable to the masses due to various socio-religious, psychological, and traditional reasons.

The good intentions of the government staff are not to be questioned, but in a programme in which there is no real participation by the rural poor leads to delays, inappropriate services and apparently arbitrary demands by the programme staff. A well-documented proposal cannot be expected from the rural poor who is seeking financial assistance for entrepreneurship development. Laxity is, therefore, needed in the governmental programmes to muster adequate participation of the masses. People are likely to be treated in patronising ways by the programme staff but the programme itself may be misconceived and harmful to the poor households struggling to survive in an economic, social and physical environment that is too complex and fragile. Moreover, the programme guidelines are not lucid and not well propagated amongst the rural masses. The level of awareness of the masses regarding various governmental programmes is very low. In this atmosphere of ignorance the economically well off people, in liaison with the implementing staff, reap the harvests of these target driven schemes. This enhances disparity in the society and creates social tensions. Enhanced money circulation in the community leads to disruption of traditional practices and the purchasing power of the poor is severely hampered.

Recognising that developmental programmes can and must benefit from ideas and resource inputs from the participants and the people themselves, it is absolutely necessary to have some form of local organisation—a society for local *eco-development*, an association for improved water use, a club for youth, mothers and the aged. These organisations are often observed to act as catalysts and break the inertia of the masses, thus bringing about social energization. Howsoever necessary, these organisations should never be imposed upon the society. When such societies are created by the project managers rather than the people themselves we often notice the process of participation lacking from the very beginning as the people do not consider these societies to be their own and these often break down. Canvassing in favour of these may however be carried out and the leaders from amongst the community should be given the opportunity to don the mantle. The project manager can represent the society in the initial stage in the capacity of a non-voting member to ensure smooth functioning.

Looking at the bureaucratic style of dealing with the people, and specially the rural people, the reasons for the stunted development of the process of people's participation are not far to seek. There is a large educational and status gap between the governmental staff and the poor. Often there are ethnic and linguistic differences, complicating communication and mutual regard. One cannot expect one to honour somebody's beliefs unless he understands his language and culture. There is an aura of superiority that exalts the so-called expert knowledge that very often deprecates what the poor know or are capable of doing. After all accumulated expertise the authors have no hesitation in humbly accepting the fact that often they had to update their views and learn from the locals, from their age old and time-tested practices. People know their surroundings and natural processes better than anyone else; though they cannot express their feelings or experiences, the logic behind their assertions is not hard to understand. It is an art to learn from the local communities and the bureaucracy needs to master it if it intends to make its programmes a success. It is this regard for the knowledge of the local people that is lacking in the bureaucratic set-up of the nation. Even well intentioned staff tends to fall into the paternalistic postures that deprecate the capabilities of the poor and perpetuate the dependence syndrome. The aim of any project activity can never be to make the local communities perpetually dependent upon external inputs. If so, the project is formulated on ill intentioned objectives and does not seek the welfare of the masses. The aim of the project activities should be to energise people so as to make the community and the economic activities self sustaining.

The participating people and especially the rural poor cannot be expected to change their behaviour and their attitude to government programmes unless the staff change their activities and attitude vis-a-vis the participating people. Blaming the participants or the rural poor should be avoided in all respects. Bureaucratic reorganisation must involve changes in individual attitudes and values, the most important being changes in job definition, performance criteria, career incentives, bureaucratic procedures, organisational responsibilities, and so on.

The problem of bureaucratic reorganisation has not been addressed in a systematic way more especially in the context of rural and eco-development. Basically, the poor performance is largely the result of the disparity between the organisation's internal structure and the operating system on the one hand and the requirements of alleviating poverty and creating self sustained, self-reliant development on the other. A strong management would not be successful unless there is a better fit between ends and means. Apparently there is a need to incorporate certain professional modules that develop such skills in reorientation of bureaucracy in the existing training programmes. There is also a need for research and consulting services which would help achieve bureaucratic reorganisation.

Inertia in Bureaucracy

Bureaucratic convenience and advantage are seldom questioned by the administrators. These values and presumptions are deeply institutionalised in bureaucratic operations and routines. Some of these assumptions are subject to question in the developmental process:

1. *Expenditure = Results*: For decades, prevailing economic theory has equated development with growth of GNP. This is a misleading notion. Enhanced money circulation does not

necessarily mean development.

2. *Education = Superiority*: This also assumes that the judgment and even the values of the educated should prevail. This assumption truncates the participatory process. In fact, formal knowledge is usually necessary but not sufficient for programme planning and implementation. There is abundance of time tested and indigenous technical knowledge that the experts are very often not able to appreciate. They are often unable to visualise the ground realities and are therefore not in a position to determine what the local people can and should contribute to the decision-making process. There is no denying the fact that local indigenous knowledge itself is unlikely to be sufficient, but it is almost always essential for an efficient and effective use of development resources, especially when the objective is to assist the poor majority. One of the purposes is to achieve a fruitful combination of expert and indigenous knowledge.
3. *Project = Development*: It has been the practice in development management to draw a sharp distinction between operating programmes and development projects. Within this framework, development is approached though a series of finite, discontinuous actions with discrete time-bound outcomes that depend on special temporary injections of external funds. Projects implemented by temporary organizations to achieve limited time-bound results are commonly defended as having a positive demonstration effect, assuming that the new concept they demonstrate will be adopted by the more permanent organisations once proven in the field. Experience however does not support such an assumption. The temporary organisations and the ideas propagated by them are more or less not accepted by the masses and by the time these come to attain some credibility the project tenure is over. These organisations are more conscious of their social acceptability and are therefore not able to concentrate their entire energies towards defending the project objectives.

Constant and widespread ecological and rural development depends more on moving whole sections of the bureaucracy towards new modes of operation than on the enclave progress too often associated with projects. It calls for a strategic style of management that sets directions, creates new visions of the possible, and builds new, organizational capabilities for appropriate response to changing conditions. It is commonly observed that lack of commitment and imagination among the personnel of development agencies is more a consequence of bureaucratic systems that treat creative behaviour as dysfunctional rather than a reflection of any inherent qualities of such personnel.

Promoting People's Participation

Steps needed by development promoters for large-scale people's participation in China in the mid-forties as quoted from mass educator (Jimmie Yen) are as follows :

1. Go to the people
2. Live with them
3. Learn from them
4. Serve them
5. Love them
6. Plan with them
7. Start with what they know
8. Build on what they have

These principles are universal and not restricted or applicable to the ground realities in China alone. When applied to the Indian context including the Himalayas these are observed to be highly applicable and give good response to the promoter of the process of eco-development. These are thus the basic principles for ensuring people's participation.

Many of the NGOs of the region that have imbibed these fundamentals are well accepted by the masses and their programmes involve active participation of the masses. Some efforts on the following lines would be attracting more popular response:

1. Organizing get-togethers (symposia, workshops, seminars, etc.) of the NGOs and successful co-operators in the Himalayas for sharing their individual experiences.
2. Organizing eco-development camps by villagers,

students, NGOs, and others in various parts of the Himalayas. This would bring about ecological awareness at the grassroots level.

3. Initiating tree plantation and nurseries by villagers, schools, NGOs, women's groups, ex-servicemen, and others concerned about the environment. Involvement of young students in these efforts is likely to have a long-lasting impact and therefore students should be encouraged to join in these efforts.
4. Conducting training courses in universities, colleges, training institutes, and Krishi Vigyan Kendras in various parts of the Himalayas for disseminating technical know-how and to bring about a happy blending of technical and indigenous knowledge.
5. Initiating group action for water harvesting, rainwater storage, microhydel schemes, improvements in traditional water mills and the others.
6. To take farmers and participants from one area (or project) to successful on-going eco-development project areas.

Raising the People's Potential

Humans are capable of doing much more than they are doing at present especially in India as evidenced by:

1. Variability of the best and the worst in government departments;
2. Outstanding success of Non-Resident Indians, especially in the USA, Canada and Europe; and
3. Variability in industrial management.

Variables in the capability potential of the people are physical, mental and intellectual, that are partly determined by heredity, background, upbringing, social exposure, education and motivation. There is a Chinese saying: "An easy operation can become difficult due to reluctance in tackling it". Conversely, one can say: "A difficult task can be made easy by the enthusiasm in carrying it out". Similarly, people's potential can be enhanced by improving their capability, especially through education, motivation, training and participation in development programmes. Obviously, voluntary agencies have a great role to play in these areas. The Ministry of Human Resource Development has initiated programmes on adult literacy and continuing education. There is also no dearth of opportunities for training in a variety of skills—though these need to be carefully programmed in the case of the people of the Himalayas. What is more difficult, however, is the problem of actual participation of the people in development.

Some of the research carried out on waking up the human potential at the Centre for International Studies, Cornell University, USA, is worth mentioning here. Assuming no upper limit to this potential, the initial willingness and capacity of people may be limited by several factors:

- They may lack time or energy for cooperative or voluntary efforts.
- Activities required to meet immediate needs may prevent them from dealing with problems that seem less pressing (e.g. soil erosion).
- They may not expect to gain from cooperative ventures, or they may distrust the motives of those proposing such ventures, or doubt the feasibility or usefulness of the proposed activities.
- They may lack the skills to correctly perform unfamiliar tasks (e.g. planting and rearing new trees, constructing check dams, or measuring grades to determine where to terrace hillsides).

To overcome these limitations:

- It is important here to advertise the long term gains that the society at large is to reap from these endeavours. Holding meetings with the village elders and youth regarding the scheme that is to be implemented, can do this.
- The lack of time mostly reflects the lack of motivation. Once motivated to a certain level the masses would set their priorities and manage time for these activities.
- The priorities should thus be set after careful discussions with the masses.

- Work should always be scheduled around the people's calendar: people should not be expected to devote energies for other works when they need to attend to their fields or are preoccupied with other social, religious or agricultural tasks. Meetings with the people should always be planned in the evenings or some other time when they are free, even if such timing is inconvenient to the Voluntary Organisations or government agencies.
- Each project should be broken into small sub - projects. Participation will be more likely in the early stages of a project if the people are brought together for a specific effort which yields visible results quickly; these shorter sub-projects can be completed during the period when farm women have small amounts of free time, and it is easier to motivate them to participate and to continue with the work when they see evidence of progress.
- The inputs needed (seedlings, pipes, cement) or the technical personnel (surveyors, veterinarians, agronomists, medicos) required should be arranged for.
- Always arrive before the people are assembled to do the work and try to participate in the work and not just supervise it. This will energise the masses and they would be associating with the work in a better manner.
- Help the people develop a vision of the alternatives and demonstrate their possibilities. They may not initially realize that they have the potential to improve the eco-system.
- Groups of farmers could be taken on trips to places where erosion has completely ruined an area, to show them what the ultimate consequences of doing nothing could be. The same farmers could then be taken to visit areas where conservation practices have been started, so that they can see the steps necessary to arrest erosion and the advantages of taking those steps. More importantly, they should be given an opportunity to talk to the people who have developed the conservation measures. The best spokesmen for land - terracing, afforestation or water control are the farmers who did the work and are benefiting from those efforts. Seeing and hearing examples of participatory effort to save the eco-system are an effective

way of creating the vision of "what could be". Such examples of small-scale efforts that have already been tried (a spring rejuvenation scheme using a kilometre-long plastic pipe, a water-harvesting scheme) have a lasting impact upon the minds of the people.

- The project staff should seek out these examples and publicize them and arrange for other farmers to visit them. It may even be a good investment to arrange for a group of farmers to visit another country if truly noteworthy examples can be found.

Project staff has to take the villagers into confidence and show them both the short and long term benefits that they and their community shall reap from the proposed conservation actions: the prospect of increased income through the harvest of trees and plants, better crop yields or reduced fertilizer loss due to contour farming, enhanced water supply through spring rejuvenation or water harvesting may prove more attractive than a call to preserve the land for their future generations. It is a human tendency to look forward to immediate gains and therefore short term benefits need to be highlighted to attract the masses. Farmers who are put at a disadvantageous position due to the conservation project (flooding their land, for example) should be given some sort of compensation by the community or provision for employment by the project. At the same time, appeals to community pride and altruism should not be ignored. Awards to farmers, groups of farmers or villages and students who implement conservation measures and contests between communities may, depending on local customs, prove effective. These awards need not be expensive, sometimes public recognition is an adequate incentive. Flags or banners for individuals or groups who have implemented projects or visits by popular figures to award certificates can both reward and spread the word.

Inspiration and Social Energy

In practical terms, inspiration is the ability of the project staff to give farmers and land users the vision for future (the vision of what they can do to improve their situation and the vision of what will happen if resource degradation goes on unchecked). This vision is a must for inspiration and the masses cannot be inspired to devote their energies for some cause without the vision of the gains that the project is likely to bestow upon them.

In this context it is important to understand the concept of Social Energy. It is known that when people are determined and put their energy to work, mountains can be moved, canals bigger than rivers can be dug, unsolved and sometimes so called unsolvable problems find solutions. Social energy is believed to depend upon the following (Uphoff 1986):

- Idea
- Ideal
- Friendship

An appropriate simplification is that new Ideas are what teaching is all about. The realm of ideas can energize people—ideas of their security, their welfare, and their common interests that can be easily converted into people's actions.

Ideals bring the best in use: some types of leaders do bring out the worst in the people, others bring out the best and that is what makes the difference in progress.

Friendship is what stimulates people to work together. Apathy is what tears them part.

Social Energy—of immense dimension—is reached when the right type of ideas, ideals and friendship stimulate the minds and actions of people.

How can Training Help?

The villages may sometimes lack skills to perform some of the tasks involved in a conservation project. Training helps in sealing the gap between what they know and what they need to know. The best form of training is to arrange for the people to participate in an existing project and to learn while doing. This is another advantage of establishing many small sub-projects: they can provide on-the-job training opportunities for others from nearby villages.

The gap can also be narrowed by simplifying the procedures or construction designs in the project, by drawing on and integrating traditional practices the people are already familiar with, and by providing small teams of more highly trained artisans to perform a limited number of the more difficult technical tasks.

Another training approach is to establish small tree plots and tree nurseries in schools and to involve students in conservation activities. If they can be shown the importance of conservation and how to do it, when they start farming they are more likely to continue with some of the practices they have developed.

To end this chapter on People's participation, the authors are tempted to quote from Towards Green Villages (Agarwal & Narain, 1989) that outlines a strategy for environmentally sound and participatory rural development. The basic premises on which this strategy is based are applicable to the whole of India, and equally to the Himalayan region. These are:

- The fundamental cause of poverty in India arises out of the scarcity of biomass resources to meet daily basic needs like food, fuel, fodder, manure, building materials and artisan raw materials, almost all of which are biomass based.
- The growing ecological imbalance is further worsening this scarcity of vital survival needs.
- The key objective of rural development programmes must be to restore ecological balance and increase biomass production on a sustainable and equitable basis.
- Since India's land mass is made up of extremely diverse ecosystems, biomass productivity can be increased on a sustainable basis only if rural development programmes were to become eco-system specific.
- Action will be best when it is planned and undertaken at the level of the settlement. If action is executed at any other level, people's involvement will be limited.
- All rural settlements must have an active institution that has legal control over its immediate environment and access to funds. The role of the government must be that of a facilitator of village-level planning and action, rather than that of a doer.

3

People's Movement for the Rejuvenation of the Himalayas

If one asks an extension worker, a researcher, a policy maker, or a social worker, as to what is implied by, and what is the scope of "people's participation" the response inevitably will be that it implies a participatory role by the beneficiaries/farmers. Further, if a person has been influenced by the modern jargon of women's role in development, he/she may mention it separately and specifically. However, this definition of "people's participation" camouflages the issue and often results in disastrous consequences, since the focus is placed only on the group of beneficiaries/farmers/women at the grassroots level. To some extent it is a safety valve provided by other groups to take the spotlight away from them. However, if one puts the same question to the beneficiaries/farmer/women one would be surprised to hear that, in addition to themselves, all the others involved starting from the top (the policy/decision-maker) going down to the field-level functionary are the participants and by implication "people". The issue indeed is that "people's participation" should encompass all those concerned with policy/decision-making processes, project formulation/implementation, technocrats, manager, middle-level/ field-level technicians, the socio-political system, the community at large and of course the beneficiaries/ farmers/women.

The participatory role of all the people involved at all levels is crucial to successful initiation, design, financing and implementation of development programmes. There are many examples where a key person at the policy level gives a firm direction to generate programmes and a field-level functionary makes a programme succeed (even though it was faulty in design). At the lowest level the failures come to our notice but the successes achieved by individuals under great odds go unsung. Yet the people who benefit do remember their contributions. It is neither possible nor desirable to review the role/commitment of each participant of a programme, but it may be worthwhile to highlight a few points here. A beneficiary/farmer will not change land-use or a practice, on which he is subsisting, unless he perceives that the proposed change will benefit him directly and immediately, for example, he will not accept erosion control measures and pay for them because they do not benefit him directly and immediately; he will not plant/protect grasses and trees on village common land since he is not sure of his share. On the other hand, if there is a project for providing irrigation and household water, then not only is he willing to participate by way of providing labour or borrowing money to pay for part of the work, but he is also keen to improve his own bench terraces.

Further, let us not forget that beneficiaries of this movement are not only the residents of the hill areas, but also the plains below. Better management in the hills will save them from annual flooding, siltation and help recharge the underground aquifers.

Project Level Technicians

For effective transfer of technological packages, the project staff must be technically competent and sensitive to the needs, aspirations and motivations of the local people. They should be committed and oriented to doing a job well and on time. A defective job (e.g. wrong disposal of surplus water or wrong alignment of a gully plug/check dam) can damage the whole programme, which no amount of publicity or funds can rectify. Similarly, terracing and all earthwork jobs should be completed before the onset of rains or sowing of crops. A farmer cannot afford to lose a cropping season: if seeds, seedlings and fertilizers have to be supplied, these must be on site at the time of sowing planting or application. Failure to perform work on time turns the farmers away, and it would be travesty of the truth to say that the people did not participate.

Supervisors/managers, apart from being professionally competent, committed, sensitive and sympathetic to the beneficiaries, should provide leadership and guidance to their staff. Leadership is acquired by professional competence. A supervisor should be competent to resolve technical issues. A supervisor at any level has to be sensitive to the needs and motivations of his/her staff and has to be a committed person. These three abilities are the *sine qua non* of a successful supervisor.

Project Directors/technocrats/decision-makers are responsible for (a) project identification, formulation, implementation and evaluation, (b) selling the programmes at the policy and political levels, and (c) dealing with a large number of staff, laying down targets, providing/arranging funds and inputs on time, and providing a congenial environment for their staff. Of course, they need different skills but the commitment to the job/programme/cause and sensitiveness to the needs and motivation of their staff are essential for the success of the programme. These prerequisites may be obvious, but often it is the obvious, which is lost sight of. Professionally competent people or committed people do not just happen — they are created by providing suitable opportunities and motivation.

Technological Issues

Agricultural land misuse

Even though the land capability classification, currently in vogue, indicates that the land suited for agriculture (mostly Class III and IV lands) is a minor fraction of the total land area, yet the land which is actually cultivated is much more. Obviously, either the land is grossly misused or the specifications for land capability classification need revision. What are the options? As regards the land capability classification system, there is not much leeway as there are physical and economic limitations to cultivation of steep slopes beyond a certain limit. The other options are: (a) bench terracing, (b) providing irrigation facilities, (c) use of modern technology for rainfed/irrigated farming, and (d) diversify by growing high-value vegetables/flowers, seeds, fruits etc. However, growing fuits can be fraught with dangers of deforestation, as has been observed in Himachal Pradesh.

Agricultural land - mismanagement/fragmentation

The size of farm holding in the hills is very small; 70 per cent being less than one hectare and only 13 per cent being more than two hectares. These small land holdings are fragmented and, therefore, mismanaged at many locations. Given this scenario, how can a farmer be expected to construct terraces, provide irrigation and use modern technological inputs? The obvious approach is to consolidate the holdings. But this is not as simple as it appears. There are many bio-physical handicaps (e.g. the field being at different elevations, terraced/unterraced, rainfed/irrigated, near/away from the water source, road etc.) and legal difficulties. The issue being complex and intractable remains unresolved. The solution may lie in the development and growth of other sectors so that the population is weaned away from the land.

Forest land

About 50 per cent of land in the Himalayas is under the control of the Government Forest Departments but it is not necessarily forested land. In Uttarakhand only 60 per cent of land under the control of the Forest Department is forested, 40 per cent of this forest is degraded/inferior. The question is how to forest it and make it produce goods and services on a sustained basis (Considering the pressures on forest land it is indeed remarkable that the Forest Departments have successfully protected some forests). This is practical and feasible as technologies are available as well as land in large contiguous blocks is also available, and is under the control of Government. The emphasis needed is on an increased pace of afforestation with a sense of a job well done from start to finish. The achievement should not be reported as "area planted" but as "area planted and made productive".

Common lands

Common lands are provided to villages to meet grazing, timber and fuelwood needs. In land use statistics, these are included in "area not available for cultivation". In addition, particularly in the districts of Uttarakhand, there are forest lands given to revenue authorities and Panchayats, which account for as much as 30 per cent of the total forest land. Over the years the condition of these common lands has become deplorable due to the breakdown of social cohesion, and means and sanctions for the maintenance of these. These do not generally contain forests nor do they grow sufficient grass to support cattle. These lands are highly degraded and a source of sediment and cause of damage (due to gullying) to neighbouring fields, water courses, roads and property. The extent of damage done is to be seen to be believed. In the pockets that have maintained the age old customs the common lands are observed to be serving their designated purpose. These lands are suited for supporting good grass cover and trees. There are indigenous grasses/bushes/trees which, if given the opportunity will grow naturally. The basic problem is that of management. There is no other solution in a democratic society than that the people themselves provide a "Social Fencing" and appropriate management to regulate the use of this common resource. The issue is how would this be achieved. Uttarakhand has a long and outstanding tradition of social fencing of the common lands that were often revered and associated with local deities and were not disturbed. Increasing authority of government agencies have disrupted this age old system. Can sociology and social action resolve this issue under the changed scenario?

Carrying capacity

The carrying capacity of land is a subjective issue that is often debated. There is no direct evidence as to whether the carrying capacity of the land in the Indian Himalayas has been exceeded. However, general circumstantial evidence is observed. The situation is also not uniform throughout the Himalayan region. It appears quite critical in Uttarakhand but not so critical in Arunachal Pradesh. Sikkim could be considered to be well within the carrying capacity of the land. Other states fit in at various levels between these two extremes. However, it is clear that in the entire region wherever man has intervened, there are pockets where the carrying capacity has been exceeded. To that extent, the entire Himalayan eco-system in India is subject to stress and strain.

What are the options?

These are rather limited. For example, the need for restricting human and cattle populations is already known. No practical economically viable and socially acceptable suggestion has however been put forth for achieving this. A suggestion has been made to transfer forest land to villages for agricultural and non-agricultural production. This is an approach of horizontal expansion, which could be very dangerous, as whatever little forest is left might also be lost. Secondly, there is no guarantee that production will increase; there is every likelihood that the fate of this transferred land could be the same as that of other common lands. A tried option is the migration of the people. This is already taking place in a limited way. However, migration is not a solution since there is no land available either in the Himalayas or in the plains. *So the only option left is to optimize land use and increase its productivity on a sustained basis in conjunction with population control.*

Transport system

If any single source of sediment generation, instability of hill slopes, cause of landslides (man-made), erosion and gullying and forest degeneration is to be identified, it will be generally agreed that this is the vast network of roads constructed in the Indian Himalayas.The extensive network of Himalayan roads has been a mixed blessing. It is necessary for the development which has taken place in the hills as well as in the plains. But the lack of attention to ecological considerations has played havoc with the eco-system. Even as we enter the 21st century correct lessons have not been learnt, though the techniques of aligning and constructing roads on eco-friendly scientific basis and stabilizing the slopes are well known.

Perhaps the issues are not technological but socio-economic and political. People want roads, and politicians are there to oblige them. Money is allocated for road construction without any consideration for allocation for conservation/stabilization works. Further, road alignment is changed to suit the "convenience" of those who matter. In the process a road is constructed which costs more in terms of environmental damage and maintenance.

Not that these facts are not known; these are widely known, discussed and debated. What is needed is action to ensure that within the given allocations the roads are aligned and made on scientific principles, with provisions for drainage, slope stabilization, etc. There is another angle to this issue. The best of roads can easily be damaged with consequent cyclical ecological disturbances if the surrounding forest land, grazing land etc. are not properly used. In the prevailing situation, the road engineer damages the forest/cultivated land, the forester damages the road/cultivated land and the farmer damages forests/roads and nobody really cares. This lack of concern must stop. *Coordination and cooperation is the need of the day.*

The people of the Himalayas have contributed their energies and material resources for various social movements to local, regional as well as national causes. Comprising a major portion of the work force in the Himalayas, women have overwhelmingly participated in these movements. Having come under British colonial rule in 1815 after the Anglo-Gurkha War this region remained overwhelmingly passive during the first war of independence in 1857 when northern India revolted against British authority. In 1915 the deposed ruler of Tehri Garhwal, Sudarshan Shah was elevated to the throne of the Protectorate State and other parts of the region came under the colonial rule. The condition of the peasants was alike both in the Protectorate State and in British Kumaun. In many aspects the areas ruled by the British were better off as the middle class had free access to modern education and thought. This was reflected in years to come when under the influence of modern, democratic thought this region was actively involved in the freedom struggle, and gave birth to a series of freedom fighters and contributed towards the cause of India's freedom.

Both the British and the native ruler of the Protectorate State of Tehri exploited the natural resources of the region. The British in the name of protecting the forests started expanding their authority over the forests and in 1893 all the lands except revenue and common lands of the people were brought under the control of the British. Three categories of forests ware defined and the people had no rights over A category, over category B people's rights were limited while C category was open forest. This was looked upon by the masses as an attempt to encroach upon their life support system. The traditional hill economy is woven around the forests that provide fodder, fuelwood, timber, and a rich variety of minor forests produce. Religion-magical beliefs of the people also revolved around forests. Religious and customary sanctions were often invoked for the management of the forests. The gradual extension of government authority over the forest areas and the desire of the forest officials to exercise closer control over the forests and use of forest produce deeply disturbed the hill economy. One of the results of this gradual appropriation and erosion of the commons has been a continuing pattern of agitations by local communities in various parts of the Himalayas. Whereas in the Kumaun region there were a series of local protests over British administered forest management policies, a large number of people were prosecuted when forest fires followed the drought of 1921. These protests ultimately resulted in the establishment of Van Panchayats (local village forest councils) in the early decades of this century. West of the Ganges in Tehri Garhwal state the situation was however markedly different. Here the Tehri kings, aided and abetted by British forest contractors and consultants, embarked over the same period on centralisation of state control over the forests. Traditional forms of forests and successive representations were unheeded and culminated in the massacre of protesters at Tilari in 1930. The momentum of this appropriation process and its associated institutions continued during the early decades after Independence.

After achieving freedom the people did not know what to do immediately; as most had expected that all their hardships would, be gone once the colonial rulers departed. Nothing like that ever happened and the new masters replaced the departing ones and the lot of the common people remained the same or deteriorated even further. There was further centralisation of the forests and the limited rights granted to the natives were further curtailed. The forest policy of 1952 reduced the privileges granted by the arrangement of 1884 to the status of mere concessions. This fact is highlighted by enhanced resource crisis after independence that led to the giving up of their intensive traditional agricultural practices in this region. The rights and privileges of the individuals can well be taken away for the larger good of the society but it should be done only by creating a regime of awareness and an informal public opinion. Nothing in this direction was done by the authorities of free India and the people of the Himalayan region largely felt alienated.

The green, blue and white revolutions that transformed the economic status of many rural communities of the nation in the post-independence era failed to make any appreciable impact on the rural life of the people in the Himalayan region. Little headway could be made even in the field of horticulture in the hills of Uttar Pradesh; a field in which this region held a competitive advantage. The state of general environment in the region also deteriorated and the hills were colonised by moneyed people mostly forest contractors and builders from far flung places who supported by disparity in the purchasing power between them and the masses in the hills bought vast interests in land and capital market. It was these people who are mainly responsible for deforestation and defacing of the green face of the Himalayas. The resentment against these people came to the forefront and this was the main concern of the masses after getting independence.

The economy of the hills was hijacked by these big players and the educated youth of the hills were unable to get employment, nor could they start self reliant ventures and most remained underemployed. To add to the deterioration in the environment, the rural masses of the region were deprived of basic necessities such as fodder, fuelwood and timber that usually used to percolate from the nearby forests, in the name of saving the forest resources. The movements be it *Chipko,* or the quest for a separate state of Uttarakhand are driven by this resentment that had an economic background. At the same time some organisations took the challenge of regreening the Himalayas and motivated the masses to plant trees in their surroundings. These groups though successful in the area of their influence have not been able to make a dent on the overall scenario due to the lack of resources and infrastructure and mass movement. Emanating from the grassroots level and an expression of the quest of the masses to have the basic rights of free access to basic resources, *Chipko* evolved as a women's movement against depleting natural resources of the region, that added to the drudgery of the hill women, together with commercial exploitation of the resources. The *Chipko movement* spread a lot in the seventies. Agitated by blatant exploitation of the resources that triggered a chain reaction of landslides, floods, drought, mass wastage and denial of basic necessities of life to their sons, womenfolk of the region took up the challenge of saving the forest in an innovative but peaceful manner of well disciplined *satyagrahis* of the Mahatma. The movement found able leaders amongst the masses and in many parts of Garhwal the *Chipko movement* has played a leading role in organising and linking protests in favour of local control over hill forests. The northern branch of this movement located in Chamoli district has protested against the commercial working of forests by lumber contractors from the plains, and lobbied with success for a policy of development in which local cooperatives are given primary responsibility for the sustainable working of the local forests. On the other hand, the southern branch of the movement located in Tehri district, while rooted in the similar pattern of local protests over the seventies, has explicitly opposed any working of forests except for purposes of subsistence. None the less it has lobbied successfully for a ban on commercial felling above 1000 metres.

The Himalayas are characterised by a partial and incomplete development of markets for reasons including the physical and social characteristics of mountains such as inaccessibility and marginality. The subsistence of local communities requires collective regimes for the management of forest, pastures, and water. These resources are generally managed as commons, not so much because the nature of the natural resource demands it but because it enables individual households to pool risks within the settlement. Although observers argue that the *Chipko movements* are not literally defunct, their energies sapped by excessive adulation, these early local protests were essentially concerned with social and economic policies that affected communities largely dependent upon local resource regimes. At various times these protests opposed centralised state policies for natural resource management, regional investment and tourism development.

Of late some groups are worried about the deteriorating resource management scenario in the Himalayas; they see afforestation and watershed management as the key to the rejuvenation of the Himalayan environment. They advocate these issues to be taken up like mass movements but limited resources keep their sphere of influence limited, though they are doing their level best to promote the cause of a greener and self reliant Himalayan region. Trees for Life (TFL), a national organisation devoted to the cause of promotion of trees of all sorts had been engaged in the previous decade in tree plantation drives in the various parts of the Himalayas. It has introduced new horticultural plants such as almond, chestnuts, walnuts and pecan nuts in the region and is also engaged in promoting improvement of the local plant varieties through grafting drives. Besides this it has also been promoting native wild forest flora. The Himalayan Consortium for Conservation (HIMCON) has taken up the challenge of rebuilding a prosperous Himalayan region through the holistic approach of Watershed Management, concentrating mainly upon water management as it sees water to be the main dynamic entity capable of affecting the quality of all other resources. In its endeavours it has followed the policy of catching the water where it falls. For this a network of rain water harvesting structures have been erected. Scientifically considering all the parameters affecting recharge of groundwater it has brought about the free movement of water so as to maximise infitration. To add to it through its drive of spring rejuvenation it has brought life back around a number of hitherto dried up springs. The work of HIMCON does not end with this and it has worked consistently to improve the quality of life of the people of this terrain through a series of measures aimed at bringing about self reliance amongst the masses. To name a few it has initiated: Seed Banks that loan seeds to the farmers in whatever quantities they demand during the sowing period with the condition of return at the time of harvest, Health Banks that bring medicos and nurses to the masses with the capital contributed by them, and Self Help Groups that cater to the financial exigencies of the masses. All these are being managed by the Mahila Mangal Dals of the villages concerned and the intervention of HIMCON in the management of these is minimal. HIMCON wishes to take the mantle of good work to various parts of Uttarakhand and for this it is looking for partners for this expansion as this exercise is beyond its managerial capabilities.

Some groups working for the welfare of the masses are concerned by the reducing water availability in the Himalayan region. These groups are working to bring awareness amongst the masses in the judicious use of water and the need to conserve the same in whatever possible manner through *padyatras* and meetings. Besides awareness building these groups are propagating water harvesting and water conserving agricultural and horticultural practices.

Depletion of biodiversity of the region is a cause of concern for many groups and individuals working in this region but nothing has so far been done to agitate the masses and give the protection of biodiversity, the shape of a people's movement.

"Some groups see economic backwardness at the root of most social problems and therefore they are promoting the cause of income generation in the rural Himalayas. Horticulture, sericulture, medicinal and aromatic plants, fruit processing and other such activities are being promoted in various parts of the region by these groups but because of the lack of an organised, effective and aggressive marketing strategy their efforts are not making adequate headway. The people of the Himalayas well understand the deteriorating environmental and resource availability of the region, and are concerned for the same and at the same time are taking positive and corrective measures to set things right. This is reflected in the little acts of benevolence done by innocent children of the region and till this continues and expands there lies a hope for a better tomorrow."

A man of
integrity
is accepted,
Believed,
Trusted and
Befriended
by all.

4
Towards Self-Reliance in Himalayan Communities

Strategy for Human Development

India's achievement in various fields of human development such as health, literacy, environment and quantum of schooling for children, can be rated as only very meagre, comparing quite unfavourably with other similarly placed developing countries. Why has the state in India failed to satisfy even the basic needs of its people? Why has it also not been able to discharge the obligations placed on it by the country's Constitution? In this context, we discuss some aspects of state functioning and management of programmes, some historical antecedents of political processes and administrative behaviour and some structural, behavioural and policy issues. These could help us in understanding the underlying factors responsible for poor human development performance and also in suggesting an alternative development strategy for improving the situation in the country.

Recognising the advances in many fields of development in India, the overall Human Development performance in the country in the last 50 years from Independence can only be rated as very low. Despite the Constitutional Directives and Fundamental Rights and despite promises made repeatedly, the situation obtaining in the fields of elementary education, literacy, health care, employment and in such other basic areas such as environment has been rather pathetic and highly disappointing. The state and its various organs have thus failed even to discharge their minimum Constitutional obligations to the people.

The state agencies in India have been tightly controlled by the 'elite' who have been historically and even educationally conditioned to be insensitive to the needs of the lowly placed labouring people. They have been motivated more by the traditional values of inequality and social power than by the liberal values enshrined in the Constitution of India. The functionaries in India have tended to show caste-like rigidity, inflexibility and lack of entrepreneurship while discharging their public duties. The administration in the post-Independence period has continued to impose and reinforce negative self-concepts and dependency syndrome on the common man. The lives of vast sections of the Indian population have thus continued to be mired in shameful conditions of illiteracy, ill health, malnutrition and abysmal poverty.

Under such conditions, human development would require not just some literacy and any casual work but inculcation of positive self-concepts and capability. The people have to be helped to move away from dependent pawn-like behaviours to initiative and actor-like behaviours. Participation in organized collective action in people's movements as well as in self-initiated development action would greatly help in promoting and reinforcing such positive self-concepts. Public activism is also important for pressursing and activising the unwilling government to act for the welfare of the people and to decentralise and democratise the administration. Repeated electoral verdicts in the past few years indicate, on the one hand, an increasing articulation of pressing socio-economic issues in this respect and, on the other, people's yearning for greater social and political empowerment.

Creative Interaction of the People and the State

Economic programmes and structural changes such as strengthening of rural infrastructure; investments in agriculture and rural development; egalitarian land reforms; stress on self-reliance and mobilisation of internal resources as against dependency on foreign investments; interventions designed to promote new enterprises and competitiveness for excellence and quality at the workplace; empowerment and activisation of PRIs and municipal bodies for active participation in planning and in development and similar other superordinate policy goals, all have the potential for raising the morale of the people, thus releasing their productive energy to actively participate in obtaining various goals. Kerala's state-sponsored people's campaign for decentralised planning is a good example of creative interaction between the people and the state.

Creative interaction between the people and the state thus has the potential for motivating the various state agencies as well as the public. This could directly contribute to promoting the desired psychological and social environment for sustainable alternative development. Such development involves a process of social and political empowerment with the long-term objective of rebalancing the structure of power in society.

Creative and meaningful interaction between people and the state thus helps in people's empowerment and democratisation in the wider society. As the assertive power of the people increases and as they become more and more concerned with social achievement goals, they would also activise the state for similar achievement goals, thus accelerating the process of democratic governance and sustainable human and economic development in the country.

It is in this context that we wish to launch a People's Movement for Himalayan Rejuvenation. Experience of some Movements given below indicates that such a People's Movement can yield positive results.

Emerging Mass Movements : Towards a Qualitative Psychological and Physical Change*

1. In the last few dacades, several salient issues have motivated the people for mass mobilisation. Single issues have tended to spill over other interrelated issues, thus creating conditions for a qualitative change in people's thinking. In West Bengal, for instance, the peasant's movement following the Tehbhaga agitation and the mobilisation of different castes and classes in rural areas in favour of redistribution of land became an important contributor to the future land reforms in the state. These in turn motivated the people to strive for greater agricultural production even without the benefit of a technological breakthrough as was available in the case of Punjab. In Kerala also, several movements such as the library movement and the people's science movement paved the way for land reforms. Such movements energised the people as well as the official machinery.

---

* Psychological Strategy for Alternative Human Development "India's Performance since Independence", Prayag Mehta, Sage Publications, New Delhi, 1995, pp. 169-185

2. There have also been several movements in various parts of the country around issues pertaining to environment, rights of livelihood, forest rights, human rights and social justice. Such movements tend to spill over and multiply their impact on people as well as on the establishment. The anti-liquor movement in Andhra Pradesh is a good example of such spill-over and qualitative psychological change. Similar changes have also been obtained by Total Literacy Campaigns, in which millions of women have participated, as these campaigns got linked with issues of livelihood and social equality (Sengupta and Roy 1996). Movement for protection of trees, fodder, fuel and forests have got linked with protests against land submergence and have snowballed into a strong movement against large dams. Anti-price movement in several states also got linked with movements for land and against the nexus of landlords, officials, contractors, politicians and money lenders and also against 'liberalisation' and TNCs.

3. The *Dalit* movement against atrocities and social oppression has evolved into a bigger movement against the caste-ridden Brahminical social order and for democratisation of the civil society. The movements against child labour and bonded labour have tended to get linked with issues pertaining to child health, nutrition, corruption in high places and with government's mis-governance in general.

4. The anti-arrack movement, literacy campaigns in various states, the movement for protection of trees, fodder and fuel and similar other movements highlight the emergence of militancy of women in civil society. Their cry against alcohol and for prohibition has been *Nasha Nahi, Rozgar Do,* thus, linking their anti-arrack movement with demand for adequate water, medical facilities, employment and other basic public amenities. Women tend to perceive the local shopkeepers and moneylenders as a symbol as well as a cause of their miseries. Such militancy has been observed in Andhra Pradesh, Karnataka, Kerala, Haryana, Uttar Pradesh, Madhya Pradesh and Maharashtra and during the Nav Nirman movement in Gujarat in the seventies.

5. The age-old proverbial tolerance and silence of the deprived people is thus, unmistakably and increasingly, being broken. Even at places where there has been no perceptible movement or agitation, the labouring people, including the tribal people in remote villages, have been articulating their deep-felt problems and needs.

6. Studies of Total Literacy Campaigns, adult education and

some related rural development programmes also reveal the changing self-image of the labouring rural poor. Millions of people including a large number of women have been activated into movements by such campaigns which have provided them with a new sense of identity and reinforced their sense of assertion and hope. They have been participating in various cultural activities such as *Kala Jathas* in which songs and other items are linked with basic issues of their livelihood and with the need for resisting oppression in whatever form. Such campaigns and cultural activities have thus enthused a large number of educated girls and rural youths to serve as volunteer-instructors and raised their level of political and environmental consciousness.

7. One of the urgent requirements in our present situation of poor human development is to pressurise the state to fulfil its Constitutional obligations in order to provide basic services to all people. Since it has been indifferent to meeting such needs, it is necessary to force it to change direction and to show greater concern for the quality of life of vulnerable people. People's movements and organisations alone can weaken the various inhibiting forces and help re-energise the state organs and public institutions for these important tasks. It is essential to enhance the assertive role of the common people if sustainable human development has to be achieved. Social mobilisation, as discussed above, plays an important role in this respect and contributes to changing the social and political pyschology of the common people and enhances public activism. Needless to say, such efforts need to be well planned and organised. All this has led us to make a Proposal for People's Movement for Himalayan Rejuvenation.

People's Movement for Himalayan Rejuvenation

1. *People's Movement for Himalayan Rejuvenation in the Central Himalayas—Uttarakhand and Himachal*

The Himalayas are one of the youngest and most fragile eco-systems on Earth. The Himalayan mountains are regarded as the water towers for mankind living in the region. Though gifted with rich flora, fauna, minerals and natural resources besides a rich cultural heritage, the people inhabiting these mountain are among the poorest in the world. These mountains are revered as the abode of gods from times immemorial. This relationship that provided special sanctity to this terrain and saved it from over-exploitation through a series of socio-religious sanctions certainly had utilitarian overtones. Our predecessors well understood the important role played by this mountain system in conserving the ecosystem of a larger area. Besides providing stability to the monsoon climate of the Indian subcontinent, the rivers emanating from the mountains give rise to fertile plains. At the same time unchecked exploitation of this fragile terrain was well understood to trigger a series of disasters, such as floods, siltation, erosion, land slides and mass wastage. The essence of this symbiotic relationship has been greatly diluted over the years. The Himalayan mountains have been pushed to the periphery of mainstream thinking and are considered as just 'hinterlands' of the plains.

The importance of the mountain eco-system is once again being recognised the world over and these are gradually occupying a central place in development intervention. The well-being of the mountains has come to be recognised as necessary for the well-being of the plains. The importance of the mountain eco-systems is reflected in the first ever Mountain Agenda that came into being in 1992. Now the year 2002 has been declared as the International Year of the Mountains.

Since the sustainability of the mountain ecosystems is essential for the sustainability of the whole globe, the need for a strategy and Action Programme to assist and promote the rejuvenation of the fast deteriorating Himalayas is being felt by mountain scholars, revolutionaries and local residents.

2. *Land slides and mass wastage*

It is a common phenomenon that natural erosive forces subdue any topographic expression. Man-made activities however accelerate the pace of these erosive forces manifold. The ill effects of this phenomenon are observed in :

- increased frequency of landslides
- increased rates of erosion
- adverse changes in land cover and depleting forests and pastures
- diminishing biodiversity of mountain eco-system
- depleting fertility of lands and thus depleting yields
- increased rates of surface run off.
- drying up of springs and resultant water scarcity
- out migration
- deteriorating quality of life of the masses.

The Consequences of Erosion

Deterioration in the Himalayas is shown in a typical catchment in the chart attached where are depicted the following :

1. Deforested Land
2. Cultivation on steep slopes
3. Devastating landslides and soil erosion and gully erosion
4. Fish catch is reduced in shallow waters
5. Siltation of reservoirs with consequent reduction in lifetimes of hydroelectric plants
6. Mud banks leading to reduce navigability of rivers
7. Urban slums grow as rural population migrates to the city
8. Crops grown on large unproductive fields
9. Badly managed pastures

Prevention and Repair
What can be done?

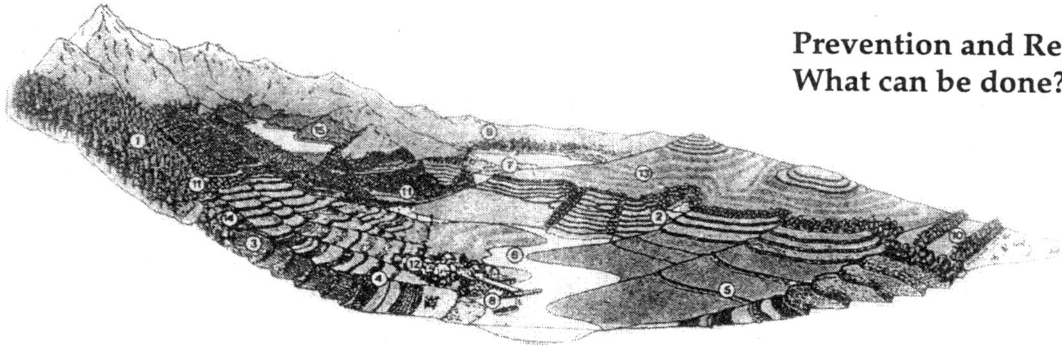

2.3 *Prevention and repair—what can be done : as defined in the chart attached*

1. Reforested land
2. Gully erosion halted by check dams, trees planted on gully banks
3. Steep land is bench terraced
4. Contour cultivation practised on lower land
5. Bunds are built to control surface run-off
6. As erosion stops, flooding is reduced
7. New reservoir supplies power to nearby villages
8. River navigation improves fish catch increases
9. Urban services improve as population migration stops
10. Shelter belts reduce wind erosion, pastures are improved/upgraded
11. Absence of landslides and floods improves road communication
12. Rural services improve as villages expand
13. Crop rotation practised in strips along contours
14. Tree crops grown on eyebrow terraces on steep land
15. Forested slopes prevent siltation of reservoirs.

3 *Visualised Plan of Action for Himalayan Rejuvenation*

It is being overwhelmingly recognised that the resource crisis in the Himalayas is deepening and the quality of life of the masses is detoriorating despite all material progress. HIMCON has been working in this region with the participation of the masses and has come to formulate a comprehensive strategy for regenerating Himalayas on emerging principles of watershed management and sustainable development.

At the beginning of the programme, besides undertaking a massive awareness drive on various issues concerning the masses it is necessary to undertake a detailed exercise of natural resource assessment through satellite remote sensing applications. Integrated study using GIS and remote sensing data can also be put to use for assessing the mass wastage scenario. This exercise has proved fruitful for better resources management the world over.

Extremes of atmospheric precipitation in the mountains are recognised to trigger a series of erosive processes. It is therefore necessary to manage and reduce flow of surface water. This would be affected through: Checkdams, checkwalls, gully plugging, contour bunding, conservation agriculture, afforestation and planting of trees for fruit, fuel and fodder and grassland development. In non-accessible areas this could be achieved by aerial seeding.

The repletion of sub-surface water would be brought about by various water harvesting structures, while water availability can be improved upon by a series of roof water and other harvesting structures.

Agriculture including horticulture and animal husbandry is the mainstay of the hill economy, therefore a package of seed bank, grafting, composting, and planting would be resorted to. The seed bank scheme developed by HIMCON in Tehri Garhwal district under which seed material is given to the farmers on the condition of replenishment has been very popular.

To improve health amenities the trained nurses of HIMCON are working in unison with the masses through health banks and mother and child centres towards which the people contribute funds. To add to it adoption of medicinal plants is envisaged to show positive results in times to come.

Fuelwood is the main source of energy for most of the rural people in the hills. Large scale energy plantations with adequate fencing (bio and social) has therefore to be undertaken on community lands. Besides this briquetting and alternate energy programmes have to be taken up in the region. In addition a series of income generating activities are to be promoted in this region. Above all environmental and adult education needs promotion in the Himalayan terrain.

This work is to be undertaken with the support of 3H Rotary programmes in three years times in Tehri Garhwal District. It is also expected that some grant may be obtained from UNDP which plans to launch a "Sustainable Development in the Central Himalayan Programme". HIMCON is promoting and is deeply involved in the "People's Movement for Himalayan Rejuvenation" with special emphasis on UP Himalayas (Uttarakhand).

People's Movement aspect is being envisaged as follows:

1. Vision ——> Work Together
2. ——> People's Organizations as follows.

Local Panch-ayats	Mahila Mandals	Youth Organi-sations	Schools	NGOs	Ex-servic-emen	Others

3. Human Values as binding force and guiding principles

4. Examples of People's Movement are CHIPKO and Trees for Life Movement which need to be evaluated and brain storming with the People's Organizations mentioned above are required.

5. Movement towards sustainability

Principles and practices of sustainability

Human Resource Development

- Health & sanitation
- Literacy
- Entrepreneurial training learning to work together

Promotion of renewable energy sources (Green sources) MNES to help & cooperate

Income generating activities
- — Ecotourism
- — Horticultural activities and conservation cropping
- — Forests & forest produce
- — Medicinal & aromatic plants
- — Grasses, fodder & animal husbandry
- — Sericulture
- — Apiculture
- — Nut and fruit revolution

OUTPUTS OF THIS PROJECT (NEXT 5-10 YEARS)

Central Indian Himalayas can be and must be hopefully rejuvenated—a resource that is not replaceable

— Minimum 10,000 new jobs / entrepreneurs for Uttarakhand / Himachal during years 2000-2005

— Income generated over 10 years: crores of additional income per year during and after first five years. These benefits are both non-quantifiable and quantifiable.

* Non quantifiable in terms of a movement which can save, rejuvenate and transform the mountain region starting with Uttarakhand and Himachal
* Quantifiable in terms of entrepreneurship, training, and generation of wealth from presently wasted resources of land, water, forests, horticulture, medicinal plants, climate, etc.

5
Himalayan Eco-System : Conservation, Development and Management

The Sixth and also Seventh and subsequent Five Year plans for the first time brought into proper focus the importance of agriculture and rural development in India. These plans clearly defined the importance and urgency of the Himalayan eco-system conservation development and management. High priority is to be given to flood control, soil and water conservation, environment, forestry, afforestation, hill area development, and, above all, people's participation.

The participating states of Jammu & Kashmir, Himachal Pradesh, Uttar Pradesh, Assam and northeastern states thus included in their plans, action programmes and projects to meet the above needs. The programmes are in the framework of the National Plan and, according to the guidelines given by the Planning Commission to the states. The central and state government operate these action programmes which need to be integrated, monitored, regulated and evaluated for optimum results with greater participation and interaction of the people.

Four key points are to be considered in large-scale operations, such as the Himalayan Programme.

Integrated Approach

Technical means and measures must be sound and coordinated with one another. While there is a lot of water in the Himalayan rivers, there are many areas that are often water-starved and others that are flooded. While immense hydro-potential remains, forests are being over-exploited for the energy needs of the people, the conservation and watershed management measures must encompass tree planting and engineering structures, improved agriculture and conservation cropping, range and pasture management, including animal husbandry, etc. Integrated approach is needed rather than a sectoral approach.

People's Participation

Large scale participation of people, essentially the rural population of the Himalayan watersheds, is extremely important. Over 50 million people live in the hill areas and could benefit from such programmes. In this context, special attempts have to be made to involve the youth and students both from rural and urban areas. This has a great employment-creating potential that must be utilised urgently. Public opinion and enthusiasm have also to be mobilized for such large-scale people's participation, which could reach up to 10 million people. Programmes have also to be developed at the suggestion of the people who benefit as it is they who have to maintain the forests, orchards, range and pasture, water-development structures and, in short, the whole eco-system.

Involvement of NGOs and Civil Society

Although the Government of India and state governments are earmarking the equivalent of 1.5 to 2 billion dollars, or about Rs. 2,000 crores, these funds would be adequate provided non-Government Organizations, voluntary agencies, ex-servicemen groups, schools and colleges are involved as the development schemes could be completed at a much lower cost provided they work in an overall master plan and are full participants in a people's programme.

Apex Body

Monitoring, regulating, evaluating and even additional fund-raising for such a huge and challenging programme should be entrusted to a definite focal point. It is for the Prime Minister to decide on the location of such a focal point. It is proposed that Himalayan Eco-system Programme Coordinator be entrusted under the aegis of the Department of Environment and Forestry with involvement of the Ministry of Agriculture and Ministry of Water Resources and Ministry of Human Resources.

Water

The life-blood of agriculture, it is a constituent for economic development of a region and has a special place and significance in the life of the people of the Himalayan region. The Himalayan watersheds are dependent upon atmospheric precipitation for all its water supply. Rains though abundant, are not uniformly distributed and the terrain conditions promote quick runoff of the precipitating water to lower altitudes. This flowing water cannot be brought up without an expense of energy and therefore every effort should be towards conserving it at the higher altitude for as long a duration as possible. This would maximise recharge of subsurface waters and the water so harvested would be available easily for diverse use.

If allowed to flow unchecked water is a malefactor destroying life of the people, their property and crops with devastating floods.

Floods and Droughts

Floods are a menace and a bottleneck to the realization of the optimum use of resources. They occur practically every year in varying degrees of intensity and it is essential to mitigate their destructive capacity though it is almost impossible to control them totally. This is evident in the floods that occurred in India in 1975 which promoted the senior author to prepare a comprehensive note for the programme of development and utilization of land and water resources of the Himalayan Region.

Heavy rains in the catchment areas of the Ganges, the Brahmaputra and their tributaries have caused these rivers to inundate low-lying areas and destroy paddy and jute crops. Floods have affected almost the whole of northern India and Pakistan, and have also not spared Bangladesh from their wrath.

Droughts have been observed as a setback to the welfare of the people as a flood-drought-flood cycle. Drought brings near famine conditions for the people. Now that drought-prone areas have been identified and remedial measures contemplated some worthwhile action can emerge.

The Governments of India, Pakistan, Bangladesh and, to some extent, Nepal have spent billions of dollars in the previous years to contain these floods and droughts but with limited success.

Both India and Pakistan have built several reservoirs to store such flood waters for irrigation and other uses with positive results. In the Ganges and Brahmaputra river systems—international in character—it is essential that the riparian countries work cooperatively for the development and management of these rivers and their watershed areas.

The subcontinent of India has had to tackle the excessive rainfall problem in the Asian region. The deforestation in the highlands of northern India, Nepal, Bhutan and Pakistan has increased the rate of erosion and the silt load of the rivers as well as caused greater damage to this area which is subject to high rainfall and, therefore, can no longer absorb the river water for irrigation, as the Indus can.

To tackle all this a programme called "Himalayan Region Land and Water Resources Conservation, Development and Utilization" was prepared with the major aim of breaking the cycle of floods-droughts-floods, and for better conservation and utilization of land and water resources in the region. The realization of the objectives of such a programme will not only stabilize and protect the ever-degrading land resources and increase production of food and energy, but also create a dependable socio-economic climate for its people and dignified employment opportunities for coming generations. To stop the cycle of floods-droughts-floods, or at least to reduce their intensity to a manageable extent in this region, it will need a Himalayan effort. The main features of this programme are:

Programme Area

An area of about 2,600,000 km^2 with hydrological boundaries of the Indus, Ganges and Brahmaputra rivers and their tributaries is formed calling it the Programme Area. This can be divided into two hydrologic units—the Indus river Basin (about 1,00,000 km^2) and the Ganges and Brahmaputra River Basin (1,600,000 km^2). The Indus River Basin is located within the national boundaries of China, Afghanistan, India and Pakistan. The Ganges River Basin is located in Nepal, India and Bangladesh and that of the Brahmaputra in China, Bhutan, India and Bangladesh.

Potential of the Area for Land and Water Development

The annual average run-off figure for the three-river system are 207 billion m^3 for the Indus, 374 billion m^3 for the Ganges and 670 billion m^3 for the Brahmaputra (for the Ganges and Brahmaputra combined 1044 billion m^3) with a total for three of 1,251 billion m^3. At present only about 10-12 per cent of this potential is utilized for agriculture. A rough estimate for irrigation water requirement for the arable land will be about 1,200 m^3. This amount is almost equal to the annual average river flows. It cannot be assumed that all the surface water will be regulated for this purpose. There will, however, be at least an amount of groundwater equal to the surface flow which is of the order of 4,000 billion m^3.

This analysis indicates that if half of the total surface and ground water potential is regulated and /or utilized according to the needs of agriculture and soil and water conservation, the full agricultural potential of the area could be realized. In terms of additional food production potential due to double or triple cropping, this may run into well over a hundred million tonnes per year which will provide food to people of the region, and support livestock development to meet the requirements of the region. The potential of the watershed area for forest resources development is also very great. The region also possesses a huge potential for inland fisheries as well as aquaculture, especially combined with other agricultural activities.

The hydro-power potential of the area also appears to be colossal. The sources of the gigantic rivers of the area are at very high elevations in the Himalayas and the rivers accumulate the bulk of their water resources at still relatively high altitudes and possess high energy potential—roughly 4,000 billion KWH annually.

The realization of the above potential will require a huge investment of about US $ 200,000 million with the present money value. The amount required for irrigation, drainage and flood control systems, land preparation for agriculture and soil conservation measures, is almost the same as that for hydro-power schemes.

The whole programme may take 30-40 years to implement and

during its implementation it will provide employment to nearly 100 million rural youths, benefiting about 700 million people in the South Asia region. This programme, though vital for humanity, will certainly have special appeal for the countries located within the region, although in different principal values. To Bangladesh, it would provide the long desired and dreamed of flood relief, and security to produce more; to India and Pakistan, a final halt to the historical vicious circle of droughts-floods-droughts. To Nepal it will be a relief from hill-land degradation as well as surplus energy for trade. To Bhutan, it will be the same as for Nepal. Finally, to China, it would mean a huge availability of cheap and renewable energy to be utilised for domestic purposes and to be traded with her neighbours.

Preparation of a Master Plan

Several studies have been made so far for the development of the resources within these three basins, and several programmes have already been implemented to control floods, to provide irrigation water, to generate hydro-power, etc, although limited as compared to the potential.

Before launching a programme for further studies,* a thorough review of all-accessible studies and reports will have to be made with a view to assessing them from the objective standpoint and identify gaps requiring further studies. The main follow-up work will be organized on the basis of this review.

In view of what has been stated above immediate efforts for planning should be concentrated on the Ganges and Brahmaputra area. Mainly on the basis of the existing data, and with some field reconnaissance work as well as completed topographic, hydro-meteorological and land capability studies, an Indicative Master Plan should be prepared. This plan will include several projects in order of priority and a well-described programme for further studies to prepare detailed projects for pre-investment studies and implementation.

The Master Plan should indicate different types of projects required whether single or multi-purpose consisting of soil

---

* International Centre For Integrated Mountain Development, (ICIMOD) Kathmandu has conducted lots of studies and some action programmes in the Hindukush Himalayas.

conservation and hydraulic works.

National Efforts

National effort towards controlling floods and fighting droughts and for full conservation and development of land and water resources started long ago. It will have to be continued to the extent the national boundaries permit. Under a coordinated programme and with cooperative action and spirit among the countries concerned, the national effort will no doubt be more fruitful and have a long-lasting impact on multiple cropping, increased food production and the well-being of the area.

International Efforts

International support may prove useful to ensure a coordinated approach and cooperative action bearing in mind that the actual work will be carried out by the countries directly concerned utilizing their capacity and resources to the maximum extent towards the development of the land and water resources of the Himalayas. International effort could play a catalytic role in programme implementation and also provide a link with major extra-budgetary sources to supplement national resources.

The Cultured
Give
Happiness
Wherever
They go
They Uncultured,
Whenever
They Go !

6
Towards Betterment of the Himalayan Watersheds*

A Watershed is a natural geohydrological unit, water precipitating within which leaves its boundaries through a common exit in a concentrated flow. All natural and anthropogenic activities in the limits of the watershed affect each other and have a definite bearing on each other. It has been debated and shown over and again that better resource management can be achieved by taking the watershed as the unit of development. Lately the government and other funding agencies have accepted it as the unit for the development of the hilly terrain and future work is sought to be undertaken through watershed development strategy, primarily through schemes for integrated development of resources within the limits of the watershed through people's participation.

National Issues

Awareness

Awareness of a problem—that something needs to be done, awareness that if something is being done, it must be correctly implemented to achieve the goals set—is perhaps the foremost requirement for resolution of the problems. Regarding land-water-vegetation systems, it is the Government, the line/sectoral departments, socio-political system, people at large, farmers and users of land who are to become aware, active and responsive. In India the problems of watershed degradation have received considerable attention.

At government level, this is evident from the extensive

* Dr. K.G. Tejwani. Part of a paper for the International Workshop on Watershed Management organized by ICIMOD at Changdu, Sichuan, China in 1985.

development research and training programmes initiated and implemented. Recently CAPART and Ministry of Rural Development have floated detailed guidelines for the projects to be implemented through watershed approach in the hilly areas of the nation. These projects are to be implemented through the NGOs with active participation of the masses.

At the people's level, the Chipko movement in the Himalayas is a classical example of the people, and more so the women who bear the brunt of the hard work connected with farming, and fetching fuel, fodder and water, initiating a movement to conserve their surroundings (Kunwar 1982). This movement has both economic and ecological overtones. People in the Himalayas are also aware of the problem of degradation of the production base and disappearance of water and presumably wish to act. However, perhaps they are enmeshed in a socio-economic-cultural environment that does not permit them to be effective.

Population pressure

Population continues to grow unabated at an explosive rate in the fragile mountain eco-system as well as in the plains. If mobilized properly this can prove to be an asset. Although a considerable proportion of the population has indicated a capacity to absorb, adapt and benefit from modern technology, there are limits within the system to support an increasing population. Population control is the "key issue" in fragile mountain eco-system. 'If any single programme determines the success or failure of developmental activities it is population control, population control and population control.' Visualising the importance of this the state government of UP has launched a massive World Bank aided programme Family Planning Programme, SIFPSA, that is to be implemented with the involvement of the NGOs. Time would tell the efficacy of this programme.

Regional Issues

Development Strategy

Watershed management, however important, cannot be made a development activity by itself, particularly when large numbers of poor agrarian people are living in the watersheds. Watershed management has to be a part of the overall development strategy for the Himalayan region. All mountain watersheds in general, and the Himalayan watersheds in particular, have inherent bio-physical and socio-economic constraints which impinge on the pace, quality and growth of development. The major constraints identified are isolation, poor infrastructure facilities, an ecologically fragile natural system, wide variations in agro-ecological conditions within very short distances due to permutations and combinations of altitude, slope and aspect conditions, and limited availability of good agricultural land that places a natural barrier to increasing food production.

Recognition of these constraints has led to the formulation of specific strategies for the development of the Himalayan areas. The National Plans suggested a multi-dimensional Area Development Approach to accelerate development of backward areas including Himalayan hill areas; it also recognized that in hill areas investment is high compared to the returns, therefore more central assistance has been allocated to meet specific needs and problems.

People : Upland/lowland Relationship

The terms "Upland" and "Lowland" are used to identify the hills and plains. If the people of the upland manage catchments and use water wisely they obtain good quality and sufficient water for longer periods of time, besides decreasing the rates of wastage. The people of the lower reaches also reap benefits from these acts; the siltation rates in the reservoirs are reduced and the threat of flash floods is mitigated. If the people of the hills misuse and mismanage catchments the water gets polluted (with sediment) and the inhabitants of the plains have to face serious problems in terms of resource management, flooding and other related issues.

Every individual wishes to survive, and only when this is assured does one consider other issues. This fact of life is also applicable to the relationship between the people of the hills and the plains. The economic security of the hill people must be assured before they can be persuaded to perceive that their lives are interwoven with those of the people living in the plains. They should perceive that they are equal partners in the development of the hills and the plains. This perception will not come automatically; the people in the plains must also realise that their development and growth is intrinsically linked with the ecological and economic developments in the hill areas. Unless this interdependence, based on common goals and respective roles, is appreciated at the policy, decision making, planning, and implementation levels, the pace of development and growth and commitment to programmes may not necessarily achieve the goals envisaged.

As far as water and forest resources are concerned, it is much more beneficial that their generation, utilization, maintenance and conservation start upstream with benefits flowing downstream for the good of all. Fortunately this has been realized and what is needed now is vigorous implementation of programmes based on this perception.

Institutional Issues

Research

Since watershed management is a combination of many and varied field techniques, it requires strong research, demonstration and technological package for application in the field. Two centres were responsible for work in the Siwalik hill region (at Chandigarh) and the Himalayan watersheds (Dehradun). In addition, there is a network of Universities, Central Research Institute, and State Research Centres working in the Indian Himalayan region. All the centres and universities are making important contributions to research and demonstration. Much has been achieved at the institutional levels and many innovative techniques of resource conservation and management have been evolved in the post-independence period. What is lacking is the timely and effective transfer of the same to the end users. For this serious efforts are required at bringing the end users, NGOs and the researchers on one platform.

Training Programmes

Watershed management as a multi-disciplinary programme needs skilled technicians and professionals for implementation. Further it requires options of alternate land-use and structural works needing investment. If the work is incorrectly done, investment is wasted and great damage caused by programme failures. It is therefore, essential that trained, fully oriented and committed personnel do the work. While a lot has been achieved, a lot more needs to be done (Vohra 1975; Tejwani 1979, 1981).

Looking Ahead

Are we catching up?

It is good to know that (a) the problem of watershed degradation in the Himalayas is recognized; and (b) large-scale watershed management and afforestation programmes have been initiated and are being implemented at an increasing pace. However, the question which is yet to be answered is : "Is enough being done ?"

Despite all that has been done and achieved it can be stated that it is just the beginning in the right direction and enough is not being done. It must also be remembered that apart from afforestation most of the earth work programmes—gully plugs, check dams, etc. have a limited life of, say 10-15 years. If an area has not been well stabilized, some of the works will need to be redone. On balance, currently the rate of degradation is higher than the rate of restoration/afforestation.

It is imperative, therefore that we carry out perspective planning so that at least in the next decade, the pace of improvement becomes greater than the rate of degradation and the coming generations find an environment suitable for their overall growth.

Remedy vs. Prevention

Many multipurpose projects are coming up in the region. These are all being planned and designed assuming that the inflow of water and silt will continue to be the same in quality and quantity as observed in the past.

It is only subsequent to project implementation when apprehensions of variations in design assumptions, likely to adversely affect the life and stability of reservoirs and structures, are confirmed that remedial measures of catchment treatment are thought of. This is a very short-sighted policy having dangerous consequences since:

- The country does not get the designed benefits both in quality and quantity from the investments made.

- The country loses more capital in higher costs of operation, repair and maintenance than originally provided for.
- Dam sites which are very rare are lost within a shorter life span.
- The cost-benefit ratios are never attained, and if costs are realistically allocated the project may in fact have negative cost-benefit ratios.

It is imperative to take a firm policy decision that hereafter the catchment reservoir command area will be surveyed, planned, constructed and managed simultaneously. Indeed it is wiser to plan and implement catchment area programmes in ADVANCE of reservoir construction (Tejwani 1984). Once this decision is taken, it is not to be varied/changed on any account whatsoever. This view of the authors is supported by the past experiences and it may be more economical and beneficial to adopt it as a policy. It has been reported that if soil conservation and watershed management practices are included as a part of the project from planning and design stages, and silt discharge is planned to be reduced by 25 per cent, the percentage increase in utilization of water can be 1.49 - 1.79 and 3.02 - 3.81 over a design period of 50 and 100 years, respectively. In another case study, it was observed that a pre-planned 25 per cent reduction in sediment would help by reducing the height of the dam from 32.6 m to 32.0 m thereby reducing construction costs by 5-6 per cent. In addition, there will be less submergence, reduced costs of rehabilitation, less loss of land resources and forests, and reduced evaporation losses due to reduced surface area of the reservoir (Sinha, 1984).

Institutions — Coordination vs Integration

Watershed management is a multi-disciplinary programme. At the national level CAPART and the Ministry of Rural Development are extending projects in this field to the NGOs. Some states have separate soil conservation departments, some undertake work in soil and water conservation through agriculture and/or forest departments. As work in watershed management gains momentum, the issue often arises as to how to coordinate/integrate the work of different departments. This is discussed here with respect to allocation of responsibility (and therefore funds) so as to ensure that the work is undertaken in a concentrated manner. There is a consensus of opinion that, as line departments in the states have been long established and have many functions to perform, it is better that they continue to function independently. However, as regards watershed management programmes, they should attend to all the activities and establish within themselves a competence to work on all land-uses. This approach is possible and has been resolved where programmes are large. If a decision is taken that each department will implement its sectoral activities, it becomes necessary that all related departments coordinate their work in the same watershed simultaneously, to complete the work in the stipulated time and to achieve effective results.

There are other issues of coordination between agriculture, forest, roads, electricity and irrigation departments. It is well known that forest/irrigation departments, as also people by their activities cause damage to roads; while roads/power departments cause damage to plantations, water courses and bench terracing undertaken by other departments. Everyone goes merrily about in their sectoral pursuits. On balance, in some situations perhaps more damage is caused than good. Obviously, there is great need and urgency for cooperation and coordination between various departments.

Who Pays for the Work and How Much?

Soil conservation and afforestation works do not pay immediate returns on the investments made, neither to the farmer nor to the community. Often, the benefits accrue far away from the site and may be indirect. It is also necessary that investments be made. The issue then is : Who pays?

- If a farmer or an individual in the upland watershed is to pay, then for which type of work, and how much should he pay ?
- What are the obligations of the people who live in the plains towards supporting the upland watershed programmes? Do they pay directly?

As regards contributions from the plains for restoration and maintenance of upland watersheds, there is an excellent example from Colombia where a percentage of income from power generation (4 %) is transferred for the rehabilitation and development of watersheds. This mechanism needs to be explored, experimented and adapted to the Himalayas. The Ministry of Finance and Ministry of Power are requested to consider it very seriously and actively. There may be serious negative effects if efforts are not made in this direction.

Our Present Work
May Be
Great
Or
Small,
Yet,
The Important Thing
is to
Do it well

7

Little Traditions of the Region

Religion is commonly perceived as pertaining exclusively to the spiritual domain while science and technology are viewed as systems pertaining exclusively to the material domain. Issues of material development and progress have therefore been left to the complete charge of scientific experts while religious beliefs have been left to guide the inner spiritual development of private individuals. An in-depth and unbiased investigation of the religious and cultural heritage reveals that these have, over the centuries, provided knowledge of nature and rules of natural resource utilisation that have enabled ancient societies to survive materially.

A re-appraisal and re-investigation of the relevance of these systems as guides to man's relationship with the environment, are important from the point of view of material survival. Destruction of resources and the erosion of life support systems leads to destruction of livelihoods and thus to migration. Religious traditions have a dual role in the search for peace in contemporary times. At the level of resource use these can provide the value framework which makes for prudent and hence, sustainable use of resources and thus creates the material conditions for peace. At the level of social conflicts, these can prevent the social consequences of resource degeneration from taking on a communal and sectarian form, by reminding the religious communities that all religions teach peaceful co-existence.

Ours is an ancient civilisation with a continuity extending over millennia. The earliest recorded thought found in the *Rig Veda* begins with a vivid description of five elements (*panchatatva*) — earth, water, energy, air and space—that constitute our universe and provide the life support for man and animal and the base for all forms of vegetation and all forms of human activity. These elements are defined as the manifestation of the absolute and man is ordained to conserve these elements for his eternal prosperity by scrupulously performing his duties prescribed in this regard in the various religious texts.

The *ashrams* of the ancient sages represent systems of ecological management marked by the most rational husbandry of natural resources, partnership between man and animal, sound balance between material satisfaction and spiritual and cultural pursuits and community life that ensured health, happiness and harmony for all the constituents.

The *Yagnyavalka Smriti* spells out man's obligations towards protection of the plant and animal kingdom for his own survival and prosperity. Shankara, Madhwa and Ramanuja — all the three schools of philosophy are in unison in stressing the importance of conservation of natural resources and their judicious use by man for satisfying his material needs.

No religion justifies the most destructive attitude modern man has developed towards his environment. All urge man to treat nature as a God given gift. Hinduism expresses the firm belief that the natural environment in which man is placed is created by God himself. *Akasa* (space) is the first creation of the Lord, and the Brahman in the form of *akasa* created *marut* or *vayu* (air) and *vayu* in that form created *tej* or energy. The other element *apa* (water) and *kspiti* (earth) are further creations. It is affirmed that the Lord alone, residing in these various forms of *akasa, vayu, tej, apa* and *kspiti,* created the further entities. The Supreme is immanent in every one of these and these are not mere inert and independent entities.

Of the four purusharthas, *dharma, artha, kama* and *moksha, dharma* denotes righteousness or the proper utilisation of the resources to fulfil or satisfy the needs and desires of the humans. If man goes on increasing his own needs than he requires more and more resources to fulfil his needs. *Dharma* etymologically means the stabiliser, the society becomes stable only on account of this. Overutilisation of resources to fulfil the innumerable needs and wants is prohibited by *dharma*. In fact, *dharma* restricts the utilisation of the resources only to satisfy the basic needs of man.

The waters of most of the rivers is considered holy. Every *Srivaishanava* is to chant several *mantras* and *slokas* while taking a bath. The holy water of the celestial Ganga is to be kept in the house of every *Srivaishanava* so that it can be given at the time of leaving this mortal world. Therefore elementary rules against pollution of water were already formulated in our ancient texts.

The ever increasing ecological crisis in all parts of the globe is an indicator of the inadequacy of contemporary scientific beliefs in providing the basis for sustaining the present forms of economic development and natural resource utilisation. The rich philosophical and cultural heritage of the Indian tradition provide a set of religious beliefs that cannot be called totally irrational and devoid of any material basis. Through religion many social customs that were created, only ensured in-built ecological restraint. Though not explicitly, but implicitly, the social and religious customs provided the basis for a sustainable and ecological use of natural resources. The heritage of India, undoubtedly holds in store important sources to respond to the ecological crisis emerging in modern India.

In Uttarakhand the indigenous populations had struck a fine tuned balance with nature. These people never overexploited their natural environment. The sons of the soil well understand the fragile ecological relationship and have been for centuries living in perfect harmony with nature. Through centuries of experience these people had learnt to thrive on minimal available resources. Many socio-religious sanctions were woven around nature and even today the little tradition of the region diverges from the main dictums of Hinduism. *Jagars,* animal sacrifice, spirit and nature worship are imbibed deep into the little tradition of the region and the cultural *digvijay* of Shankaracharya failed to obliterate these. Woven around these are many sanctions that protected the natural environment of the region since ancient times. The intricate relationship between water and the floral cover was well understood and the protected forest cover was therefore maintained on the higher reaches (the recharge zones of the natural springs) and often local deities (*devatas*) were installed at such places. These were thus looked upon with reverence and special attention was paid to protect their sanctity. Leave aside lopping, even shoes were forbidden in these sanctuaries to keep them pollution free. The concept of social fencing is deep rooted in the culture of the land. The places where water was collected were considered auspicious. Many important rituals were associated with these places and deities were often installed here (*naulas* and *dharas*). Even today the newly weds are taken to the household *naula* to get the blessings of prosperity.

With the onset of consumerism and reducing dependence upon the society, the sacred feeling that was the result of the development of the nature-man-spirit complex through the inter-dependence of centuries has been disrupted. But the appeal to the indigenous communities can be effectively made through the use of these motifs and such an attempt is bound to have far reaching impact upon the environment of this region.

We close this Chapter on Traditions of the Region from an extract of what Dr. Karan Singh wrote as a Foreword to Discovering Himalaya Series No. 3, "Vedic Philosophy for Himalaya Eco-System Development."

"Ancient Indian civilization was based upon nature worship, as it was an "aranyaka" of forest civilization. Our ancient scriptures, namely, the *Vedas,* appeared in the forests and the mountains. The most beautiful descriptions of the reverence of nature are to be found in these texts. The Bhumi Suktam in the *Atharva Veda* is the most impressive and eloquent testament of ecological values that can be found anywhere in world literature. These verses from the *Atharva Veda* were chanted thousands of years ago in the sylvan glens of the Himalayas and on the banks of our sacred rivers. These and similar spiritual texts from diverse cultural traditions throughout the planet earth express a world view which is informed by the spirituality inherent in Nature and teaches the holistic and harmonious relationship between humanity and Nature. Through the long passage of time, this glorious vision has dimmed and we are now mired in the malign effects of man's thoughtless interventions in Nature's processes. The reverence for natural phenomenon that was deeply ingrained in the Indian psyche has been eroded. We have to revive the spiritual traditions and those of other religions if we are to survive."

Dignity of Labour
Consists in Service
Without Devotion,
Knowledge is Tasteless,
Without Knowledge,
Devotion is Mere Empty
Idol Worship

8
Resource Management through Indigenous Knowledge*

India has a long and outstanding tradition of systematic exploration and development of natural resources. Hydrology was advanced in the past and *Vrihatsamhita* of Varamihira gives a vivid account of the various techniques employed. Similar other texts describe ways of natural resource management. Even today many unsung entrepreneurs are busy devising means of better resource management. With the disruption of the traditional system of education most indigenous knowledge has however been lost. Archeological excavations at various places have brought forth well developed systems. Many villages in the remote hilly regions still use the age-old systems of natural resource management and the very existence of these practices even in the present times reflects their sound knowledge base.

Lying in the vicinity of the famous Hindu shrine of *Jwalaji* at Jwalamukhi, the area around Khundia in Kangra district (31°40' - 32°25' N & 75°35' - 77°5' E) in Himachal Pradesh, is locally referred to as *Changar*. Though not recorded in any of the political maps the boundaries of *Changar* are well engraved in the minds of the local populace. *Changar* in local parlance is a water-starved land. The indigenous people of this rugged terrain through experimentation, imaginativeness and scientific temperament have evolved means of overcoming their physiographic handicap. This area comprises of 427 sq km and lies in the basin of the Beas river and encompasses 99 panchayats and 570 villages.

This region falls in the sub-tropical climatic zone. The summers

---

* The fieldwork for this study was undertaken by the second author (PR) and was aided by SPWD, New Delhi and ERA, Khundia. The authors acknowledge personal asssistance from Shri Pankaj Kumar & Dr. A. Chandan.

are hot and dry; winters cool and dry, while the rains are heavy. Though the average annual rainfall in this region is around 1200 mm, it is not well distributed around the year and most of it is confined to the rainy season. These extremes in climate often enhance the rates of erosion in this region. The soil profile in the region is generally shallow and erosion by the forces of nature often exposes the hard bedrock (sandstone), referred to as *sappar*. Large unproductive tracts of *sappar* are often encountered in the region and most land falling under the land classification *gairmumkin* (5 to 21 per cent in the sampled villages) represents *sappar*. The reasons for the formation of wasteland are soil erosion, steep and rocky slopes, overgrazing, deforestation, infestation by weeds, and proliferation of bushes. The rocks of the region generally fall under the Siwalik Group and the rock types encountered are sandstone and pebbly sandstone with minor clays, mudstone and siltstone. The sandstone is generally coarse grained, grey to reddish grey in colour, has good porosity and is capable of holding vast volumes of water. Harder varieties of sandstone are also seen along with minor clays. Both confined and unconfined aquifers are found in this region.

Water and the Indigenous Genius of the People

The availability of water has always affected the settlement pattern. In *Changar*, the northern slopes are well habitated while the southern slopes are sparsely populated. When people first inhabited this region some sources of water would have been existing in the vicinity. These sources were subsequently tapped and developed, while the others were designed through long experimentation. The tools, implements and the techniques used by these people are lost with the passage of time but the structures developed by them clearly show that the people had a well developed hydrology discipline that guided them to set forth the roots of the sound traditional system of water harvesting in *Changar*. May be through intuition, but these people could locate the sites for these structures very effectively. The efficacy of their deep knowledge is testified by the very fact that even after the introduction of tap water through the Department of Irrigation and Public Health (IPH) a major part of the drinking water requirements are still fulfilled by these age old structures. No doubt in many circumstances these are unable to provide adequate supply, specially during the summers, but then this can be attributed to the neglect of these structures over the years and indiscriminate tapping of resources by the IPH at higher locations that has ultimately resulted in the lower yields of the downslope structures. No one has really cared to undertake scientific study of these traditional means of water harvesting to assess their efficacy in the present scenario. An attempt in this direction would have provided water to the masses in a cost-effective manner. It is indeed an irony that even after fifty long years of independence and pumping of huge national resources the situation in the water sector is far from satisfactory and even then the traditional genius is not being recognised as a potential alternative. The need of the hour is to review the situation and pay due attention to the traditional water harvesting systems. The scenario is the same everywhere in the Himalayas and mammoth schemes are being introduced to supply water to the masses. Lengthy pipelines are not suited to the fragile terrain of the Himalayas and moreover, recurring costs of maintenance and pumping put a question mark on the economic viability of many a scheme in this region.

Everywhere the people develop some innovative practices that can rightly be termed as the tool of adaptation. In *Changar* the topography is rugged, the northern slopes though gentle are largely *sappar*, the southern slopes are steeper with some grasslands and vegetal cover. The climate, diurnal temperature fluctuations and topography of the region favour high rates of erosion and evaporation. Through centuries of experimentation and hard work the people of *Changar* have devised methods for water harvesting for various uses; methods that are well suited to the ground realities of the area.

Drinking and Household Purposes

Bawari

Bawari is the main source of drinking water in *Changar* (Plate 1). This is a generally a square structure with flights of stairs on all the sides. There is a natural seepage of water within the structure. The source is generally roofed and a wall is erected around it to ward off animals and also to prevent used water from polluting the water source. This structure is similar to the traditional *naulas* of the Kumaun Himalayas. Smaller and larger variations of *bawari* are called *bouru* and *naurh.* Provision is made for washing of clothes in the vicinity.

The Peepal tree is regarded as purifying and some sort of worship stones are often observed to be associated with *Bawari* and this is the *Changarian* example of nature-man-spirit complex. Those worshipped are *nag devata* and the ancestors.

The traditional method of locating the *bawari* site is lost and despite a deep probe nothing can be commented upon this aspect. The people however attribute it to guess work and experience of the local masons that dictated the selection procedure.

The *bawaris* actually surveyed in.the field were observed to have noticeable discharge even during the middle of May (Table 8.4). The data on the discharge of some of the *bawaris* is given in Table 8.1 indicates that on an average daily discharge of 14,400 litres can be expected from each *bawari.* This data raises vast hopes towards making the community self reliant, considering the number of *bawaris* each village of the region does have (Table 8.2).

Table 8.1: Data on the discharge of some bawaris measured in the field

Location	*Discharge per minute (in litres)*	*Discharge per day (in litres)*
Chillag	3	4320
Bal	4	5760
Salihar	15	21600
Gal	18	25920

These structures were traditionally built with the contributions from the community whose responsibility was also to maintain them regularly. However with the introduction of tap water and the disinterest of the state department to take charge of these structures these institutions have been neglected and consequently many have silted (Plate 1), or have been covered with vegetation (Plate 2) and thus their discharge has decreased considerably.

Khatri

With depleting water resources rainwater harvesting is gaining ground everywhere at present. Rai‧ ‧ater harvesting structures are however not very common in the H..nalayan terrain. The generally fractured and foliated strata of this region does not favour this

Plate 1: Silted Bawari is the testimony of human neglect

practice. *Changar* is however an exception and rainwater harvesting is well developed in this region. *Khatri* is the traditional rainwater harvesting structure of *Changar* and is carved out in the massive, hard sandstone (Plate 3), but those constructed in pebbly sandstone are also observed. The rock types chosen for hosting these structures are free of structural weaknesses and are less permeable. This helps water storage for prolonged periods. Evaporation losses in *Changar* type of climate are extremely high and it is essential to devise some means for countering these for successful storage of water. The best-suited answer to this problem could be subsurface storage and this is what is widely practiced in *Changar*. *Khatri* is a subsurface structure with a small opening on the surface. Stairs are carved out in bedrock and these lead to the underground storage space, generally a cube of 10 feet. The stairs are generally ten in number and each is one foot high. Water percolates into *khatri* by seepage from the overlying strata, and is subsequently used for household purposes. Most *khatris* observed were designed to collect water from seepage in order to retard siltation and also to ensure water quality.

Plate 2: Breakdown of social mechanism of maintenance has led to the growth of vegetation in Bawari

Plate 3: Khatri : Rainwater harvesting structure of Changar

Direct runoff is not allowed into these structures and diversion channels are made above the entrance of the structure. *Khatri* water is not generally used for drinking. These structures are also called *talai* and *kufri*.

Table 8.2: Account of the water sources in some villages of Changar

Village	*Number of families*	*Bawaris*	*Khatris*	*Taps*
Fareha	14	1	3	
Rihari	15	4	2	3
Bamdiara	20	1	2	1
Thatti	14			1
Bahalan Kurd	22	1	5	3
Bahalan Kala	5	1	2	2
Lihas	12	1		
Daklehad	24	3	1	
Kwali	27	2	4	3
Karal	13	1		
Rihari	9	5		1
Fulwari	8	2	3	2
Jol	9		4	
Upper Mora	8	3		2
Tiala	16		4	4
Badog Lahad	26	2	4	2
Sudra Lahad	20	1		2
Silah	13	2		3
Ambada	67	4		4
Average per village	18	1.8 ~ 2	1.8 ~ 2	1.7 ~ 2

Source: ERA, Khundia

On an average the *khatri* has a storage capacity of around 30,000 to 1,00,000 litres. The evaporation losses from these are minimal and the water is stored for long duration and is replenished by occasional rains. These serve the household requirements of the masses in the region and can rightly be designated the lifeline of *Changar*.

The number of drinking water sources in the villages for which data could be accessed are given in Table 8.2. From this data it is clear that considering the average size of the family to be around seven, the average population of the villages is around 126. Considering the average water requirements to be around 40 litres, the daily water requirements of the villages is about 5,040 litres, that can be made available easily from the surrounding *bawaris* and *khatris*.

Irrigation Purposes

Chappri

These are small depressions in the hill side (Plate 4) generally at the slope break. Water collects in these during the rains and is used for feeding the animals and for irrigation later on. Besides providing water, *chappri* enhances recharge of groundwater, retards quick runoff and thus erosion. Disruption of *chappri* has led to the depletion in the yields of the downstream *bawaris*. These structures are also observed in the Garhwal Himalayas, where these are termed *chaal*. These are generally clay lined; *pukki chappri* is also observed in *sappar* (Plate 5). While enhancing the storage capacity of the *chappri* care has to be taken to ensure that the clays at the base of these do not get disturbed so that there is no leakage of water.

Khu

At many places in the *Changar* the water table is relatively shallow. It is at these places the sub-surface water is utilised for irrigation by digging wells at specific locations. Water is generally lifted from these wells by load and bucket method. *Khu* are generally stone lined, while the undeveloped wells are called *dungali* (Plate 6). These are traditional dugwells of *Changar*. The traditional genius utilised for locating the depth of the water table could not be traced. In some cases the water was reportedly struck accidentally and these sites were later developed into *khu* or *dungali*.

Tank

Tanks are used for harvesting the rainwater and also for storing the diverted water at appropriate locations so that it could be conveniently used for irrigation. These are generally stone and cement lined. At present many farmers use them for storing the water lifted from the nearby channels.

Plate 4: Chappri at slope break

Plate 5: Pukki chhapri in sappar

Plate 6: Dungali with load and bucket arrangement to lift water

Bundhs

These are generally constructed at the slopebreak in seasonal *nalas* for storing the rainwater for the lean periods. The storage capacity of these structures diminishes soon due to siltation and lack of proper management strategy. Construction of a series of bundhs along the slope could store a huge amount of water besides enhancing the recharge of the springs in the downstream area.

Some More Options

In the changed scenario the village community is exposed to many new options that were not known before. There are taps that provide water but the social acceptability of taps in the rural areas is relatively low. People that have access to tap water were observed to collect drinking water from the nearby *bawari* whose water is considered pure. With the growth of technology handpumps are being installed almost everywhere. The water from the handpump is considered pure and is used for drinking purposes. LDPE tanks are also being used to harvest water during the rains. The shallow soil profile and the rocky substratum however create problems in the construction of these tanks. Due care should be taken to reduce the evaporation rates from the tanks. Locally available abundant supply of bamboo can be used for this purpose in a cost effective manner.

On an average there are two *bawaris* and *khatris* in every village. Daily drinking water requirements of the village average around 5,040 litres. The two *bawaris* alone can supply 28,800 litres of water daily. Average rainfall in the region is 1200 mm and there are around 18 houses in every village. On an average the covered area of each house is estimated to be around 40 sq m. If the rainwater on the roofs is harvested with the help of split-bamboo pipes and collected, it augments the daily supply of water by another 2367 litres. These data show that the villages of *Changar* have a substantial daily surplus of water that comes to 26,000 litres. There would still be a huge surplus water for routine household needs even after satisfying the animal population of the village. We have not yet added to this surplus the water from other sources like *khatri, khu* and the others. This excess water can be used for irrigating the nearby fields. This data shows that the ancestors in *Changar* devised a technique that can sustain the entire population without any problem. The problems have been created by the enhanced dependence upon tap water, breakdown of the social mechanism for the maintenance of the traditional structures and failure to make innovations in the management of the available resource. For a sustainable solution of the water related problems of *Changar* in a cost effective manner the traditional water harvesting structures have to be incorporated in the routine preview of IPH.

People's Initiatives for Wasteland Reclamation

During the summer the diurnal temperature variations in *Changar* are large. These extremes in climate often enhance the rates of erosion in this region. The soil in this region is generally shallow and erosion by the forces of nature often exposes the hard bedrock, referred to as *sappar* (Plate 7). As in the hills elsewhere the area that is available for production is under severe pressure from various quarters and in order to enhance the biomass production the population is under pressure to enhance the area under production. Any strategy that could reclaim the *sappar* land could add to the biomass production of the area besides enhancing the rates of recharge and decreasing the erosion rates. Not that the people of the area have not made any attempt in this direction; they do realise the seriousness of the problem and are trying their best to reclaim the land. There are many un-narrated success stories hidden in the region and what is needed is to learn from these experiences and to devise a large scale assault on this problem.

Sappar is devoid of any soil and therefore vegetal cover and thus exposed to blunt erosion by the forces of nature. The movement of water has smoothened these surfaces further. Having been deprived of vegetal cover these surfaces are exposed to direct solar radiation and the diurnal temperature variation is high.

Any developmental task in this region has to focus on the problem of *sappar* that constitute a major portion of the wasteland. If a method could be devised to bring these surfaces under cultivation the available land area under cultivation can increase significantly. Not that the people are not taking initiatives in this

Plate 7: *Sappar* with trees growing behind the retention walls erected by the people

direction. The brains of the people are constantly working to upgrade their environment. As is common, the hill folk are uncompromising and laborious; so are the people over here and we salute their ingenuity. We have to learn from their experiences and devise a model that can be replicated and is capable of bringing these *sappars* under vegetal cover in a short time and of course in a cost effective manner. Such an effort would result in the following:

- decreased rates of erosion
- decreased run-off
- decreased wasteland
- increased productive land
- increased fodder and fuelwood supply
- increased recharge and hence the water availability

The *sappars* are generally observed on the bedding slopes of the country rocks (Siwaliks). These are therefore found more frequently on the northern slopes, rather than on the southern. This example goes against the conviction that the northern slopes are more thickly forested than the southern ones.

Fishing Sediments with Retention Walls

Many examples were gathered from the villages of *Changar* where the people both in their individual and collective capacity have erected retention walls in the concave slopes of the barren tracts (*sappar*) to collect the sediment from the runoff. Over time erosion products have been caught up behind these walls and consequently the vegetation has propagated over the wasteland. A most impressive example was observed in Balera village. This village has an old co-operative farming society and the reclamation work has taken place with the efforts of the society. It was in 1960 that two retention walls were erected in the concave slope of *sappar* above the village. These walls were two metres high, 30 metres long and were constructed with locally available stone. Encouraged by the positive results of their effort two more walls of similar dimensions were erected in 1965-66. The slope of the *sappar* here is 32° and approximate distance between the walls is 25 metres. Over the years these walls have been silted with the sediments eroded by the action of the moving water; as reported it took around 20 years for these structures to fill. As at present an area of around 300 square metres is reclaimed by these efforts (Plate 8). Encouraged by their collective endeavours small walls have been constructed by individuals in the vicinity of their houses in Balera and the sediment caught up supports trees (Plate 7). This amply reflects the level of motivation of the people and their belief in their own destiny.

At Dhatti it is the individual zeal of an innovative farmer, Purushottam Chand that has reclaimed the *sappar* by erecting the retention walls. A large area has been reclaimed by him. Similarly on the left bank of Drugh Khad near Jarundi *sappar* has been reclaimed by erecting retention walls.

In many cases the wall that was erected for rain water harvesting has outlived its purpose and land has been reclaimed by siltation. Same was observed at several places: Balera, Lahru Chamar Kuli. In the latter case breakdown of the social arrangement of raka system (watchman) led to the abandonment of the once fertile land due to infestation by animals. Over the years the irrigation system has been silted. In the reclaimed marshy land *Bacopa monariai* (*brahmi*) was observed to be thriving (Plate 5).

Pitting and Plantation

The technique employed by Shaligram, a weaver by profession, of Bal village is rather innovative and relatively result oriented. Unfortunately he was given a *patta* in an absolutely degraded *sappar* land. The attitude of the officials did not discourage the ingenious spirit of Shaligram and using his innovative approaches he converted the wasteland into a farm and even constructed a house out of the revenue generated from it.

He literally dug out bench terraces out of his sloping lands (>30°). Mixing the ground rock mass with the soil imported from the surrounding field he planted grasses on it. Once the fertility and moisture holding capacity of the soil was regained, he started to raise a variety of crops on these lands. In the steeper tracts he has made pits in the *sappar* and filled these by the soil brought from the surrounding fields. The mulberry trees planted by him in these pits are thriving and he is quite encouraged by the results. He is confident that his strategy can bring large *sappar* areas under tree cover. The technique no doubt gives quick results but has the

Plate 8: Wasteland reclamation efforts at Balera

demerit that only the pitted area is reclaimed. Moreover the pits do not catch the sediments running down, unless specifically directed by some earth or stone work.

An Integrated Approach

The gestation period of the retention wall method is long, it is not well suited for the convex slopes while pitting covers only the area pitted; an integrated approach is therefore needed. Any single strategy is not capable of reclaiming the area quickly and in a bid to multiply the effects we have to blend various techniques together. Retention walls serve the purpose on the concave slopes and the height of the wall and the distance between these is a function of the slope. But all slopes are not concave and in such areas pitting can be mixed with staggered trenching. The pits however may not trap the sediments and therefore retention walls can be erected in small concave enclaves.

In order to reduce the gestation period and bring large areas under vegetal cover the strategy of Saligram can be employed behind small retention walls. Capital investments in this strategy would be rather low and the results would be quickly observable. This strategy can be blended in the reclamation plan. Under this strategy the depth of the foundation of the walls can be considerably reduced as after filling with imported soil the area does not have to face the direct vigour of running water flowing over it.

Overall plantation of taller plants might not give the desired results and therefore it is advisable to introduce local pioneering species in the staggered trenches and on the retention wall together with some bushes and grasses. In the pits and in the land reclaimed behind the retention walls taller plants can be introduced.

These efforts are designed to change the barren face of *Changar*. The ideas expressed are based on the innovations of the local people and further innovations are always welcome.

"The indigenous knowledge of various parts of the nation needs documentation and promotion, and the ingenious spirit of the grassroots level entrepreneurs needs to be appreciated, promoted and propagated for better resource management in the rugged hills of the Himalayas. Promotion of these is easy at the ground level as the masses accept these with open arms. Moreover the technology involved, though hard to explain, is friendly enough with the end users. Promotion of these techniques would encourage grassroots level entrepreneurs and resource management would be better accomplished in this terrain."

The Mighty Himalayas
Seemed to
Symbolize
The Almighty himself,
And the Ganges
Looked as if
She were overflowing
With Milk

9
Forest Fires in the Himalayas*

Studies reveal that roughly 175 million acres of forest and grasslands are ravaged by fire each year. It is estimated that 80 acres of rain forest disappear every minute in the world and less than one-third of the world's original rain forest remains. The amount of destruction caused by forest fires depends upon the type of forest fire. The crown fires spread to the upper branches and consume the entire plant community. The biotic community needs to be regenerated. The surface fires burn the litter layer, but are not as destructive as crown fires. Studies suggest that the burn out of the litter layer by surface fires could avert crown fires. The ground fires consume the organic matter of the forest floor and also burn into the underlying soil itself. The creeping fires occur even in the absence of the ground cover or undergrowth mostly in the summer nights without any strong wind. Studies reveal that in India there is a predominance of ground fires as compared to the crown fires.

Fire is not new to the fragile Himalayan terrain as are other natural disasters and the fire season in the Chir pine forests begins in the first week of May or even earlier and ends in June, while in the Deodar zone the fire season starts in May and ends in June. Devastating fire has broken out in the forests of Uttarakhand (hills of Uttar Pradesh) this season (1999) and that too a bit too early (Plate 21). The region had not witnessed the usual winter rains which had resulted in an abundance of absolutely dry foliage in the forest all around with little moisture content. The stage was virtually set for a fire and accidental sparks have ignited

---

* This article is co-authored with Dr. Sudip Paul and Dr. R.K. Pant of Wadia Institute of Himalayan Geology, Dehradun and is the result of the fieldwork undertaken by the second author (PR) with the former in Garhwal and with the latter in Kumaun in March - April 1999. Authors acknowledge financial assistance from DST New Delhi and WIHG Dehradun.

devastating fires in the entire region.

Fires are regular features in this region and the devastating fires usually break out in four-year cycles—the previous in the series took place in 1995. This fire destroyed 93,000 hectares of forests. The fire this year is even bigger and has engulfed the entire region. With no signs of rains in the near future the fire has already gutted about 60,000 hectares of forests. The entire Uttarakhand region is in the grip of fire that is spreading fast to newer places. The fire is observed to begin at diverse localities and does not have geographical continuity. Such fires cannot be initiated without human involvement. The magnitude of this fire was assessed during the two stints of fieldwork undertaken in Kumaun-Garhwal Himalaya in March-April 1999 during which both crown and ground fires were observed in the region; the latter however predominated.

There was a cover of thick smoke all around in the region and visibility had dropped to less than a kilometre, specially in the morning hours. The scenic beauty of the Himalayan terrain, snow clad mountains and lush green valleys, were nowhere visible and even the slopes across the valley were barely seen. The abundance of dust and ash in the atmosphere scattered sunlight and the sun was observed as a red ball for most part of the day. The region had not experienced bright sunlight for weeks together. During the morning hours breathing was hard and eyes itched in the smoky environment. Day time temperatures in the hills were observed to shoot up abnormally and the glaciers had begun to ablate relatively early.

Fire had driven the wildlife out of the forests in search of safer grounds. Tigers were encountered in the region on the road side even before dusk. Deprived of food these animals were reportedly preying upon the cattle population of the region and even threatened humans living in tents after the earthquake disaster (March 29, 1999 with epicentre at Chamoli).

Both the masses and the officials well understand the implications of the fire, that usually has a devastating effect, upon their day to day life and upon the environment. But the irony is that significant efforts from any quarter are not forthcoming to control this fire. A majority of the people as well as the administration have turned a blind eye to the blazing woods and fumes. The indifference of the villagers is understandable for they have been alienated and their traditional rights over the forests have been largely restricted by a series of legislations that have provided the forest officials with sweeping powers that they use to cow down the villagers. Forests that once used to be the abode of the local gods and around which were woven the fabric of socio-cultural and economic life of the local communities have been handed over to the forest department with scant regard to the needs and emotions of the local populations. These communities, having lost the rights over the management of the forests are not bothered about the welfare of the same and have turned a blind eye towards the flames. Enlightened ones in the region however agree that this attitude of the people is suicidal for it would lead to rampant shortage of fodder, fuelwood, water, timber and minor forest produce but they fail to gather enough support.

The fire was spreading to newer areas at an alarming pace and was observed to appear at diverse places. This had complicated the problem and the damage was observed with each day that passed by. The forest officials were not taking this fire seriously and were busy issuing statements playing down the scale of damage being done and highlighting the components of their World Bank aided project for fighting forest fires. There seems something seriously wrong that warrants probe into the causes of fire.

Causes of the Fire

Local People

The traditional belief of the locals that productivity of the grasses increases after a fire very often leads to firing of the grazing fields in the hills. This is the explanation that the forest department has been giving over and again for the present fire. The fire so initiated by the villagers in the lust for reaping more fodder, no doubt suppresses weeds but the quantum of real gain is debatable. To add to it such fires sometimes do spread to the forests but are generally supervised and restricted to the grazing lands. However the fires appearing in the regions that are inhabitated cannot be attributed to such a misadventure.

To add to it the masses have a lot at stake and they are dependent upon the surrounding forests for fuelwood, timber and fodder supply. They well realise that in the wake of a big forest fire in the surrounding forest their females have to devote more time and energy for firewood and fodder collection and further the water sources are going to be depleted. The villagers do realise these facts fully and therefore it is logical to assert that the villagers are not guilty in initiating these fires for they have nothing really to gain from them and their stakes are high in case fire breaks out. They are however guilty of consciously turning a blind eye to the blatant destruction of the forest resources.

Natural/Accidental Reasons

Many a big fire starts accidentally or owing to human neglect. In the present instance the fires were observed to appear at diverse locations and the probability of all these being accidental is extremely less.

Many people in the region attributed these fires to earthquakes and believe that these were initiated by the friction caused by boulders rolling down. This view was also held by some forest officials. Some people in Okhimath tehsil stood testimony to the fire appearing near the rockfalls just after the earthquake. Some fires may well be earthquake induced as quartzite boulders (most rockfalls are observed in quartzites that are pervaded by a number of secondary weaknesses) rolling down have the potential of initiating fire amid dry foliage but the region was in flames well before the first tremor occurred on the night of 29th March 1999 and at many places the fire was observed to appear at places that have no rockfall record.

Some people in the region claim that the fire was spreading to newer locations by rolling pinecones which had caught fire. This argument seemed sensible. Fire might have spread through this mechanism but the burden of blame cannot be solely put upon pine as nonpine forests on hilltops were also observed to be on fire.

Survival Strategy

Every population group is charged with a very strong survival instinct and innovative techniques are used in adverse circumstances. After the earthquake disaster of March 1999 the shelters of most people in the region were rendered unsuitable for habitation and the people were forced to stay out in open. In this situation both human and cattle populations were being threatened by wild beasts and fires are known to ward off wild animals. Armed with this logic some people in the region, specially in urban centres were claiming that these fires were initiated by local villagers affected by the quake in order to ward off beasts. This argument was also propagated by forest officials, fails to explain fires in the regions that are inhabitated or not affected by the quake (Kumaun Himalayas), as also those fires initiated before the earthquake.

Conspiracy or Cover-up Measures

Some of the people in the region hold a strong opinion that the fire is a well planned conspiracy against the Himalayan people and they assert that there exists a strong lobby that is bent upon teaching a lesson to the hill community and with this background they see this fire as a part of their accumulated resentment. However neither could anyone explicitly figure out any group working towards this end nor could they point out individuals working for these groups. Many in the region however claim having seen someone alien initiating fires. Unless there is proof and the local populations are totally blameless it would be unwise to put the burden of blame upon a third party based upon rumours. Moreover there seems to be no such party that is to gain.

Some people in the region claim that the fires are being initiated in a well-planned manner by the forest department itself as a face saving exercise to cover up the blunders in undertaking plantation in the region. This line of thinking is hard to write off easily but the fire is not restricted to newly planted areas alone and is spreading to well forested regions as well. May be it brings forth additional grants but it is a risky exercise in which the officials would not like to involve themselves. Though logical and based upon the experience of the masses and the attitude of the forest department this assertion is hard to digest.

There is however no denying the fact that the forest department machinery was not engaged in any sort of fire fighting exercise in the region. They were rather busy trying their best to dilute the magnitude of the fire and attributing it to other causes (earthquake/human neglect/traditional firing practice and the others). Leave apart fires in remote areas no one even cared about the fire that broke out in the forests surrounding the district headquarters of Rudraprayag on April 14th 1999. Everyone reacted to the fire as a routine phenomenon.

Mischief of the children

Many people in the region argue that these fires were the product of child play but this does not explain the fires in the uninhabitated areas. Children can set fire to an area for the sheer joy and excitement and the same can spread to forested areas, but seeing the magnitude of devastation it would be unwise to put the burden of blame on children alone.

Consequences of Fire

Whatever be the reasons of this fire this is a hard fact that fire occassionally breaks out in the forests of Uttarakhand and Himachal Pradesh and the effects are very destructive. A forest fire is injurious to forest productivity, wild life, soil, and the regeneration of new plants. The usual damage to a tree is burning of the bark and sometimes, the cellular plant tissue layer. This results in reducing the organic life of the tree. Consequently the chances of getting attacked by insects and fungi increase. This affects the quality of plant growth. Destruction of the organic matter also affects the structure of the soil. The nitrogen content in the soil gets depleted and the soil becomes hard and starts to crack, which affects the pace of regeneration. The losses that may be the result of a fire of this magnitude is enumerated below:

Biodiversity Loss

Loss of biodiversity is a cause for concern around the globe and rampant fire in the ecologically sensitive zone of the Himalayas is bound to threaten the genetic biodiversity of the region. Reports regarding the death of many a rare species have already started to trickle in and the list may well be quite long. The fire could take heavy toll of the smaller insects and other creatures that may destabilise the ecological balance. To add to this problem it is reported that the multipurpose evergreen oak trees across the region are mysteriously drying up. The reasons for this are yet to be probed but it might well be the nature's early warning to the habitants of the region to stop interfering with the Himalayan ecosystem.

Economy

As a result of the fire, fuel and fodder would become scarce in the region. Commercial fuel alternatives are unheard of in the region and competition for the left over would intensify. Besides causing inter-community conflicts this would lead to commercial selling of fuelwood and fodder (a phenomenon hitherto unheard of). In times to come people would have to invest more on fuel, fodder and timber. This would have negative repercussions on the economy of the region. Reduction in fodder would mean parting with the cattle population that would lead to instability within the agricultural linkages and hence would have a negative impact upon productivity and thus the economy.

Water

Recharge of aquifers is a function of the time for which the water stays on the surface of a particular piece of land. In the absence of foliage (burnt down during fire) the water would flow in an uncontrolled manner leading to less recharge and enhanced erosion. Forest fires are already known to have a negative impact upon the water resources of the hills. As per present statistics adequate quantities of tap water are not available to the masses and the women of the region have to spend long hours in fetching water, specially in the summers. The scenario is likely to deteriorate with the current fire and this would enhance the burden of the female populations. In the aftermath of the Chamoli earthquake most people in the region have reported that the discharge from the springs has increased. This implies that the subsurface channels have widened and the same are depleting at a faster rate. This, seemingly a good sign (water at present has appeared at places that have no record of seepage) can cause severe scarcity of water in the region in the approaching summers for most reserves would be depleted before time and during the summers even the perennial springs would dry up.

Landslides

Bereft of foliage and litter due to fire, rainwater is bound to flow downslope unhindered. This would lead to enhanced rates of mass wastage and reduced rates of groundwater recharge. To add to it the earthquake has fractured the region and lubrication due to water entering these fractures has the potential of causing devastating landslides. Such fractures were observed above Akhori, Senagarponga, Oring and Sari (to name a few). In these situations the region is exposed to the threat of severe mass wastage and preparatory exercise is warranted to ensure that nothing like a Bheti (Madhyamaheshwar valley that caused damming of the river and ravaging of three villages) slide is repeated in the region.

Green House Effect

Large scale deforestation coupled with forest fires which result in the release of green house gases is a dominant contributor to global warming. The chopping down of the trees and their burning increases the carbon dioxide and carbon monoxide as well as methane that interact with hydroxyl resulting in a loss of ozone. Scientists estimate that from 1850 to 1980, between 90 to 120 billion metric tons of carbon dioxide was released into the atmosphere from the tropical forest fires. Burning of tropical forests contribute to 2-4 gigatons or 30 percent of carbon per year. These emissions have a significant impact upon atmospheric chemistry, clouds and earth's radiant energy and influence climate on regional and global scales. Biomass burning contributes to about one-fourth of the global emissions of green house gases. The recent fires in Indonesia are said to have released as many green house gases as all the cars and power plants in Europe emit in an entire year.

Enhanced carbon dioxide and ash particles in the atmosphere would be affecting the local climate of the area besides depleting the ozone layer. Premature ablation of the Himalayan glaciers is a warning signal and should be taken seriously.

Health

Exposed to the smoke of the traditional hearth the females of the region are chronic eye and lung patients. Being exposed to heavier doses of smoke and dust in the aftermath of the fire this vulnerable section of the people of the hills is liable to succumb to eye and lung infections.

Productivity

Enhanced rates of erosion together with depleted water supply would lead to reduced productivity of the region. Despite bumper crops across the country the crops have failed in the hills for want of rains. This trend would impoverish the already poor populations of the region.

Tourism

The Himalayan region is a hot favourite amongst nature lovers and excitement seekers. Tourists flock to this region in large numbers and livelihood of thousands of people depends upon the influx of tourists. The deteriorating health of the general environment of the region would discourage people from venturing into this region. This would have a negative impact upon the economy of the region.

Forest Resources

In the wake of the fire there would be a crisis of timber, fuelwood and fodder in the region. The earthquake has rendered a large number of houses in this region unsuitable for habitation and a large volume of timber is needed for carrying out rehabilitation work. The fire is bound to add to the timber scarcity in the region. Apart from loss of minor forest produce which provide livelihood to many, this region which is starved of commercial fuel alternatives would be facing a severe scarcity of fuelwood in times to come.

Some Solutions

Whatever be the cause of the fire it is a harsh reality that there has been an immense loss to the society, government and to entire humanity. A multipronged strategy is required for controlling and wiping out the four-year fire cycle from the Himalayan region. Given below are some suggestions that could help in minimising the damage if not in obliterating fire as such.

People's Participation

Lack of people's participation in the management of the forest resources has alienated them and it is required that the masses be involved in the same. In the policies of governance of forest resources the Forest Department officials must realise that the forest actually belongs to the people of the region and that it is their duty to seek people's cooperation in the management of the same.

With active cooperation of the local communities it would be easy to detect fires, as also to control them. For this purpose the Forest Department may initiate youth groups as Fire Brigades, that would bring about awareness amongst the masses regarding the consequences of fire, would keep vigil on the surrounding forest and also help in controlling the spread of fire. More than infrastructure and finances a strong will to part with some authority is needed for this task.

Fire Lines

Fire lines were traditionally drawn to check the spread of fire. These are broad, cleared strips all around, as well as running criss-cross inside the forest at suitable intervals. These are kept clean of inflammable material during the fire season and act as barriers for advancing fire. The practice of maintaining fire lines should be revived in the Himalayan terrain in view of the recurring fires and the remoteness of the terrain that deters other fire fighting practices.

Controlled Burning

The practice of early and controlled burning of dry foliage and litter, resorted to by the Forest Department should be given priority and this work should be finished well in advance of the fire season.

Briquetting

Briquetting of biomass for commercial production of charcoal bricks should be promoted in the region as this practice has the potential of clearning the forest of inflammable material. The Forest Department can provide soft loans for this purpose to the local youth who would be gainfully employed in return. Improved methods for briquetting can be evolved to fulfil some of the fuel and heating needs of the people.

Fire Fighting Infrastructure

The economic constraints in India have hindered acquisition of sophisticated fire fighting equipment and the traditional practice of beating fire with bushes still continues. However, after the devastating 1995 fire the Forest Department acquired some costly communication and other fire fighting equipment. It is an irony that most of the money so invested seems to have gone down the drain as it has been reported during the 1999 fire that most of the equipment was found to be non-functional. The Forest Department should make sure that all the equipment so acquired is functional before the onset of the fire season and always kept in readiness.

It is hoped that with the participation of the masses the forest fires and the story of the four-year fire cycle is not repeated in this region again.

Work
Without
Faith and Prayer,
Without
Sincerity
Are Like
Artificial Flowers
Without
Fragrance

10

Tree Plantation : Fencing for Regeneration

As Frank Llyod Wright has said: Wood is a friend of mine. The best friend on earth is the tree. When we use the tree respectfully, we have one of the greatest resources of the earth. Therefore a tree whether fully grown, or a sapling, should be carefully safeguarded. For regeneration and for protection of tree saplings, it is essential to safeguard the area against cattle and human encroachment.

There are various ways of protecting trees; bio-fencing, trench fencing, wall fencing, barbed wire fencing, and social fencing. Though recorded at the end social fencing is the most potent and lasting of all. Social fencing is the practice of guarding the trees by mutually agreed actions of the people/community.

Bio-fencing

There are several plants that by their very nature can act as a barrier hedge for most cattle (and also humans). The best part of this type of fencing is that the fence in itself is of plants and adds to the greenery. It is also most cost effective.

Cacti (family *Cactacae*) of which about 1,600 species are known are useful as barriers. None of these species has poisonous or even noxious fruit when eaten in moderate quantities. The cacti with the widest distribution are the Opuntias, or more specifically the Platyopuntias (those with flat, fleshy "pads" or "joints"). Opuntias have numerous uses; their fruits are edible and contain nearly eight percent sugar, these have been used fresh and dried in making sweets and fermentable liquors. Its numerous seeds are nutritious and can be used as animal feed after grinding. Quite a few species of Opuntia are cultivated for hedge or fence around fields because they thrive in the poorest and driest soils and are very easy to propagate (just break off a pod, put in the ground and sprinkle water). Their spiky nature provides good protection against livestock.

Cereus is another important group of useful cacti, broken up into subtribes, Hylocereus, Echinocereus, and the others. Most species are not edible, but some are well known for their fragrant and beautiful flowers and sometimes large, sweet fruits. Some are arborescent with spiny ribs, others are slender, trailing or climbing type and can be used as live for bio-fencing.

Agaves (that belongs to the family of Amaryllidaceae) are succulent (with a lot of moisture) with clumps of fleshy sword like leaves. These leaves can pierce and hurt the intruder when they try to ignore the barrier made by agaves. Agaves are resistant to wind, drought and fire. Flowering may take upto 10 years, and once accomplished, the foliage clump dies, usually leaving behind suckers that make new plants. In Mexico, the agave plants are said to have some 400 possible uses besides being used as cattle barrier hedge.

Sisal hemp (*Agave sisalanerigida*) is native to Mexico but is also cultivated commercially in other parts of the world, including India, for hemp fibre. These fibres are used for making ropes, nets, hammocks, cordage, mats, and other such products. The waste is used in making paper and paper board in India. It can also be composted into an excellent fertilizer due to its high mineral content. The leaves may be fed to the cattle and the juice used as an insecticide. In Hawaii, the tall woody flower stems are used as permanent fences.

The leaves of *Agave cantale* (Bombay aloe) yield about four percent fibre that is extracted on a commercial scale in India. The fibre is used for making cordage, twines, nets etc. The plant grows well as a hedge and is useful in checking erosion. Aloes are succulents of the *Liliaccae* family. These drought tolerant plants usually have very showy flowers and are used primarily in landscaping and as houseplants. The drug aloe is extracted from several aloe species. The leaves are cut across and the juice extracted and dried. The active principle is aloin that is used to treat intestinal worms, to encourage menstruation, and as a cathartic. Barbados aloe or medical aloe (*Agave barbadensis*) has a mucilaginous fleshy stem that produces a gel used for treating burns, bites and inflammations. The gel is best used fresh from the plant or as its commercially available medicinal stable extraction (of aloe).

Ringal is another species that can be used for bio-fencing. It is a local hill bamboo and supports ringal-based cottage industries.

Trench Fencing

Digging of trenches around plantations by manual labour or by machine is called trench fencing. The depth and width of the trench fence to be dug should ensure that it is not negotiable by cattle, goats, and the others.

Wall Fencing

Walls are often used as fence. The wall should be of sufficient height and thickness to act as an effective barrier. A wall may be made of (i) brick with mud mortar or cement mortar, and may have soil or cement lining, (ii) stone or (iii) mud namely, a soil and water mixture with some straw for binding to make it adequately strong.

Dry stone walls are common in the hills of Uttar Pradesh and act as an effective barrier to protect the plantation areas.

Barbed Wire Fencing

For this purpose wooden or iron poles are fixed into the ground and then secured by barbed wires, preferably in four parallel lines. This is however not recommended for mountain areas as it is costly, wood demanding and the steel poles are too costly and easily manipulated by graziers and others.

Social Fencing

Training and education play an important role in social fencing. The principle here is to tell the people that protection of forest / trees is in their own interest as trees provide wood, food, fuel and fodder, besides protecting the eco-system. Social fencing has existed in all societies in some form or the other. In the Himalayan terrain many practices aimed at protecting the forest wealth are observed. The most common is attaching the forests to some local deities and these are thereafter looked upon with reverence and are protected. These practices have however been forgotten, mainly due to alienation of the people from the fruits of the forest. It is the most effective form of fencing, but the masses should be motivated and assured of certain rights on the forest that they are protecting.

In actual practice, fencing can be a combination of two or more of the above systems depending upon the situation. This is left to the discretion of the people concerned; the target being Complete Protection.

Reflect !
Strive on
History is full of instances
Wherein, victory would have been
To the vanquished,
If only they had
Battled a Little Longer !
We Often Fail
For Lack of Perseverance
In Our Efforts.
We Leave our work half done
In our impatience;
Every job demands
Its quota of efforts.
Never give up too soon;
Strive on
Until You win

11

Agro-horticultural Interventions in Uttarakhand : Strategy for a Greener Tomorrow

The hill region of Uttar Pradesh, popularly known as Uttarakhand, produces a large variety of horticultural and agricultural crops. Some specific areas in Uttarakhand like the Ramgarh belt and the Chamba belt are well known for their apple and tomato crops. Likewise certain pockets in Rudraprayag, Chamoli and Pithoragarh districts are known for their citrus crops. In much the same way in certain pockets in Tehri and Uttarkashi districts seasonal and off-season vegetable crops such as potato, ginger, chillies, peas and variety of pulses are grown. Apart from these agricultural and horticultural crops that constitute a part of the staple diet of the nation as a whole, there are certain specific agricultural produce like *manduan, jhingora, kodon, chaulain* and certain spicies like *jambu, rai, timmar, gandhraini, bhangira* and *bhang* that add flavour to the local ethnic food. It is reported that these traditional ethnic crops are rich in a variety of minerals and vitamins. However as the sturdy hill folk are assimilated into the national mainstream these traditional ethnic agricultural crops are losing their importance and are not grown as widely as before. This might affect the genetic biodiversity of the region, as these crops may well be extinct in the times to come.

Uttarakhand is home to rich biodiversity and has been traditionally renowned for its medicinal flora, a part of which adds aroma to the local cuisine and is widely in demand the world over for diverse usage. These plants were traditionally collected from the wild and traded on a small scale. With enhanced demand the pressure upon the wild output has been mounting and consequently the collection is declining. A large variety of these plants can be grown commercially in suitable climatic zones without any deterioration in the chemical constituents. Further, these wild varieties do not require very fertile soil and can well be cultivated on marginal lands that are amply available in the hilly tract. Promotion of these would add to the economic status of the masses in the region, besides opening a wide variety of new processing, pre-processing, marketing and entrepreneurial opportunities.

The region thus plays an important role in the economy of the state by providing off-season vegetables, various temperate fruits and flowers, forest based products, medicinal plants, and revenue from tourism. Industrial growth in the region is very low and agriculture is the main source of livelihood. However, the agricultural sector by itself is not capable of providing productive and full time employment owing to the constraints imposed on its development by nature. The potential of development of the agricultural sector, particularly increases in the level of productivity, are restricted by several basic problems such as geographical and topographical conditions, small size of holdings, and lack of irrigation facilities. In addition, there is lack of awareness regarding the innovations in agriculture and improved variety of inputs. Seeds, saplings and bio-manure are not readily available to the farmers in far off places of the region. Extension work has not been taken up with vigour in the region. Whatever the reasons be, the area has many reputed institutions devoted to the cause of hill agriculture and it is an irony to see that even basic agricultural implements suited to the terrain and work conditions in the hills are lacking.

Realising the importance of good quality planting material and seeds TFL/HIMCON has started an innovative Seed Bank scheme in the area around Ranichauri in Tehri Garhwal. Under this scheme the farmers are provided with adequate quantities of seeds during the sowing season under an obligation to return the same at the harvesting season. Other farm inputs are also being made available under this scheme. This scheme is being operated through the Mahila Mangal Dals and is becoming self sustaining with the collections surpassing the distributed material. This has led to the introduction of good quality and commercially important crops in the area, that were until now not grown owing to the high input costs involved. TFL/HIMCON is also introducing new high value horticultural crops and medicinal plants in the region. Kiwi and almonds are being promoted together with geranium, brahmi, aswagandha, shatavri, kuth and kutki. A four acre mother nursery called *Swastha Vatika* has been set up at Ranichauri to cater to the needs of the masses. A geranium oil extraction unit is also being installed at this site. The people of the region are reaping the benefits of these initiatives and it is proposed to undertake promotion of cottage industries in the villages in future involving women for pre-processing medicinal plants.

As a result of the prevailing climatic conditions and topography in Uttarakhand, the region has the potential to support a wide variety of temperate and subtropical fruits, medicinal plants and flowers. The elevation of the region ranges between 300 and 7000 metres above sea level and the temperature ranges from 16° to 40° C; going to subzero during winters in several pockets. Subtropical fruits like mango, litchi, banana, locat, citrus, guava, papaya, strawberry and others can be grown between 300 and 1400 metres and temperate fruits like apple, pear, peach, plum, apricot, cherry, kiwi, walnut and others can be successfully grown between the elevations of 1000 to 3000 metres above sea level.

Horticulture Guide for Uttarakhand

The importance attached to the development of horticulture in Uttarakhand is not only limited to the creation of employment opportunities and increasing the income level of the masses; it also provides permanent green cover to the soil besides acting as soil binder thereby preventing soil erosion to a considerable extent. Plantation of trees also helps in bringing back the nutrients that are actually lost and cannot be used by the field crops as a result of leaching to the deeper zones of the soil. Moreover the cultivation of fruits is labour intensive and requires a significantly larger labour force as compared to the cultivation of field crops starting from the stage of tree plantation to marketing. Thus the intensive development of horticulture in Uttarakhand could be a viable alternative strategy of development of the region. This would at the same time check the migrations of the able bodied workforce and provide gainful employment opportunities within region. Analyses have shown that the cultivation of horticultural crops (apple) provides 77 per cent more mandays of employment and returns which are 53 percent higher as compared to the cultivation of agricultural crops. However the production of apples per tree or per acre of land is found to be three times higher in neighbouring Himachal as compared to Uttarakhand, while the rates of return are four times higher in the case of the former than the latter. The prevailing differentials in the returns and productivity between these two hilly areas are by and large the result of lower level of productivity or yield rates of the trees, low levels of investment at different stages of production and marketing, lack of awareness of different marketing channels and systems and the disposal of a major proportion of produce through the contractors under the pre-harvest arrangement system in Uttarakhand.

Participatory research and development and on-farm research are important for bringing about a change in the agricultural practices in the region. Efforts in this direction should be initiated by the government, and research scientists, extension scientists/ workers, social scientists and ultimate beneficiaries have to be brought to a common platform. The on-farm research is intended to bring relevance and excellence in technologies and packages of practices. In fact all field development efforts should be like action research where promotion and observation can go side by side. For agriculture, there cannot be better experimental stations than the farms of the villagers, where besides agroclimatic considerations, the socio-economic situations can also be evaluated in the generation of technologies.

Women play a key role in hill agriculture with their involvement exceeding 80 percent. They undertake all the farm activities other than ploughing. Agricultural implements thus need improvisation to suit the terrain and the nature of the workforce. The whole strategy should revolve around the active participation of the people, particularly of women, in the fulfilment of their basic needs.

The following four initiatives are considered to be the pillars for supporting sustainable agriculture in the hilly terrain:

- Research system in the area for generating appropriate technologies
- Educational institutions for appropriately trained manpower
- Training: both short and long term for keeping the local

people abreast with latest inputs
- Extension system for farm advisory services

The extent to which the Himalayan hills are endowed with these infrastructures, will partially explain the status of development in these areas. Farm technologies are the basis for good education, training and extension and therefore research infrastructure is a basic prerequisite. Krishi Vigyan Kendras (KVKs) need to be promoted in the region. These are down-to-earth grassroots level organisations operating on the principles of teaching by doing and learning by doing. In KVKs farmers are imparted skills by participatory methods by sharing work experience, rather than conventional lectures. The field level extension functionaries are also trained in KVKs, besides farmers, farm women, school dropouts and farm youth. By design KVKs do not offer any formal certificate or diploma course so as to discourage white-collar job seekers. At present there are only a handful of KVKs in the entire Himalayan region and these are taking a relatively longer time to develop as they have not been able to get required trained manpower. The manpower recruited is largely ignorant of agricultural practices suited to the hills and the basic ground realities and is not motivated to take up the cause of the people. A mechanism for manpower development in the hills from amongst hill people has therefore to be evolved and promoted on priority basis.

No amount of agricultural and horticultural inputs can bring prosperity to the region unless strong and organised marketing of the produce is ensured. At present distress sale of the output of the commercially important agricultural and horticultural output from this region to the wholesalers from Delhi, Tanakpur, Haldwani, Bareilly and Saharanpur is common. On an average primary producers of the crop hardly get 15-20 percent of the price which the ultimate consumer has to pay for the same articles. The *modus operandi* of these big players is quite innovative and their interventions in the region start well in advance of the cropping season. They provide working capital to the farmers and get proprietary rights over the crop. The formalities of organised financing deters people from seeking loans from these sources and the finance available buys the produce at throw away prices.

Due to the linked marketing network that dictates prices, the local produce is also not cheaply available to the people in the remote regions where the purchasing power of the people is well below the prices dictated by the forces of market. The local population has to buy the produce re-transported from the mandis in the plains. The local people are not in a position to retain their crops till the time they fetch better prices, nor are there proper warehousing facilities and more importantly the food processing industry in the region is in its infancy. If developed it has the potential of deterring distress sales.

Barring a few, most of the produce from the hills is perishable in nature. Organised marketing of this produce is not being undertaken and the mediators supplying the same to the markets in the plains, reap heavy profits and the growers are barely left with anything. Difficult terrain conditions and inaccessibility cause a large portion of the crop to be destroyed. Fruit processing/ preprocessing units in key areas that produce large volumes of horticultural produce can be economically viable and bring home ample returns to the local artisans.

The fruit processing interventions undertaken by the Garhwal/ Kumaun Mandal Vikas Nigam are fraught with bureaucratic hassles and are not aimed at helping the lot of the primary producers. Rather than a stationary processing/pre-processing plant the region requires a series of mobile units that can cater to the demands of the local producer in a decentralised manner. No study has however been undertaken to access the economic viability of these units.

This background stresses the need for integrated efforts towards accessing the potential of fruit processing endeavours in the region and also to access the condition of the uphill primary producers. These endeavours need to focus attention upon the following:

- To demarcate the areas which have a seasonal excess of agricultural and horticultural produce, together with the assessment of the produce that can be available locally for processing/pre-processing.
- To study in detail the economics of horticultural crops in the region: for this data pertaining to the returns of the horticultural produce would be procured and the condition of the primary producers would be adjudged against the prevailing market prices.

- Support prices for various agricultural and horticultural produce are generally declared in adjoining Himachal Pradesh. The effect of the same has to be studied in the wake of the formation of the new state.
- The Government of Uttar Pradesh does not render any support services to the produce of its hilly region. The impact of these services upon the economy of the artisans has been studied, comparing the farmers from the region with their counterparts from Himachal.
- The traditional fruit processing practices have to be documented and the present status of the fruit/vegetable market and the gains that the local growers are reaping have to be studied.
- The economic viability of setting up a fruit processing/pre-processing unit/mobile unit has to be worked out together with the study of the economics of similar units currently operating in the region.
- Based on the studies so carried out a detailed plan for the popularisation of different horticultural species in different belts can be made.

We may
Often
Give
Without Love
But We Can
Never
Love
Without Giving

12

Landslide Hazards in Uttarakhand : The Tragedy of Kali Valley*

Landslides are a common feature in the Himalayas and often, during the monsoons, many parts of the area are cut off from rest of the world and the people inhabiting the hills have to face severe hardships. Not only are the remote areas affected; townships like Almora and Nainital have witnessed colossal losses in the past. An overwhelmingly large number of such events result from man's own acts, particularly his reckless plunder of natural resources, triggering off the havoc. Whatever the cause may be, when there is a landslide the locals have to bear the brunt. In the course of adaptation to their harsh environment the people inhabiting the fragile hilly terrain learnt by 'trial and error' to cope with these. They have also developed a symbiotic relationship with nature that guided them to settle at safe locations. But the increasing pressure of population and human interference with the landscape has significantly increased the frequency of the slides, often deceiving the instinct.

It is through the process of terrain evolution that a stage has been reached where most of the hillslopes in the Himalayas have been stabilized for normal habitation over prolonged periods. Records show disastrous consequences of human interference. Despite designating ourselves an intelligent species we do not seem to be learning from our past experiences and are busy manoeuvring these fragile slopes at an enhanced pace, which is leading to

---

* This article is co-authored by Dr. R.K. Pant of the Wadia Institute of Himalayan Geology, Dehradun and N. Juyal of Physical Research Laboratory, Ahmedabad and is the result of scientific investigations undertaken by the second author (PR) under the leadership of Dr. R.K. Pant in Kali Valley. The authors acknowledge financial assistance from Department of Science and Technology (Government of India) for this work.

colossal loss of human lives, effort and property.

Many natural processes and anthropogenic activities cause the movement of rockmass. Some of these are as follows:

Excessive Precipitation

Water destabilises earth materials in three ways: (i) the extra moisture can increase the weight of the total mass thereby creating a downslope movement, (ii) penetration of water to slip zones can provide lubrication and facilitate mass movement, and (iii) the filling of soil or rock openings with water increases pore-water pressure that in turn reduces grain-to-grain strength and lowers resistance to movement. All the three processes however act in unison to cause the landslides.

Hillslope Disturbance

Reckless engineering activity on fragile hill slopes destabilises these and causes landslides. The menace of debris disposal in such constructions causes further land degradation. The likelihood of landslides is increased whenever the hillslopes are steepened, such as it occurs with road construction, construction of buildings on sloping terrain, and in quarrying and mining.

Vegetative Changes

Landslides are aggravated by deforestation that exposes the soil to direct impact of the rainfall. Related effects are soil erosion, removing topsoil needed for agriculture, and increased dust as the windbreak effect of trees is lost. Change in the vegetal cover also alters the hydrologic regime of the region. This might result in creep, slump and slides.

Pore Water Changes

Many human activities increase water content within the earth materials, thereby changing pore-water conditions. This might be through unmanaged drains, changes in water level of the reservoirs or others, but the added water lowers the rock and regolith strength and can become critical in determining the threshold of stability.

Earthquakes

Violent shaking of the earth surface often triggers landslides. The rock mass that is in a destabilised position and is waiting for a little push marches downslope during the earthquakes, thus compounding the misery.

Recent landslides across Uttarakhand have once again brought to the forefront the vulnerability of the hill people and the fragility of the Himalayas. It has at the same time brought out severe lapses on the part of the administration that has no disaster relief methodology and as a result, the relief work gets hampered, delayed and mismanaged. Despite categorisation of the terrain as fragile the scientists are yet to gather sufficient data for some kind of predictive modelling of the disaster that can strike the region.

The tragedy that followed from the series of landslides in August 1998 was unprecedented and exposed the reality of high profile scientists and relief managers. The landslide in the heavily populated and well-known township of Nainital at the onset of the rains was just the precursor of the events to follow. The warning signal was however not taken seriously and with the build up of the monsoon, the mountains came crumbling down at many places. A series of landslides in the Okhimath tehsil of the newly created Rudraprayag district caused heavy loss of life and property and the blockade of the Madhyamaheshwar river, a tributary of the Mandakini, threatened the habitations downstream. Damming and flooding of the Himalayan rivers during the monsoons is not new, but a concrete strategy to tackle such exigencies has not been prepared. According to the Himalayan Gazetteer, a landslip fell into the Gudiyar Tal, one of the feeders of Birahi Ganga in 1868 and drained out half the lake causing 73 deaths along the banks of Alaknanda. The same was repeated in 1893. In 1970 and 1978 landslides blocked river courses and eventually the breach caused heavy loss of life and property. Though the lake has not been breached this season, a series of landslides in the region have taken the death toll to over 100. A number of villages have been ravaged and tracts of agricultural lands have been devastated. Statistics show that the weaker sections of the society that were occupying the marginal lands were worst hit. Summary of the losses incurred around Okhimath is as follows:

- 29 villages affected
- 1395 families affected
- 9752 persons affected
- 101 human lives lost
- 422 cattle heads lost
- 411 hectares of agricultural land lost
- 10 to 90 per cent crops lost
- 301 houses lost
- 519 houses damaged
- Rs. 14 million worth of private property lost
- Rs. 27 million worth of government property lost

Immense loss was caused to habitations, agricultural fields, cattle and infrastructure facilities. More than 5000 people were forced to take shelter in the relief camps set up in the area. There was a severe shortage of supplies and a large number of tourists and pilgrims were stranded at different places. They had no means of communicating their whereabouts and welfare to their anxious relatives at home. Reports say that more than five thousand pilgrims were stranded at Govindghat alone. Despite supplies from various sources reaching the region and the army of voluntary workers, incessant rains and remoteness of the affected population hampered the pace of relief work. A large number of the people of the region that were soon to witness the wrath of snow were rendered homeless. Providing safe housing to these people is an uphill task that requires immense resources and managerial skills.

The worst was however yet to follow; the twelfth batch of the Kailash - Mansarovar *yatra* was buried under the thick cover of landslide debris amid the ferocity of Kali ravaging Malpa. More than 200 people died and the rescue work in the remote hilly terrain was severely hampered by the bad weather conditions and inaccessibility. This tragedy was highlighted in the media and nearly shifted public attention from the Okhimath tragedy. Even at Malpa no one cared for the poor locals buried or swept away by the Kali. They were sidelined in the rescue operations with VIPs of the *yatra* getting most of the attention. It may be noted that most of the locals involved in the tragedy were poor labourers and mule attendants that carry the burden of the pilgrims. These people regularly risk their lives in the rugged and hazard prone terrain of the Himalayas to make both ends meet. The death of an earning member means havoc for the dependants; yet there is no news of the whereabouts of many *Mangal Singhs*, whose dear ones are still waiting impatiently for them to return.

No doubt the loss of life and property at Malpa is colossal, but for the inhabitants of the Kali valley, natural disasters are not new, though the people have for the first time witnessed large-scale administrative manoeuvres. The administration has never cared to heal the wounds of the people in a participatory manner and vague awards were given in the past in lieu of the losses incurred. The apathy of the administration has led to the destruction of the largest and most thriving village of the region, Garbyang. This region in the pre-1962 era was one of the most flourishing tracts of Kumaun and the entire economy of the region, down to the *tarai* was intricately interwoven with the migratory traders of the region. With the disruption of trade no attempt was made on the part of the government to revamp the economy; a short sighted and narrow-minded decision to declare the border inhabitants as tribals was taken recourse to. Implicit in this arrangement is the ignorance of the authorities regarding the terrain and the people. This measure cut off these people from the cultural mainstream of the region of which they were an essential and inseparable part, besides permanently destabilising the economy of the region.

Trekking in the hazardous Kali valley (Byans valley in local parlance) used to start right from Tawaghat (Fig. 12.1), but a badly made road up to Mangati cuts short the arduous climb to Narain Ashram and one can reach Bindakoti (2378 m), via Garbha by the end of the day. From Bindakoti it is a tiring and steep descent upto Lakhanpur along the Kali. The path ahead follows Kali through a narrow gorge, where one has to often revert back if mules are coming from the other direction. This region witnesses frequent rockfalls and there are virtually no safety measures. Though the authorities have denied having undertaken any blasting operations in the region to construct a road, the sound of heavy blasting often filled the atmosphere and added to the horror of the journey. Malpa itself is situated on the landslide debris and the Kali was actively undercutting the entire area that once occupied the Kumaun Mandal Vikas Nigam (KMVN; the organisers of the Kailash-Mansarovar Yatra) camps. The village was situated at some higher location. It was a threatening view of the Kali from the overhanging rock mass near the KMVN camp. There were no safety measures

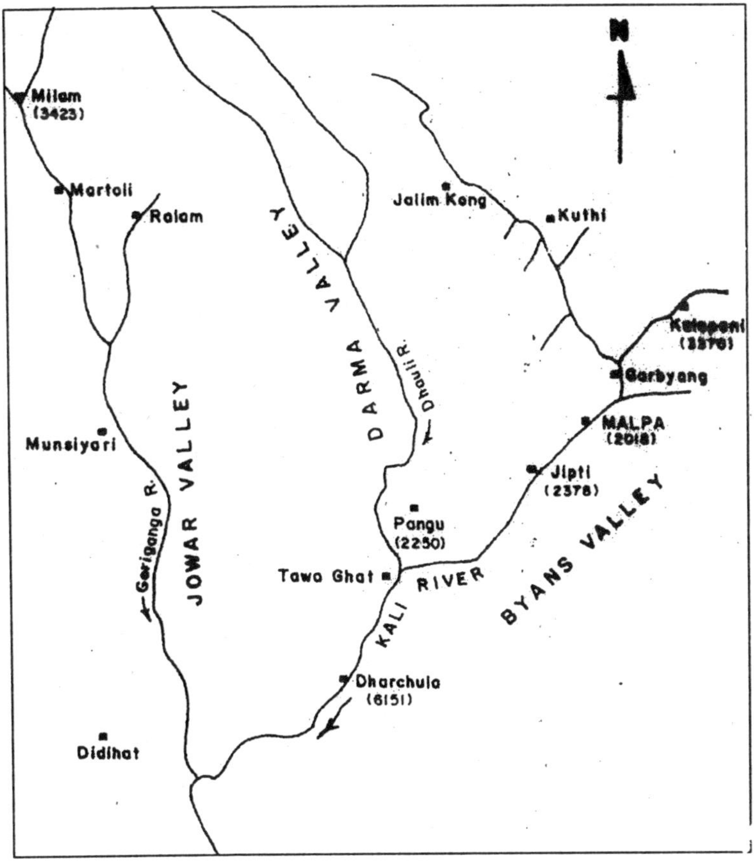

Fig. 12.1 : Location map of Kali valley

taken and had it not been the landslide the undercutting would have resulted in a tragedy in times to come.

Ahead of Malpa huge lacustrine deposits are encountered at Lamyari that stand testimony to the fact that the river course at this place was once blocked by landslides, resulting in a lake in which these sediments were laid down. Active deformation is observed in these deposits that stands testimony to the creeping mass. Blockade of the river course in the valley is not new and Trail (Himalayan Gazetteer) observes that the frequency of mountain slips (*paira* in local parlance) render the preservation of the road an object of constant toil for the locals. By accidents of this type, the course of the river is sometimes completely blocked for two or three successive days, and every part of the pathway within its reach, is swept away by the accumulated torrent and not an atom of soil is left on which to found a new road; on forming the latter a deviation from the old line and level becomes necessary in consequence. The passes, taking their whole extent, may be said to be barely practicable.

Ahead of Budhi, across the Chialekh pass (3350 m) where the Kali was blocked by morainic deposits in the past is situated the village of Garbyang that once occupied a vast expanse of flat ground overlooking the river. The lacustrine deposits forming flat ground at Garbyang provided a vantage point for the people whose economic activity revolved around flourishing trade with Tibet (*Hundes* in local parlance) with a strong backing of livestock. Today the surface is broken into various undulating terraces with irregular surfaces often dipping away from the riverside. The houses with ornate woodwork have tilted and many have been consumed by sinking ground and appear at different levels. The administration has done nothing to restore the village and has devised an easy alternative of relocating the people to an alien land around Sitarganj (in *tarai*). This amounts to the alienation of a culture. This approach is not new; these people who were basically traders were in the past granted tribal status as a poor substitute for their economic loss. Most fertile valleys (e.g. Johar) in this part of the Higher Himalayas are deserted as a result of the mass exodus of people to far off lands subsequent to the disruption of trade. This reflects on the short sightedness and apathy of the authorities to the problems of the locals.

The houses at Garbyang were observed to be ornate and double storied (Himalayan Gazetteer); subsidence so evident presently (Plate 9 and 10) was not observed then (in 1883). There is however an account of the Chhindu village near Garbyang that was swept away by the Kali. The villages of Jakti and Siti belonging to the Garbiyals upstream of Garbyang were also observed to be

Plate 9: Land subsidence is taking toll of the houses at Garbyang. The entire ground floor has been consumed and upper edge of the door is observed at ground level

Plate 10: Architecture of the houses being modified by sinking ground

unhabitated and seemed to be destroyed by landslips (Himalayan Gazetteer).

The locals are truly aware of the fact that the land on which the village is situated is reclaimed from an ancient lake. They firmly believe that their deity *Namjung* made a small opening at the base of Chialekh, towards the western side of the valley allowing the lake to drain out. It is said that Garbyang village once occupied a flat surface that is terraced today. The ground started sinking sometimes after 1962 when the trade with Tibet got disrupted. The exact date of the commencement of the sinking process is however hard to ascertain.

Garbyang is a basin with a NE-SW trend comprised of a flight of lacustrine terraces formed by land subsidence. The village is located towards the northern flank of the basin. The relict lake deposits (varves) are terraced and these run parallel to the valley (E-W). The morphology of the terraces suggests that these are tectonogenic with sharp vertical breaks. The degree of preservation is good towards the west while towards the central part and in the east these merge together. The central part of the terraces is undergoing extensive slumping. The axis of slumping coincides with the concavity of the Kali meander that has been pushed towards the north due to the avalanching of colluvial debris from the southern mountain range.

Four distinct episodes of tectonic disturbances are observed in the *in situ* varve succession at Garbyang and are attributed to seismicity in the region, caused by movement along a Tethyan Fault. Radiocarbon chronology suggests that the lake had come into existence much before 40,000 years BP and was in existence till 10,000 years BP. The four tectonic events are restricted between 36,600 and 28,600 years BP.

Deformation in the mass which had slid down was observed on the right bank of Kali to the south of the *in situ* section. These folds are the manifestations of the drag along the slide plane and are similar to those observed at Lamyari. These deformations are the product of gravity gliding alone and the mass has been sliding down from N-NE along the weak plane parallel to the valley walls. Such weak planes were also observed in Garbyang village, where along an E-W oriented fault plane the sediments have sunk as much as 4 metres at the eastern end. The displacement at the western end is however of the order of 20 metres. This plane is observed for

150 metres and is associated with the Dharchula earthquake of 1980. Erosive forces have not yet concealed the scrap and the surface is still fresh. Houses that were once at one level are now observed at different levels across this fault line (Plate 11.

The Kali river flowing E-W is eroding the varve deposits from the base and thus the mass from the north is moving down. This movement expresses itself in the folding of the sediments. This movement is threatening the very existence of Garbyang village (Plate 12). The pace of this movement can be checked by protecting the northern bank of the river by mechanical measures.

Another episode of river blockade in the Kali valley is witnessed around the Kali - Tinkar confluence, upstream of Garbyang. Thick deposits are observed over here along the Tinkar and the village of Chhangru (in Nepal across Kali) situated over these deposits houses a number of caves that reportedly have remains of an entire population. Locally called *Chhangru Rakha* these caves have a large repository of artifacts and remains of the people killed suddenly, as suggested by their postures. The cause of the deaths is buried under the veil of myth that says that the village is cursed and as the households exceed fifty the tragedy would be repeated. This keeps the families undivided and well within fifty.

In the wake of landslide tragedies that have occurred in the region, scientific institutions and the state government have set up teams to review the situation and probe the causes of the slides. What is however needed is a thorough study using modern techniques and extensive fieldwork. Backed by the data so collected high hazard prone zones in the region have to be identified and a mitigative strategy should be worked out taking into consideration the views and beliefs of the locals which have so far been considered redundant by the experts and bureaucrats alike. It should be remembered that before independence the locals managed their affairs drawing from their experience. The road to Kailash-Mansarovar, as the legend says was constructed under the personal supervision of the *Kasdesadhipati* (king of *Kasdes*) Baz Bahadur Chand (1638-78), to facilitate trade and administration (Himalayan Gazetteer).

The entire Kali valley is vulnerable and inaccessible and requires serious studies immediately. Existing studies indicate that there are many places in the valley that warrant quick measures

Plate11: Houses that were once at one level have attained different levels due to differential ground subsidence across a weak zone running E-W.

Plate 12: Ground subsidence is taking its toll and rich cultural heritage of Garbyang is being razed to the ground

on the part of the government, so as to avoid repetition of the tragedy in future. Apart from the pilgrims en route to Kailash Mansarovar the safety of the habitations of the region needs to be given due importance; the villages of Garbyang and Lamyari need particular attention.

Over the years the attitude of the bureaucracy has alienated the masses in this region. There is an urgent need to rebuild the confidence of these people in the governance of India. These people value their tradition and braving all odds large families gather regularly in their ancestral houses even today to participate in the baptism (*badani pooja*) of the eldest son during the monsoons. These people care a lot about their surroundings and are willing to participate in every effort of the government to conserve its ecosystem. They are not satisfied with the award of land in alien regions and want their own lands to be rescued by immediate and collective endeavours. The efforts have however to be initiated by the government.

In the wake of massive losses incurred in Uttarakhand, experts are attributing the present landslides to diverse causative factors; deforestation and overexploitation of the resources, past earthquakes that weakened the rocks, subsurface anomalies and so on. The enthusiasm of the scientific community, together with their concern for the region and its people is worth appreciation but they must ensure that their predictions so closely followed by media and the people alike do not cause a sense of insecurity and panic. Deforestation and overexploitation of the resources however need to be given a second thought, at least in the Kali valley. The entire valley has been depopulated and the traffic even after the resumption of trade in recent years has never reached anywhere near the past levels. In the earlier times thousands of sheep, mule and yaks used to frequent the track along with the people engaged in trade. Now the quantum of trade is severely reduced and there is no pressure upon the resources. Deforestation is not observed in Byans valley; the slopes are pristine and whatever happened was a natural phenomenon; may be triggered by excessive rainfall/ cloudburst.

Besides thoroughly probing the causes of the slide, a comprehensive strategy for relief and rescue also needs to be prepared keeping in view the fragility of the region that often destroys conventional infrastructure. The bureaucracy should be well versed with the relief and rescue operations that they have to undertake. In any event of tragedy the locals, well acquainted with the terrain can be the best rescue workers. As reported the surrounding villagers reached Malpa the same day, but for the lack of proper anchoring equipment they could not approach the site of the tragedy. Had these people been provided some emergency rescue equipment the death toll probably might not have been so high.

At the same time the pilgrims and trekkers should be adequately briefed of the risks involved in the trek and should be encouraged to adhere to safety norms and carry along emergency rescue equipment. Infrastructure and communication facilities should also be provided en route in remote areas.

It has been flashed over and again by the media that a new route to Kailash-Mansarovar is under consideration; but it may well be remembered that this is not the pilgrim route alone. It is the traditional trade route of the region and the foundation of the once thriving trade of Uttarakhand. Even today an overwhelmingly large proportion of the locals is engaged in this trade. Before actually considering these suggestions the government should have a concrete plan for providing alternative livelihood to these people and ensure that the region does not witness another post-1962 scene.

People's participation can play an important role in evolving a viable solution to the problem. This would not disrupt the economy of the region and at the same time losses would be minimised.

God
Is Not an
'Object'
To Be Found
Outside
Stop
Searching
"Discover"
Him
Within

13

Air Pollution : The Case of Dehradun

Described in the *Rig Veda* amongst *panchatatva* (*Kspit* : earth; *apa* : water; *teg* : engergy; *vayu* : air; and *akasa* : space) and regarded sacred and life giving, AIR is being polluted at an alarming pace and is a cause of concern to the present day population as it has wide ranging ramifications that threaten the very existence of life on this planet. Air pollution is defined as the presence in air of chemical elements or compounds in sufficient quantity to constitute injury to health or life over short or long time periods. The problem of air pollution is mounting in the present age and even the smaller towns are not spared. Situated in the foothills of the Himalayas, Dehradun, a small township of northern India, is known for its beautiful climate impressed by which the British established a number of premier organisations and training centres over there. With mounting population the natural environment of Dehradun is showing signs of decay. Lime kilns, vehicular pollution, dust from unpaved roads and large scale captive power generation are the main reasons for air pollution in the city. The population of the city has risen alarmingly and it has put severe pressure on the natural resources of the region. The city was never planned to support the mammoth population it has today and the entire infrastructure is on the verge of collapse.

Access to abundant limestone reserves in the vicinity and ease of transportation led to the establishment of a large number of lime kilns in the area. Armed with outdated technology that took as long as three months for calcination these kilns polluted the natural environment of the city. In the year 1995 as many as 114 lime kilns were operating in and around the city and none was fitted with pollution control devices. After the landmark decision of the apex court in World Savior v/s Union of India it was made mandatory for the kilns to adopt pollution control measures. At present the number of kilns is reduced to 59 and all of them have installed pollution control devices (tar traps and wet scrubbers); moreover the improved technology adopted by the kiln operators has reduced the calcination time to 72 hours.

Despite stringent measures set by the pollution control authorities there still remain certain constraints. There are no means of checking the pollution during the charging of the kiln that is done manually. Power supply in the town is not regular and it hampers the operation of the pollution control devices. Power is required to ensure that the emissions from the kiln are pollution free and regular power failures leave the kiln operators with no other option but to discharge the untreated emission into the atmosphere. Captive power generation using generators are not permitted as it would add to the pollution. To add to it the maximum permissible limit for suspended particulate material (SPM) from the chimney exhaust is set at 100 μg/cu m, that is well above the maximum permissible for sensitive areas. The cumulative effect of a number of kilns operating in the vicinity is that the SPM concentration in the area is rendered much higher than that is permissible and the controlling authorities have no regulatory powers. The upper limit for the SPM therefore needs to be lowered.

The kilns burn huge volumes of fossil fuel (~3 metric tonnes of steam coal is required to be burnt for producing 5 metric tonnes of lime), but still these are not the sole culprits for all the atmospheric pollution in the city and as brought out by the sample surveys most people consider vehicular pollution to be the prime cause of atmospheric pollution. When asked to point the single culprit, the choice of all invariably fell upon the *Vikrams* (Diesel operated autorickshaws). The city of Dehradun has more than 1.3 lakh vehicles, out of which the *Vikrams* account for a mere 2500. The people of Dehradun agree that the city does not have an efficient transport system and banning *Vikrams* would adversely affect the movement of the masses.

The majority of the roads in Dehradun city are badly maintained and most are unpaved. Considering the number of vehicles in the city, the condition of the roads is miserable. This accounts for enhanced SPM concentrations in the atmosphere. The seasonal data of SPM levels testifies this fact for the SPM levels show fluctuations with the distribution of rains and are particularly low during the monsoon months. To add to these problems, the city faces severe power crisis. Captive power generation is therefore rampant. Almost all the commercial and government establishments resort to generators, besides a large proportion of the upper middle and upper income households in the city. This adds heavily to atmospheric pollution. Moreover the seasonal influx of people during the summer months also adds to the problem.

The pollution figures for the city are available in terms of SPM, NO_2 and SO_2 that the State Pollution Control Board is monitoring (Fig. 13.1, 13.2). From the data available it is hard to place the blame upon a single source of pollution. In case of diesel vehicles, the experts claim, the problem is more of SPM while the NO_2 and SO_2 emissions from these are insignificant (their concentration being low in diesel itself, ~ 0.5%). In the case of petrol driven vehicles the SO_2 and NO_2 emissions are particularly high while the SPM emissions are within tolerable limits. As the pollution data clearly show that the NO_2 and SO_2 levels in the city are within tolerable limits, the experts hold the diesel vehicles mainly responsible for the atmospheric pollution in the city. This is an important conclusion in the light of the fact that most diesel vehicles are commercial vehicles and their maintenance is generally poor. This causes them to emit higher levels of pollutants.

Seasonal fluctuations in the pollution data from the two monitoring stations at Dehradun city (Raipur Road that has most of the kilns in the vicinity and the Clock Tower that is the main market of the city) for the year 1996-97 show the following facts:

- SO_2 levels at the two monitoring stations show similar trends (correlation coefficient 0.4) except for the season between July - October. The SO_2 concentration is generally high at Raipur Road except in the months of March, July and September.
- The SO_2 concentrations at both the stations are well within the acceptable limit of 30 μg/cu m.
- The trend in NO_2 levels at the two observation points is mostly similar (correlation coefficient 0.54).
- The NO_2 concentrations at Raipur Road are generally high except for the months of October and November.
- At both the stations the minimum concentration of NO_2 is observed in November. However, the maximum levels are observed in April in Raipur Road and in January at the Clock Tower.

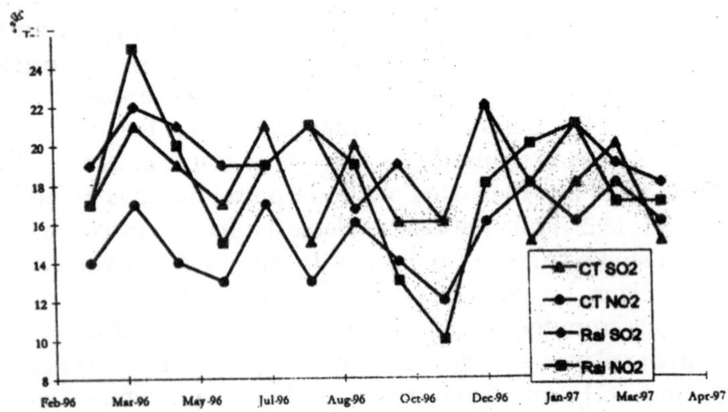

Fig. 13.1: NO_2 and SO_2 levels (in µg/cu m) at the two observation points; Raipur Road (Rai) and Clock Tower (CT) at Dehradun during 1996-97
(*Source*: U.P. Pollution Control Board, Dehradun).

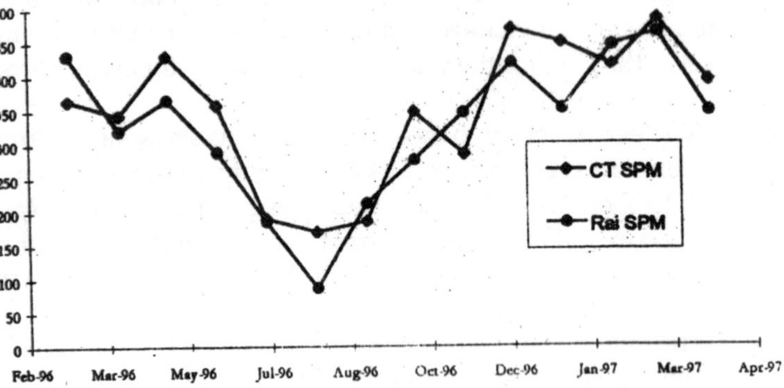

Fig. 13.2: SPM levels (in µg/cu m) at the two observation points; Raipur Road (Rai) and Clock Tower (CT) at Dehradun during 1996-97
(*Source*: U.P. Pollution Control Board, Dehradun).

- The NO_2 concentration at both the stations is well within the acceptable limits of 30 μg/cu m, the concentration at Raipur Road however reaches as high as 25 μg/cu m in April.
- SPM concentrations in the city are high all through the year and always above the 100 μg/cu m limit. The SPM concentration is generally around 400 μg/cu m and peaks in March when it tends to touch the 500 μg/cu m threshold. In the months July to September the SPM levels are generally low and fall below the 200 μg/cu m mark.

Unprecedented growth in the population of Dehradun town is the single factor that is contributing to the mounting atmospheric pollution in the city. Consumption of fossil fuel is attributed to the growing population and increases the pollution levels considerably. To add to it the emission levels for chimney exhausts are particularly high.

Dehradun is a closed valley between the Siwaliks to the south and the main Himalayan ranges to the north. The experts hold the opinion that the enclosed valley configuration deters dissipation of pollutants and inversion phenomenon during the nights causes enhanced concentration of the same in the atmosphere. Keeping in view these physiographic compulsions the natural environment of Dehradun needs special attention and polluting practices in the valley need an immediate check.

During the course of the study the experts and the people approached have come forward with some suggestions that could help in improving the natural environment of Dehradun city. These are summarised below:

(1) The population of the city of Dehradun has already crossed the threshold limit imposed by the carrying capacity of the infrastructure. Unless infrastructure is streamlined the growth of population should be checked. This can be done by shifting some of the government establishments out of the city and developing satellite townships in the vicinity.

(2) More efficient and less polluting transport alternatives should be provided for the city.

(3) Pollution control measures need to be employed in a stringent manner in the city and all movement of polluting vehicles should be curbed.

(4) The prescribed upper limit for the kilns operating in the surroundings should be lowered.
(5) The power supply to the city should be streamlined and those resorting to captive power generation should be charged adequate fees so as to invest adequately on improving the situation.
(6) The road network in the city needs overhauling. All the roads should be metalled and regularly maintained.

The Secret of Success
Behind All Men of
Achievement,
Lies in the Faculty of
Applying their Intellect
In all their Activities,
Without being misled
By any Surging
Emotion or Feeling.
The Secret of
Success in Life Lies
In Keeping the Head above
The Storms of the Heart.

14

Mining and Environmental Degradation : Case of Sirmaur District in Himachal*

The reported minerals from the Himalayas include magnesite, dolomite, gypsum, talc, limestone and other precious and semi-precious stones. These are being plundered at an alarming pace. Armed with sophisticated technological know-how man is leaving no stone unturned in scarring the beautiful landscape of the Himalayas. The Lesser Himalayan belt is gifted with high-grade limestone - dolomite - marble reserves that have been mined since antiquity. With the coming of roads the gates of this El Dorado were flung open to exploitation and the pace of exploitation accelerated with the inflow of mechanisation and capital. Environmental awareness however brought forth many representations against these operations. The apex court cried halt to this exploitative and environmentally unfriendly mining practices and the operations came to a grinding halt in the Doon valley. The persons engaged in the trade, having tasted the gains that emanate from the exploitation of the resources of the Himalayas could not however be cowed down by a single stroke of the pen. All their attention was thus focused upon trans-Giri where the operations were not banned. This caused heavy inflow of mine hunters to this land. Closure of mining in the surrounding Doon valley thus accelerated the pace of mining in trans-Giri (sandwiched between the rivers Tons and Giri in Sirmaur district of Himachal Pradesh and bound by 77°35′E & 77° 50′E longitudes and 30° 30′N & 30° 40′N latitudes). Conscious of the fact that the wrath of the apex court could push them out of business the players decided this time to make the most of the opportunity available. More than a million

---

* This article is co-authored by R.C. Lakhera of the Indian Institute of Remote Sensing, Dehradun.

tonnes of material is being legally mined in the region annually. Authentic sources however claim that an even higher volume is being mined illegally. To add to it vast volumes of the material is wasted in the haste. Environmental and mining regulations are violated in broad day light and these incidences are not reported, owing to pressure from various quarters. The villagers find themselves helpless when confronted with the neo-rich and the mining mafia. They no doubt feel sorry for the mindless exploitation of the resource but have no option but to be silent observers to the worsening quality of their lives. Mining has disturbed the vital forest - land - water - agriculture linkages. The lands are increasingly becoming infertile and productivity is sharply on the decline. Water availability has been reduced over the decade and a number of springs have virtually dried out.

Deforestation in the terrain owing to mining operations has adversely affected :

- Fodder and fuelwood availability
- Water availability
- Erosion rates
- Rates of degradation of agricultural lands

The womenfolk now devote more time for fodder and fuelwood collection than a decade before. Though a few people of the region have amassed huge wealth, life has become difficult for the common people who have now to toil harder to make both ends meet.

A large cement factory of the Cement Corporation of India is situated at Rajban and as many as nine mini cement plants, besides a large number of crushers are operating in the region around Sataun and Poanta Sahib. These are depleting the existing resources and are adding to the air pollution leading to a deterioration in the quality of life of the masses of the region.

Population density of the area is low and is concentrated around some centres. The sex ratio in the villages favours the masculine gender and the literacy rates in the region are generally low (Table 14.1).

Table 14.1: Population and literacy figures for trans-Giri region

Population					*Literacy*				
Male	%	Female	%	Total	Male	%	Female	%	Total
16206	54.19	13702	45.81	29908	6579	40.6	2250	16.4	8829

Landuse

Being a direct expression of the terrain condition landuse gives an important indication regarding slope instability, erosion and mass wastage. The nature of terrain and the diversity of the climate (Saxena *et al.* 1994) have influenced the landuse in the Himalayan terrain. The vegetal cover has a considerable effect on erosion and weathering intensities. Shallow landslides are generally associated with areas having very sparse vegetation (open scrub). There are numerous examples from the Himalayas where cutting down of the trees triggered landslides. Removal of the vegetal cover leads to accelerated erosion and shallow slides. Faster erosion and greater instability of the slopes are found in barren rock or soil surfaces as well as in the sparsely vegetated areas. On the other hand thickly vegetated areas are generally less prone to mass wasting processes owing to the well developed root system that bind the soil particles, thus enhancing the shearing resistance of the slope material, except for the cases where deep seated failures take place. The anthropogenic activities (engineering activities, quarries, fires and the others) greatly increase the chances of slope failure. Cultivated land behaves differently with different crops planted. The standing crops that require stagnant water sometimes result in increased pore water pressure in the soil mass underneath, resulting in mass movement.

Comparison of the landuse data of SOI toposheet (1966) with the SPOT imagery (1996) reveals that the vegetal cover in the region has been shrinking. This can well be attributed to the accelerated pace of mining operations in the region in the recent past (late nineties). These operations have shown a perceivable adverse impact upon the quality of life of the masses and their access to basic natural resources (water, fuel and fodder) has been severely hampered by these operations. The landuse pattern has been correlated with the slope and aspect maps prepared from the elevation data of the SOI toposheets.

Moderately high and high slope classes account for 79 per cent of the total barren land in the area (Table 14.2). Interestingly enough these are the slope classes that also support good vegetal cover (52 per cent of the dense forests and 76 per cent of the sparse forests). This is due to the fact that the mankind has exploited gentler slopes and vegetation remains on higher slopes only.

Table 14.2: Relationship between slope and landuse classes in trans-Giri

Landuse type	*Slope category*	*Area (sq m)*	*% of the landuse type under slope subtype*
Agriculture land	Flat ground	16519600	29.40917
Agriculture land	Gentle slope	8385600	14.92854
Agriculture land	Moderate slope	2618000	4.66-718
Agriculture land	Moderately high slope	23025200	40.99082
Agriculture land	High slope	5424000	9.656125
Barren land	Flat ground	2045600	8.98454
Barren land	Gentle slope	1474000	6.473999
Barren land	Moderate slope	792800	3.48208
Barren land	Moderately high slope	12376000	54.35699
Barren land	High slope	5586000	24.53443
Barren land	Steep	493600	2.167955
Sparse forest	Flat ground	2102000	7.653767
Sparse forest	Gentle slope	2300400	8.376178
Sparse forest	Moderate slope	1043600	3.799939
Sparse forest	Moderately high slope	14968400	54.50269
Sparse forest	High slope	6935600	25.25379
Sparse forest	Steep	113600	0.413638
Dense forest	Flat ground	30619200	31.14771
Dense forest	Gentle slope	11137600	11.32984
Dense forest	Moderate slope	3762400	3.827342
Dense forest	Moderately high slope	38888000	39.55924
Dense forest	High slope	12810800	13.03193
Dense forest	Steep	1085200	1.103932

The correlation between slope, aspect and vegetation types shows that southerly aspect (SW, S & SE) accounts for most of the barren land (65%), while the northerly aspect (NW, N & NE) accounts for only 16 per cent (Table 14.3). The vegetation is more or less uniformly distributed along all the slopes and the northerly aspect accounts for a higher percentage of the dense forest.

These data indicate that the steep slopes with southerly aspect have comparatively lesser vegetal cover. This is in conformity with the observations in other Himalayan sectors and is attributed to the intense insolation on these slopes. It is evident that the area has witnessed marked increase in the wastelands, while the forest cover has shrunk considerably.

Table 14.3: Relationship of the different landuse classes with the slope aspect

Landuse type	*Aspect*	*Area (sq m)*	*% under the defined landuse type under aspect subclass*
Agriculture land	North	5616000	10.73797
Agriculture land	Northeast	6823200	13.04617
Agriculture land	East	6198400	11.85153
Agriculture land	Southeast	6772400	12.94904
Agriculture land	South	10248800	19.59603
Agriculture land	Southwest	6815200	13.03088
Agriculture land	West	4783200	9.145628
Agriculture land	Northwest	5043200	9.642756
Barren land	North	1208400	5.451888
Barren land	Northeast	1859600	8.389879
Barren land	East	2580800	11.64369
Barren land	Southeast	5566400	25.11369
Barren land	South	5168800	23.31986
Barren land	Southwest	3640400	16.42424
Barren land	West	1387200	6.258572
Barren land	Northwest	753200	3.398181
Sparse forest	North	702000	2.612968
Sparse forest	Northeast	1900000	7.072136
Sparse forest	East	3152000	11.7323
Sparse forest	Southeast	4950800	18.42775
Sparse forest	South	5543200	20.63277
Sparse forest	Southwest	4965600	18.48284
Sparse forest	West	3801600	14.15023
Sparse forest	Northwest	1850800	6.889005
Dense forest	North	14015600	15.55761
Dense forest	Northeast	12101600	13.43303
Dense forest	East	9809200	10.88842
Dense forest	Southeast	9886400	10.97411
Dense forest	South	10975600	12.18314
Dense forest	Southwest	9532000	10.58072
Dense forest	West	10709200	11.88744
Dense forest	Northwest	13058800	14.49554

Plate 13 : Environmental degradation in trans-Giri due to unplanned mining operations

Mining Operations

Unplanned mining and quarrying activities in the region are having an adverse impact upon the environment of the region (Plate 13). Both the development of the quarry site and the approach to it take a heavy toll on the forests. In the unplanned hasty road constructions for quick commercial returns least heed is paid to the prescribed environmental norms. The excavated debris is freely rolled down the hill slope. The attitude of both, the private developers and the state authorities is the same and they consider their duty to be finished once the debris is cleared off the road. Besides increasing the siltation rates in the downstream reservoirs, this causes immense loss to the forest wealth of the nation. It was observed in the area that the symbol of development, the roads, have left behind visible scars upon the virgin mountain topography. Not that the road construction should be discouraged, but better environmental norms should be adhered to.

The region harbours a large floating population of mine workers, drivers, cleaners and the support service staff. This population is responsible for the increasing instances of venereal diseases in the region. Some cases of AIDS have also been reported from the region. This is the price the poor people of the region are paying for development.

With increased pace of mining operations economic disparity has gripped the region. The peasants who were lucky enough to own lands having limestone reserves have been blessed with sudden and immense booty but the less fortunate ones have been turned into daily wage labourers. The productivity of their land has gone down while the cash economy has disrupted the long prevailing life style and the value system. The cost of living has gone up while the purchasing power has decreased. This has adversely affected the quality of life of the masses of the region.

Though communicated under the veil of anonymity by several individuals during the course of the fieldwork, illegal mining operations in the region are as much as five times the legal ones. The *modus operandi* of the illegal operators was traced in the field; the illegally extracted rock mass is first supplied to the godowns of the legal lease holders at Sataun and from there onwards it is not illegal anywhere (the check post is situated at Rajban, while a lot of crushers and chippers are operating at Sataun itself). The authorities concerned are perhaps so overwhelmingly pleased that they cannot differentiate between what is good and what is bad for the society and the environment. Remote sensing holds the key and can help in locating illegal mining operations; but for the want of political will this does not seem the judicious alternative.

Having experienced eighty springs in this rugged terrain Mohtu of Dugana village (trans-Giri) considers mining to be a curse for this region. The debris rolling down from the mine on the upper reaches of the hill has degraded more than thirty bighas of his agricultural land. Three *kulhs* (small unlined water diversion channels) so painfully constructed in this rocky terrain by his forefathers have been sacrificed to these operations. The fields are thus water starved and productivity has been affected. For seven years he has been awaiting compensation from the mine owner, but in vain.

Glistening tears in the old and experienced eyes of Mohtu very well tell the story of rampant exploitation of the resources and the people. His ideals do not however allow him to speak out vocally, but he often breaks down into tears when describing the deteriorating social norms. Though poor, his ideals do not allow his three grown up sons to work in the mines.

The old and experienced eyes of Mohtu are overwhelmed with pain when he talks of the changing moral standards in his surroundings. Under the changed circumstances the family of Mohtu has to devote more time for firewood, fuel and water collection. *Gansanis* (pasture lands) have become unsafe due to stones rolling down and flying above as a result of the blasting that goes on uninterrupted and unwarned. Even the approach to the fields and common lands is severely hampered due to mining induced landslides, specially during monsoons.

It is doubtful if the three children of Mohtu and their children would still prefer agriculture to mining after Mohtu is gone.

Discussion

The people of the trans-Giri region are particularly prone to some diseases. Statistical data on these could however not be accessed, but the practicing government and private medicos at Poanta Sahib and Sataun affirmed abnormally high incidences of leprosy, TB, stone and STD from this region. Kapur (1934) gives an account of the abnormally high rates of syphilis in the region. Leprosy to the surprise of the doctors is particularly restricted to this zone and is not reported from the cis-Giri belt. During the field survey many cases of the disease were observed. It seems particularly high amongst the females. The doctors attribute these diseases to overcrowding, poor hygiene, sanitation and lack of communication.

Apart from these, worm infestation, anaemia, diarrhoea and amoebiasis are other common diseases of the region. Some cases of cancer have also reported from the area. Except for one case of oral cancer (due to *Gutka*), all other cases are restricted to females that have uterus or breast cancer.

The people of trans-Giri traditionally practice fraternal polyandry. Due to physiographical compulsions this system was conceived ages ago to save the marginal mountain farms from fragmentation. In this system the females at their paternal houses enjoy a lot of laxity and can well have amorous relations so as to ease the tension of life at the in-laws place. This laxity is now exploited by the floating population that looks forward to easy sexual partners. Under the changed circumstances the number of sexual partners have increased tremendously and it has taken the form of an undeclared profession. This has made the population particularly prone to STD. Treating it as a potential zone for the spread of AIDS the Government of Himachal Pradesh is taking special steps for enhancing awareness regarding AIDS. Condom dispensers are provided at public places for the people to have safe sex. What is really needed is to bring about social awareness through an enhanced literacy drive in the region.

In the mountainous terrain of the Himalayas, females have to share the burden of agriculture and allied activities besides caring for the household, children, cattle, and collecting fuelwood, fodder and water primarily due to the heavy exodus of the able bodied people in search of jobs. A routine day of the females starts early at dawn and they work hard till late in the night. The health of the females in the region is not particularly good and they suffer from a number of ailments. Anaemia is rampant and various venereal and uterus diseases are not uncommon. They however, do not enjoy the luxury of visiting the nearby doctor, if at all he is available in the vicinity, for it amounts to the disruption of the routine household chores. This causes their health to deteriorate further. In the study area the rates of female literacy are particularly low (Table 14.1). This compounds the problem.

The entire population of trans-Giri is slowly creeping under the tightening clutches of the *vicious cycle of resource degradation* that is elaborated in the following sections:

- Mining operations in the region are causing rampant erosion, landslides, loss of agricultural fields by debris rolling down, reduced productivity of the fields, deforestation, pollution, reduced access to fodder, fuelwood and water.
- The peasants are impoverished due to reduced productivity. Females have to toil more for fuelwood, fodder and water collection. Water for irrigation is decreasing. The debris of mines and road construction

disrupts many of the *kuhls*.

- Agricultural output drops with depleting land productivity and people are forced to engage in minig operations to supplement their income.
- Shift of occupation reduces the farming hands and the burden of the already overburdened femalefolk mounts further. With depleting forest cover fuelwood supply falls short of demand. Shortage forces people to use cowdung as an easy alternative to fuelwood. Diversion of cowdung to the kitchens implies reduced manure to the fields. This causes further reduction in productivity.
- Less water is utilised for routine household purposes to cope with the reduced availability. Unhygienic conditions become rampant due to the lack of easy access to safe drinking water.
- To enhance their depleting incomes more and more farming hands switch over to mining. The productivity drops further, while the burden of the females mounts. The soil nutrient cycle breaks down due to prolonged low doses of water and manure.
- To cope up with the mounting stress the males engage in illegal mining and timber trade, while the females look for easy money through the flesh trade. A large floating population of drivers, cleaners, mineworkers and others provides the ready market.
- Health-related problems increase and social cohesion is lost.
- Agriculture becomes a secondary occupation. Agricultural lands turn barren. Unemployment increases and the bargaining power of the labour force is reduced due to his overwhelming dependence upon mines. The mine owners thus exploit the people further due to their absolute dependence upon the mines.
- The society is impoverished, while a few engaged in exploitative trade mint money. The honest farmer is converted into a daily wage worker.

Given above is the hypothesis that is based upon field observations. Not that the entire area has crossed the threshold; a lot can really be done if timely corrective actions are taken. It is a pity that the mine owners in liaison with the political agents are depriving people of their rightful share in the economic wealth of the region. The exploitation of the poor peasantry and environment defies all norms of the civilised world. Low levels of awareness amongst the masses, together with their shortsighted vision aids in exploitation. For the empowerment of the rural peasantry it is important that they realise the seriousness and gravity of the problem.

The mine operators within the narrow and shortsighted goal of maximising profits are debasing the pristine natural environment of the region. Apart from nationalisation, promotion of village cooperative mining societies can help in checking environmental decay and also in bringing about equitable distribution of income. This would promote social harmony and the people who are conscious of and sensitive to their environment would carry out mining operations with due regard to environmental preservation. Moreover in these mining cooperatives local people would be assured of gainful employment.

The governance of free India in accordance with the spirit of the constitutional provisions (Art. 29) framed several legal provisions to safeguard the interests of the weaker and underprivileged sections of the society. It is really pity to observe that the people of these sections, even after much hue and cry and an outvocal testimony, have been deprived of their justified claims for compensation. Despite abolition of the Right to Property from the Fundamental Rights (44th Amendment Act, 1978) the constitutional provisions clearly mention that the land where the owner is carrying out agricultural operations would be provided with compensation. It holds good for the property of the deprived sections of the society. Denial of compensation to the masses by the mine owners where the agricultural lands have been destroyed by the rubble of the mine is a blatant mockery of the constitutional provisions.

Palaro village in Sataun was surveyed in detail in order to get a deeper insight into the havoc that the mines are spreading in the region. The mines operating upslope (owned by Shri Zalim Singh Fauzi) have overrun large tracts of agricultural lands in the village belonging to both the deprived and other sections. Details of the lands degraded by these and as reported by the victims are as follows:

Table 14.4 : Mining : Loss of Farm Land

Sl.No.	Name of farmer	Caste	Land loss
1.	Sabla Ram Supa Ram	Koli (SC)	9 bigha
2.	Ganga Ram	Koli (SC)	1.5 bigha
3.	Kushi Ram	Koli (SC)	1.5 bigha
4.	Shanti	Koli (SC) - Widow	7 bigha
5.	Rukmani	Rajaput - Widow	4 bigha
6.	Shiva Ram	Koli (SC)	3 bigha
7.	Rari Ram	Rajaput	9 bigha
8.	Kanthi Ram	Koli (SC)	4 bigha
9.	Tota Ram	Koli (SC)	3 bigha
10.	Khatri Ram	Koli (SC)	3 bigha

These data may well be exaggerated, but this does not deny the fact that the mines have destroyed the lands of the peasants and they have not been provided with adequate compensation. These lands were destroyed during the 1997 monsoons by the rubble emanating from the mine. The villagers were at that time assured by the mine owner that their lands would be cleared at an early date. No action has however been taken till date despite repeated pleadings. The villagers find themselves helpless, as they do not have enough resources to move the court against the mine owner.

Apart from personal property, the rubble has affected the village pathways and even two sources of water have disappeared below the rubble. As a result, the villagers are facing an acute shortage of drinking water. To add to this problem, blasting operations with heavy charge are undertaken in broad daylight. This has severely affected the movement of villagers (specially females) for fodder, fuelwood and water collection. During the fieldwork the author (PR) stood testimony to the blasting operations around noon (at 1230 and 1300 hrs) and had to literally run to save himself from the flying stones. It was surprising to note that the stones go flying to the habitations downslope. The poor people are braving all these besides the harsh and inhospitable living conditions. No warning signals are announced before blasting, except for shouting arrogantly.

Only one single example of a cooperative mining society was noted in the trans-Giri. The people of Poka village near Sataun have formed a cooperative society and have managed to get a short term permit for extracting limestone. These operations are going on satisfactorily.

The state government should preferentially promote such societies in place of the big players, mostly from outside, who are exploiting the geo-environment of the region. It may, no doubt, amount to a loss of revenue to some extent but in the long term it would have a better impact on the society. The government should at the same time also provide working capital to such societies as it is often beyond the financial competence of the villagers to muster enough capital for developing the site and to run these operations smoothly.

Shortage of capital in the region has encouraged the practice of giving the lease area on contract to some third party. This practice needs to be discouraged. It has been observed that a number of mines are being run on contract basis and the contractor after paying his dues to the lessee considers himself morally free to carry out mining operations in whatever manner he deems fit.

The Public Works Department in the region is spending heavily in clearing the debris from the mines. At certain places these sites have been permanently destabilised and labour force is busy round the year to keep the road open for traffic. The taxpayer's money should not be diverted in this manner to cover up the folly of the mine operators. Note should be taken of the mines spoiling the public transport network and strict and prompt action should be taken against the defaulters.

In many instances it was observed that the mine owners are not paying due and adequate compensation to the villagers whose lands are being run over by the mine waste. A special tribunal should be set up to settle such cases and to compensate the villagers adequately that is, at the prevailing market price. It was surprising to note that the soil conservation officials of the state were unable to comment upon the land being affected by the mine waste. They consider it to be outside the purview of their defined duties.

In order to strengthen the local panchayat institutions, these should be empowered to levy taxes upon the rock mass being extracted from within their jurisdiction. At the same time the lessee should be compelled to invest a fixed portion of his returns for the development of the local communities.

The royalty on the extracted rock should be imposed upon the market cost of the material actually excavated and not upon the material actually taken out of the site. This would no doubt require detailed and repeated surveys of the mine sites. But this measure would reduce the wastage of the material and the excavations would be carried out after detailed and thoughtful surveys of the entire area, rather than unthoughtful blasting of the mountain and then sorting out commercial grade material.

Heavy capital penalty together with cancellation of the lease should be resorted to in cases where the operators defy environmental and mining norms. For this the judiciary, Department of Forests, Department of Industries, the Public Works Department, the Pollution Control Board and the Department of Irrigation and Public Health have to work as a coherent and effective team. Smooth functioning of this multi-wheeled machinery would be reflected in the overall welfare of the region and improved quality of life of the masses.

Disappointments
Come only to those
Who make appointments
With future.
Do make appointments,
But only with the present.
Then disappointments
Can never, never come.

He who seeks
Happiness Outside
Himself
Will never find
Satisfaction.
It is an illusion
To thinl
That
More Comfort
Means
More Happiness.

15

Environmental Degradation : Dubra Microwatershed

Driving out of the traffic and of course the pollution of Dehradun one finds oneself in an entirely different atmosphere; lush green forest, breathtaking calm and cool breeze overtake the senses. Small hamlets are clearly visible and streams often flow across the road. Suddenly one feels elevated to spiritual heights. One more bend along the road to Saklana and one is forced to release the accelerator; still one more and the pressure on the break lever unconsciously enhances and the vehicle comes to a halt. Here, across a small stream one encounters what can rightly and justly be termed as an extreme example of human greed. The entire landscape is defaced; deep scars are clearly visible from a distance; the entire hill slope stands vegetationless, covered with excavated material and rubble (Plate 14).

The once lush green forest cover is gone just because the region has deposits of high grade limestone and phosphorite. The mineral wealth of this region has been plundered in a planned and systematic manner by the mineowners/contractors in liaison with the government agencies and the people are left with just barren tracts rendered practically useless for any productive work. The local people of this mineral rich area have been given a raw deal; daily wages of Rs. 42 in lieu of their peaceful life of an agriculturist. Such scenes are plentiful around this majestic city called Dehradun but here we are referring to a small microwatershed around Dubra the economy of which stands shattered by the wrath of limestone mining. Dubra is situated hardly half an hour's driving distance from Dehradun on the way to Saklana.

This microwatershed comprising of four small villages was inhabited by happy go lucky persons whose livelihood depended on their surroundings and land. The mining that eclipsed their life

Plate 14: Land degradation due to mining at Dubra

started some 40 years ago. Ready cash lured the hitherto agriculturists into a shortsighted deal and they were turned into wage labourers in limestone quarries. Slowly all the able bodied persons were involved in mining operations. Unknowingly these people were furthering the interests of the mine owners and contractors who have been for decades exploiting their resources, their environment and the people themselves. Here we are purposely using the term 'unknowingly' because even after prolonged association with mining operations these people are not aware of the cost of the material being excavated by them; they recognise limestone by name but phosphorite is just '*maal*' for them.

Being preoccupied with mining operations the males were unable to pay due attention to the agricultural operations. Agriculture soon took the rear seat and became the headache of the women. Deprived of working hands many of the far flung fields were left fallow, while many productive and irrigated fields in the lower reaches were run over by the debris from the mine. Many a time due compensation was not paid for these devastated fields. Community forests and livestock were equally neglected. Life thus solely depended on quarrying operations. By the time these people came to realise the consequences of mining their economy was already shattered and thus they had no option but to turn themselves into silent observers of the destruction of their environment and even helped in accelerating this destruction.

Recurring floods in the downstream region together with the increasing silt load in the rivers that threatened the life of the reservoirs and made the river course shallow, forced planners to focus their attention on this terrain that had been neglected so far. Environmental consciousness hastened this process and the public interest petition led to the Supreme Court order halting limestone mining operations in this region. With this order of the apex court the life in the microwatershed came to a grinding halt. There are no other sources of livelihood at present. The land being neglected for long has significantly lost its productivity; as most land is rainfed and the weather is unpredictable; it cannot sustain the agriculturists for even four odd months. In the past due attention was not paid towards adopting other income generating programmes and mining was the only occupation. An entire generation that had been brought up as wage labourers finds itself ill equipped to compromise with the changed ground realities. The zeal for environmental protection has led to stricter attitude of the forest officials. These have adopted a totally unsympathetic attitude towards the local people and are harassing them on one pretext or the other. The local people are not even able to manage leaves for mulching the much prized ginger crop. It is becoming hard to feed the cattle. The situation is difficult to fathom. When large-scale devastation by well-off mine operators in the watershed is being tolerated, what is really wrong with the poor people satisfying their justified needs from the nearby forest? Moreover mining operations are still continuing on the community land of the villages (Koklialgaon and Danda). But here it is not limestone but phosphorite that is being mined for a Government of India undertaking Pyrite Phosphorite and Chemicals Ltd., of course through mediation of a contractor. Here the open cast mining operations are conducted unsupervised and can therefore be potentially more hazardous for the environment. Moreover when the watershed cannot sustain limestone quarrying what can really be the plea for giving a green signal to phosphorite mining, which poses a direct threat to spring water pollution in the region?

The halting of limestone mining has sabotaged the entire economy of this microwatershed. As was expected, the local people want the quarrying operations to restart as the environment is not a priority for them. Discussions with the people revealed that they hold a lot of ill will against the government but favour the contractor. Even his exploitative attitude was justified on one pretext or the other.

In the previous decades the government has been getting the royalties on the quarrying of the resources of this watershed. The contractor has also amassed huge wealth in these operations. The local people who were being deprived of their resources got a grossly raw deal. What did they really get? Wages of Rupees forty two per day! 16 per cent bonus and a weekly holiday! Is it merely for this that the future of generations to come has been sacrificed? Not one of the two parties that earned a profit out of the environmental degradation deemed it necessary to invest in the capacity building of the masses and in social infrastructure. Even today the watershed does not have a dispensary, there is one primary school for four villages, shortage of water is acute in the summers, and many of the villages are far away from the road head. An entire generation together with its social fabric, value system and social solidarity has been ruined. Today there is an exodus of able bodied people to nearby Sataun (HP) where mining operations are still being undertaken.

After halting the mining operations government agencies could have taken special care to rebuild the economy of the area. Development agencies have not taken initiatives in capacity building of the people. This microwatershed like many others urgently requires schemes aimed at eco-restoration and more importantly schemes which would help in income generation.

16

Water Availability : Nagthat*

The Jaunsar tribal belt has not been studied in great detail by environmentalists, but has been the focus of attention of anthropologists. This region, because of its polyandry, is more romanticised than it is actually understood. Situated in the heart of the Jaunsar, Nagthat (Dabred watershed) in Dehradun district lies between 77° 56' and 78° 01' E longitudes and 30° 34' and 30° 37' N latitudes with average altitude ranging between 800 and 2200 m above mean sea level (MSL) and can be approached by the motorable road diverging from the Yamunotri highway. Dabred, which is the principal stream in the region drains into the river Yamuna near Maror (on Yamunotri highway). Small streams / nalas originating in the west around Singhori, Barat khal and Chhicherar are some of the major contributors to this drainage system.

As everywhere else in Uttarakhand the lot of the women in this region is also miserable. They shoulder the burden of all the household chores besides the work outside the home (Plate 15). Though the general health of the children in this region was observed to be good, the health of the adults is a cause for concern. This may be due to the addiction to the locally brewed liquor and tobacco amongst both sexes (Plate 16 and 17). Once a tool of adaptation, that helped the people to relax after the day's hard work, liquor has taken the form of a major social evil. In addition, the water quality data of the region warrant detailed studies because water available to the masses is far below the normal levels.

Water ranks high amongst the priorities of any human

---

* This article is co-authored by Dr. D. Sati & Dr. R.B.P. Singh of ENDS Dehradun. Chemical analysis of the samples was carried out by the latter at ENDS laboratory. Authors acknowledge financial support from DST, New Delhi.

Plate 15: Burden of females in Uttarakhand

settlement and at the same time dictates the living conditions of the people. In this remote region natural springs are the only cost effective and viable means of fulfilling the needs of these people. At present females have to devote a major portion of their time in the collection of water, specially in the summer season when piped water fails and the supply is severely reduced. It was noted that females have to walk as far as two kilometres covering the rugged and steep topography to fetch water under such circumstances. Improved availability of water would provide females with ample time to devote to other productive activities. This would improve the social status of the females. Moreover enhanced availability of water could be utilised for generating energy for diverse uses.

The landuse pattern of the region was delineated with the help of the available Survey of India toposheet (Table 16.1).

Plate 16, 17 : Addiction to locally brewed liquor and tobacco is rampant in the Nagthat belt

Table 16.1: Landuse pattern of Nagthat

Type of land area	Area (in Sq. km)	(in hectares)	(Percentage)
Cultivated	13.7325	1373.25	59.4
Forest cover	1.7525	175.25	7.6
Barren land	7.6275	762.75	33.0
Total	23.1125	2311.25	100.0

Water Harvesting Traditions

Habitations in hilly terrain have interwoven with them a tale of water harvesting, and this region is no exception. The water harvesting traditions of this region are magnificent and unparalleled, though not studied in detail. At the western edge of the watershed, upon a hilltop, lie the ruins of some historical monument from which the local people proudly trace their descent. The locals attribute these monuments to King Virat of *Mahabharat* fame in whose court the *Pandavas* took shelter during their *agyatvaas*. However, not much of interest could be found amongst these ruins except the remains of a brick lined well (Plate 18).

The nature of the construction together with the provisions created in the hill for defence, certainly indicate that it was constructed by some king, but how authentic is it to associate the same with Virat is a question of debate. The bricks are Lahgori which were not constructed in post-Mughal times. It certainly puts the structure contemporary to the Mughals; nothing more can really be said with the available evidence.

It is interesting to note that all the other structures on the hill top are made of stone while the well is lined with the fire baked bricks. In the construction of the bricks very coarse sand has been used and the proportion of clay is significantly low. From its architecture the structure resembles the ones constructed for exploiting groundwater, rather than a simple rain water harvesting structure that is normally to be expected here. It was probably exploiting some perched horizon at the hill top that is made up of phyllitic rocks. The technology employed for identifying the water bearing horizon must have been highly evolved in the region for it is hard to find water in this terrain even armed with modern tools. At present the well is defunct and has been filled up with stones by the villagers whose cattle might get trapped in the well.

Besides this magnificent but defunct structure, there exist a number of natural springs in the region. The locals regularly use these seepages for diverse uses. In the vicinity of the seepage provision for drinking of cattle is mostly provided. Most of these springs are situated in the colluvium and the state of the forest in the recharge zone is generally good.

Traditions of nature - man - spirit complex interwoven around the natural springs were observed in the region. A traditional water harvesting structure with a platform in the middle was seen in Rampur village. It is locally referred to as *pokhar* or *pak-ka-dhara*. The platform is associated with *Pap devata* and the water is regarded sacred. The logic behind installing a community water connection adjacent to the traditional source of water (Plate 19) at Rampur could not be understood. The *dhara* near Bisoi is similarly referred to as *devta-ka-dhara* and is associated with the local deity Lord *Mahasu* (incarnation of Lord *Shiva*) whose wooden motif was observed at the site of the *dhara* (Plate 20).

The water source near Lacha (Lacha - 4) is considered to be sweet and healthy by the locals. They hold that the temperature of the *dhara* varies inversely with the atmospheric temperature. The water of Lacha - 1 and *Gadiakhara* in Mundhan is believed to create stomach disorders.

More than twenty-five springs were located, sampled and studied in this region as against only four depicted in the SOI maps. Most of these springs were noticed on the western side of the watershed. Many of these are however reported to be of seasonal nature and these dry up in the summer. The discharge of the streams was recorded in the field (Table 16.2).

All the villages have tap water supply that often fails and the villagers have to take recourse to the traditional springs. The water from tap water supply is either collected from the springs or from the perennial streams. The condition of the water collection tanks was pitiable and a lot of decaying organic matter was observed. When questioned people in Duna village confirmed that they do not use it for drinking for which the water is collected from the springs.

The hilly region is gifted with abundant rain but the major

Plate 18 : Brick lined well at the hill top near Nagthat

Plate 19: Tap connection provided at the site of dhara in Rampur village

Table 16.2: Discharge of the Springs around Nagthat

Water source (in brackets is the name of the village)	Discharge (lpm)	Daily water available (litres)
Upper *Naigar* (Gadaul)	7.3	10,512
Lower *Naigar* (Gadaul)	1.3	1,872
Teday Khadd (Gadaul)	590.0	849,600
Lacha-0	6.0	8,720
Lacha-1	43.0	62,525
Lacha-2	2.5	3,490
Lacha-3	2.0	2,280
Lacha-4	27.0	39,198
Lacha-5	3.0	4,320
Lacha-6	3.0	4,320
Baikhuber (Gadaul)	1.8	2,592
Hajaka (Gadaul)	29.0	42,027
Near Rampur)	2.0	2,280
Pokhar / Pap-ka-dhara (Rampur)	31.0	45,024
Upper *Jogranda* (Nagthat)	180.0	259,200
Lower *Jogranda* (Nagthat)	60.0	86,400
Duena	7.0	9,630
Devta-ka-dhara (Bisoi)	54.0	77,433
Pani-ka-dhara (Sheela)	10.0	14,400
Periyandu (Kuwasa)	30.0	43,200
Ukhniyan (Khuna Amal)	13.5	19,440
Prantkey (Khuna)	7.6	10,944
Bai-ka-pani (Kandoi)	3.0	4,320
Total		1,603,727

Plate 20: Wooden motif of Mahasu at a *dhara* near Bisoi

portion goes waste in the form of surface run off, taking along with it the fertile soil.

As per the data collected in the field as much as 1.2 MLD of water can be made available for diverse usage to the population of the area. Besides this, there exists stream water in the area that can well be diverted for agriculture. The irony is that sufficient water is not available for drinking and agriculture, while the spring water is flowing waste in almost all the areas. The productive use of this water is as low as five per cent and this is from the springs that are situated at convenient locations within the village.

The recharge areas of most of the streams are adequately forested, but there is ample scope for constructing *chaals* that have the potential of enhancing the recharge of the aquifers. The water collected in the *chaals* would be available for the grazing animals, and the effect of the same would be reflected in the lower rates of erosion.

Physico-chemical Studies

In the present investigations 27 springs and five sites for surface water were selected for detailed monitoring through sampling and testing for water quality and data analysis. The main objective of the study was to locate both ground water sources (springs) and surface water (streams/*khals*/waterfalls) for continuous assessment from the potability point of view, as these water sources are the only drinking water sources for the inhabitants of the watershed. The water samples were collected for six consecutive days between 0800 and 1200 hours and were brought to the laboratory in pyrex glass specimen bottles. Water quality parameters like pH, dissolved oxygen (DO), free carbon dioxide (FCO_2), carbonate (CO_3^-) and bicarbonate (HCO_3^-) were estimated at the spot immediately after collection, whereas water analysis relating to the other physio-chemical parameters was done in the laboratory. The temperature was measured with a mercury filled Celsius thermometer while the pH was recorded with the portable pH meter. Other parameters like DO, FCO_2, TDS, TSS, total hardness, chloride, Ca^{++} and Mg^{++} were assessed adopting the standard techniques (Welch 1984, APHA 1989). Correction coefficient among the physio-chemical characteristics of both groundwater and the surface water sources from different sources were also statistically correlated.

Table 16.3: Physio-chemical Characteristics of Spring Water

Water source (in brackets is the name of the village)	Ambient temp. (°C)	Water temp. (°C)	pH	TDS	TSS	TS	DO	FCO_2	HCO_3^-	CO_3^{--}	Chloride	TH	Ca^{++}	Mg^{++}
Upper *Naigar* (Gadaul)	11.2	9.4	6.3	225	90	315	7.8	1.5	25	-	21	42	10.4	3.9
Lower *Naigar* (Gadaul)	13.7	9.0	6.4	100	105	205	8.2	5.0	20	-	18	32	8.0	2.7
Teday Khadd (Gadaul)	13.8	12.4	6.4	150	135	185	7.0	2.5	35	-	22	40	11.2	2.9
Lacha-1	12.4	14.6	6.4	135	105	240	8.0	4.0	35	-	24	26	7.2	0.51
Lacha-2	9.8	10.6	6.4	150	110	260	7.4	5.0	30	-	23	24	6.4	1.94
Lacha-3	18.9	13.5	6.4	144	85	229	7.8	1.0	25	-	18	28	9.6	0.96
Lacha-4	18.9	14.2	6.5	185	300	485	7.0	3.0	30	-	30	32	10.4	1.45
Lacha-5	15.5	13.0	6.5	150	105	255	9.0	6.0	20	-	19	24	7.2	1.45
Baikhuber (Gadaul)	19.6	14.2	6.4	425	225	640	8.4	6.0	30	-	27	18	4.8	1.45
Hajaka (Gadaul)	19.5	13.6	6.4	400	90	490	10.4	7.0	30	-	23	28	8.8	1.45
Roagad Khadd (Rampur)	13.5	14.8	6.6	180	90	270	7.8	2.0	40	-	15	46	14.4	2.41
Pokhar / Pap-ka-dhara (Rampur)	17.5	13.0	6.5	85	95	180	7.8	2.5	40	-	24	44	14.4	1.92
Gadiakhara (Mundhan)	19.0	15.5	6.5	225	110	335	9.0	4.0	65	-	18	66	22.4	2.41
Chichrar	19.5	14.0	6.7	200	95	295	8.0	1.5	55	-	16	68	22.0	3.24
Upper *Jogranda* (Nagthat)	22.3	17.6	6.5	125	150	275	8.6	4.0	75	-	33	70	24.1	2.19
Middle *Jogranda* (Nagthat)	22.3	16.8	6.7	325	350	675	7.4	6.0	65	-	32	68	23.2	2.41
Lower *Jogranda* (Nagthat)	22.8	16.9	6.5	225	225	450	7.8	6.0	60	-	33	52	16.8	2.41
Duena	10.8	13.5	6.4	130	175	305	7.4	4.0	25	-	21	24	7.2	1.45

Table 16.3: *Contd.*

Water source (in brackets is the name of the village)	Ambient temp. (ºC)	Water temp. (ºC)	pH	TDS	TSS	TS	DO	FCO_2	HCO_3^-	CO_3^-	Chloride	TH	Ca^{++}	Mg^{++}
Devta-ka-dhara (Bisoi)	14.8	15.4	6.3	85	300	385	8.2	3.0	30	-	18	24	7.2	1.45
Pani-ka-dhara (Sheela)	16.5	13.5	6.4	185	105	290	6.8	2.0	20	-	25	26	8.0	1.45
Periyandu (Kuwasa)	19.5	14.2	6.7	145	85	130	7.4	3.0	40	-	23	46	15.2	1.93
Kulakhet (Rakhtar)	21.5	13.4	6.7	115	95	210	8.4	2.5	50	-	33	50	17.7	1.44
Timrikhet (Mehsasa)	23.5	13.5	6.8	275	85	260	7.8	5.0	45	-	22	56	15.2	4.36
Ukhniyan (Khuna Amal)	20.8	15.2	6.7	225	400	625	7.8	5.0	45	-	32	54	17.6	2.41
Prantkey (Khuna)	20.6	15.6	6.8	325	175	500	7.4	5.0	90	-	42	120	41.7	3.85
Bai-ka-pani (Kandoi)	24.6	13.6	6.8	100	400	500	7.2	2.5	75	-	35	70	21.6	3.87
Baisgar (Kandoi)	20.2	15.1	7.0	150	375	525	7.8	6.0	95	-	37	90	31.3	2.89

All values except pH in mgl-1 (ppm), unless otherwise mentioned

Table 16.4: Physio-chemical Characteristics of Surface Water in Nagthat

Source (near to village)	Ambient temp.	Water temp.	pH (ºC)	TDS (ºC)	TSS	TS	DO	FCO_2	HCO_3^-	CO_3^-	Chloride	TH	Ca^{++}	Mg^{++}
Rain water in *khal* (Lohani)	20.8	25.1	5.0	625	500	1125	10.6	33.0	20	-	41.0	56	18.4	2.41
Kafed waterfall (Gadaul)	15.4	9.6	6.4	180	150	230	10.4	2.0	30	-	27.0	36	10.4	2.41
Chipli waterfall (Gadaul)	18.5	9.7	6.5	425	225	650	10.4	2.0	25	-	18.0	20	6.4	0.96
Turiyakhara *nala* (Rampur)	22.6	12.8	6.5	550	110	660	8.2	4.0	40	-	25.0	38	10.4	2.90
Ghasia *nala* (Chichrar)	23.8	14.0	6.6	560	85	645	8.8	2.0	50	-	18.0	46	15.2	1.92

All values except pH in mgl-1 (ppm), unless otherwise mentioned.

Variation in physio-chemical characteristics of both surface and groundwater from different locations are summarised in Tables 16.3 and 16.4. In general it was observed that both spring and open water located at lower altitudes have different chemical characteristics in comparison with those located on the ridges. The water quality varies from place to place depending upon the characteristics of the strata and type of underlying rocks. The time of contact of water with the bed rock is different for different locations and this results in some variations in the water quality of the springs (Drever 1982, Kumar & Rawat, 1996).

The pH values for most of the spring water and the surface water samples exceed the permissible limit for drinking purposes (ISI 1993). In general pyrite and calcareous minerals present in the system have the greatest impact on the aqueous regime. As a result of low pH, there is a danger of heavy metals dissolving easily in the water making it toxic and thus adversely affecting the drinking water quality of these sources (Singh & Choudhary 1997).

It was interesting to record that the water from Kuasa, Rakhtar, Khuna, Chichrar and Mehsasa villages (located in lower altitudes without appreciable forest cover) and the Nagthat springs (at high altitude but without forest cover) have higher pH (6.7 to 7.0) values than the springs located at the higher altitudes with dense forest around. The possible reason for this could be the leaching of organic matter. Kumar and Rawat (1996) observed similar results while working on the natural springs of Almora. The lowest value of pH (5.0) which was found in the khal water may be attributed to direct surface runoff from pyritic minerals and evaporation.

TDS in some of the water samples and TSS in the majority of the samples were found to be beyond the maximum permissible limits set by the Indian Standards (1993). Direct mixing of the percolated dissolved substances and comparatively low volume of water might be responsible for the increased concentration of the TDS while the higher values of TSS may be due to the movement of dust particles from open crop fields and road construction sites. Out of the 32 samples analysed in the present study only six samples registered higher values of FCO_2 than those prescribed by ISI (1993).

Based on these studies it can be stated that the water of the sampled springs is adequately safe and does not pose any serious threat to the health of the masses. Better practices of water conservation need to be popularised in the area. Both ferrocement and LDPE tanks should be promoted together with a network of large storage tanks to avoid wastage of spring water. This water should be utilised through a network of *kuhls*. In all these activities people's participation should be ensured and all major decisions be taken with the concurrence of the majority.

To Give
Without Sympathy is to
Build a Temple
Without the Idol
And is as Futie as
Painting
A Picture with Black Ink
On
A Black Board

17

Strategy for Conservation and Development of the Himalayas

A CALL FOR ACTION TOWARDS INTEGRATED MOUNTAIN DEVELOPMENT

For the overall development of the Himalayan region it is essential that an independent and autonomous institute is established to work for the holistic development of the Himalayan eco-system. This institute would monitor and stimulate development programmes and would liaison between Government, Non-Government and People's Organizations and would be responsible for bringing out a "STATE OF THE HIMALAYAS REPORT" once a year and put it up to the Government to help it take decisions relating to policy, plan, funding and action programmes. Shouldered with this great responsibility it has to involve dedicated youngsters, shedding all bureaucratic hassles. A number of consultants, technical experts, NGOs, and Action Groups would be brought under one platform at this institute and would devote their energies for the common cause of the development of the Himalayas. An action for promoting self-reliance and sustained development of the Himalayas would thus be evolved.

Established at Katarmal (Almora) U.P., the G.B. Pant Institute of Himalayan Environment and Development was established with these envisaged goals and it is increasingly helping in the direction. It is however also proposed to consider a people's institution in a manner that it is free from governmental interventions and can work smoothly.

Such an institution devoted to the cause of Himalayan conservation can appropriately be called the Centre for Himalayan Rejuvenation (CHR) as its aim would be to rejuvenate the degrading Himalayan ecosystem. It is proposed to undertake the following network activities:

- Watershed management
- Eco-dharma and Eco-philosophy, human and environmental values, Revival of dying wisdom
- Health banks for the rural Himalayas, mother and child, geriatric and handicapped centre
- Sustainable society, sustainable development and sustainable farming system centre, ecology and resource management
- Self reliance of Himalayan communities including rural industrialisation
- Propagation of medicinal and aromatic plants together with the pre-processing and processing of the produce
- Eco-tourism including promotion of culture, art, music, folklore, drama, dances and handicrafts
- Training and management

Towards Self-reliance of the Himalayan Communities

People must decide what their priorities and programmes of work are for conservation and development. There should be people's organizations, Van Panchayats, Forestry Associations and local youths, women and ex-servicemen groups for eco-development and conservation and for promotion of rural employment and income generating activities. These activities may be land based, water based, and also cottage and small scale industries suited to the temper and culture of the Himalayan communities. A Himalayan Conservation Fund should be instituted by the Consortium of People's Societies.

A Call for Action — An Appeal to all Concerned with the Health of the Himalayas

Although it is already getting too late, Prevention is many times better than Cure. This strategy applies as much, perhaps much more, to a mountain eco-system as gigantic as the Himalayas as it does to human health.The "Arithmetic of Prevention" has two angles:

- How much will it cost to protect the fragile areas?
- If not protected, how much would it cost in terms of misery and "disaster relief" that has to be arranged in the name of human suffering by governments and / or public agencies?

Table 17.1 gives the estimates of damage caused by floods alone (does not include other related disasters like drought) that occurred during the period 1953-81 in the Indo-Gangetic Plain, originating from the Himalayas.

Almost one-half of the people living in the Himalayan mountain area live in poverty, characterized by poor health, malnutrition, chronic deprivation and shortened lives. This suffering and wasted potential is one of the greatest tragedies of modern times. A contributing cause of the desperate situation is the widespread loss of natural resources throughout the Himalayas. Tragically, it is the rural poor who are themselves one of the primary agents of destruction, as they clear the forests for agricultural land, fuelwood, fodder and other necessities. Lacking other means of meeting their survival needs, the rural folk are forced to steadily erode the capacity of the natural environment that supports them.

Table 17.1: Flood Damage Estimate

	Total for 1953-81	*Maximum in one year*	*Year*	*Yearly average*
Total area affected (million ha)	235.0	19	1978	8.1
Total population involved or affected (million)	795.0	70	1973	27.4
Damage to Crops (million ha)	104.0	10	1978	3.7
Damage to Crops (Rs. Crores)	7200.0	1030	1978	248.3
Human lives lost (thousands)	40	11	1977	1.4
Damage to public utilities- roads, bridges, etc. (Rs. Crores)	3400.0	582	1981	110.3
Total damage to crops/ houses/ Public utilities (Rs. Crores)	11800.0	1700	1978	406.9

This relationship between poverty and depleting resources is clear but not inevitable. Many solutions to this vicious cycle of perpetual misery are known and have been demonstrated. Given appropriate policies and institutional support and commitment and, of course, no corruption, much can be done through well-designed forestry and agricultural investment and support programmes. The evidence is clear that forest conservation and development projects can earn high enough rates of economic returns to be self-sustaining. The challenge is to put these solutions to work for the millions of the rural poor seeking a better future. To meet this challenge requires ingenuity and above all political commitment. The failure of the central, state and local governments to respond adequately and effectively to the mammoth problem of resource depletion in the Himalayan terrain has led to extremely high costs in terms of human suffering, loss of property, life, not only in the Himalayas but also in the plains. Much of the environmental damage, decline in agricultural productivity and human suffering that the Himalayan region is facing today could have been avoided had there been greater political commitment to forest conservation and eco-development. Such commitment is, of course, much in evidence today; but it needs to be supported and promoted by the local population. An estimate of the investment required to reverse the trend in the Himalayas has not been made. The State of the Himalayas - a Call for Action and many other studies and appeals have drawn the attention of the Planning Commission to this issue. The present allocations are not adequate but modifications even within the present overall figures can help to reach the immediate targets. Such modification should spell out the mechanism of involving the large number of people affected, the modalities of political and administrative commitments, and the results to be achieved within the stipulated time frame. Additional allocations may be required but the first task should be to improve the result orientation of the existing allocations.The cost of damage to crops, houses and public utilities in one year (1978) due to heavy floods was estimated at Rs. 1,700 crores. The Government appointed a Task Force on Flood Control, Soil Conservation and Afforestation. Its well prepared and documented report was appreciated by the government. The actions, however were not consistent with the recommendations. The government once again appointed a Task Force for Study of Eco-Development in the Himalayan Region, and this report by the Planning Commission itself dated March 1982 still remains partly unimplemented. The time has come, rather it is overdue, to develop the "Arithmetic of Prevention" into the "Politics, Strategy and Plan for Cure" of man-made tragedies in the Himalayas. Let us spend only a part of the cost of prevention for the cause of eco-development, afforestation and systematic involvement of local communities and people in their own self-reliant future.

Summary of Seven-Pronged Strategy to Save the Himalayas

"1. Increase production and planting of trees: Introduce regeneration planting of fuel / fodder-fruit / multi-purpose plants and trees; revive bio-fencing / social and other fencing and promote self-generation of vegetation.
2. Reduce consumption of fuelwood and cutting of forests: Harness alternative energy sources like solar, mini / micro hydel, wind, biogas and promote more efficient smokeless chulhas.
3. Impart special attention to severely damaged areas: Concentrate on critical micro / mini catchments, villages/ towns where damage is extensive, and mass wastage is in plenty. The last must be treated by special means such as *in situ* planting of juniper, other evergreen trees etc. with the help of mist chambers, and other means.
4. Revive / regenerate springs and traditional water harvesting practices: Mismanagement of water is related to resource depletion in the Himalayan terrain and should be given its rightful due. Harvest water in small-scale water harvesting structures, promote and revive traditional practices for the same, and devise innovative techniques for efficient and cost effective management.
5. Integrate Land and Water Use: Movement of water redistributes nutrients and affects the quality of the soil. When allowed to flow unchecked it causes severe erosion rendering the land unfit for cultivation, while controlled and managed flow can enhance productivity considerably. Land and water are thus interrelated intricately and an integrated approach is required to enhance productivity.
6. A Call to the People:

- The Himalayas are overburdened with population pressure. Practice family planning: Produce less children. THIS IS MOST URGENT.
- Take up the Challenge: Establish local conservation societies.
- For Survival, be self-reliant, work cooperatively and do not always depend on government assistance.
- Start forest associations, people's nurseries and special action groups of ex-servicemen, students, NGO / voluntary bodies, and women.
- Above all, be informed about your environment and the state of its health.

7. A Call to the Government:

- Promote poverty alleviation programmes in the hills with utmost urgency.
- Promote employment generation programmes through suitable training and initial support including some investment.
- Implement eco-development programmes with speed.
- Fix accountability on development bodies for any damage to the eco-system.
- Catalyze people's action."

STRATEGY I

INCREASE PRODUCTION AND PLANTING OF TREES

The Problem

Pressure upon the forest resources is mounting owing to the rising demands for fuelwood, wood for housing, fodder, raw material for resin, pulp and paper industry, and land for agriculture. These have contributed in different ways towards deforestation in the ecologically fragile Himalayan terrain. In addition, a lot of forest wood is required for marketing of apples and other fruit crops that need packaging into crates.

It was in the colonial rule that the traditional rights of the people over the forest wealth were taken away in the name of better forest management. The governance of free India has followed the footsteps of the departing masters and after fifty years of Independence people have been totally alienated, and traditional systems of management and social fencing have been shattered. Consequently, the agricultural-forest-fodder-fuelwood-cattle linkages have been severely affected and the quality of life of the masses has been adversely affected.

Between the Kali and Tons rivers Uttarakhand region has 34,35,922 ha of forest land (63.69 % of the total land area). According to conservative estimates about 20 per cent of the land area demarcated as forest land is devoid of any vegetation. Agro-forestry interventions in this vast land area can reduce the burgeoning pressure upon the forests. Shortage of fuelwood is more acute in mountain areas (as in semi-arid/arid areas), where the productivity of natural woodlands is on the lower side and the risk of over-exploitation of the environment is the greatest. Fuelwood deficits are particularly common in and around population centres in mountain areas. In addition, several other factors are contributing to wood scarcity in the Himalayan region. For instance, many rural people do not perceive a fuelwood crisis because they have access to freely available alternatives like animal dung and crop residues. They are not aware of the efficiency of use of these alternatives, for which they pay no cash price directly (but pay much more indirectly through reduced fertility of their land) they therefore do not utilize the available alternative of bio-gas which can provide fuel, fertilizer and a pollution-free environment. There are no doubt problems with the existing bio-gas technology at higher altitudes, but it can be taken care of with research for better alternatives. In most parts of the Himalayas, disincentives that seriously affect tree plantation are low fuelwood prices and problems of land and trees tenure (and right) some of which are in the process of solution. In many cases where there is open access to wood resources, traditional systems of management are breaking down. Social fencing and bio-fencing are no longer providing adequate protection.In some parts of Himachal Pradesh and the hill districts of Uttar Pradesh it is becoming increasingly clear that progress in agriculture depends on controlling deforestation. Regenerating the vegetative cover by adopting farming practices that compensate for shortened fallow periods can restore the tree cover and enhance the net output of annual crops and a variety of perennial tree crops. Experience has shown that it is easier to motivate people to plant trees than to divert them to other activities like tending and protecting the planted trees. It is necessary therefore that regeneration of tree planting should go hand in hand with social and / or bio-fencing.

Success Stories

Chamoli district has gained considerable prominence due to the Chipko Movement, the tree planting programme and People's Nurseries through the efforts and leadership of Shri Chandi Prasad Bhatt. Aware of the problems of increasing deforestation, the menace of landslides and of the unprecedented floods of 1977 in the Alaknanda, Chandi Prasad Ji organized the women and men of neighbouring villages and demonstrated that people can take their destiny in their own hands. Chamoli district (headquarters Gopeshwar) has witnessed heroic efforts in tree planting, regeneration, water harvesting, nursery operations, bio-gas, smokeless chulhas and other related programmes.Inspired by the Chipko Movement, the Gram Sewa Sansthan in Gongad Patti of Tehri Garhwal launched a massive campaign for forest and water conservation in the region. With the active participation of the villagers, specially women, lopping was discouraged in the forest around the villages, massive plantations were undertaken, the traditional system of social fencing was revived and a series of chaals (water harvesting structures at the slope break that augment recharge) were made. Consequent to these efforts many springs have been rejuvenated; water is now easily and abundantly available, the villagers do not have to walk for long distances for fodder and fuelwood collection as the forest around the village has been regenerated and is being exploited in a managed manner. As a practice, the people lop the forest in a cyclic manner so that it is not overpressurised and gets adequate time to regenerate. Trees for Life (TFL)/ HIMCON, Ranichauri has been undertaking massive afforestation drives in the Chamba block of Tehri Garhwal. Besides promoting medicinal, aromatic and horticultural species the organisation has been propagating mutipurpose trees in the area. A number of nurseries for preparing planting material of bhimal, khadik, gurial, burans, and other indigenous varieties are being run with the cooperation of the people. The movement is gaining momentum and the Mahila Mangal Dals of the region are actively participating in the endeavours of the organization.

Need for Improved Development Planning

As clearing of land for agriculture is an important contributing cause of deforestation in many parts of the Himalayas, the role of agriculture and livestock needs to be reassessed to ensure that they promote sustainable development. The potential for integrating fuelwood production, agro-forestry and soil / water conservation techniques in farming systems need to be systematically reviewed for each of the sub-regions of the Himalayas.

Recommended Action Programme

- Promote tree planting around family homesteads and cultivated areas by removing legal and other constraints and disincentives on farm-tree planting.
- Develop low-cost technologies for direct seeding, seedling production by schools and non-governmental organizations, people's nurseries, etc.
- Encourage tree seed collection by individuals, school students, and other government and non-government groups, because often it is the lack of seeds / saplings which hampers the nursery and tree plantation programmes.
- Encourage local support and participation in tree planting by increasing the use of fast-growing, multi-purpose tree species that meet the people's immediate needs.
- Promote Village Van Panchayats with committed leadership for tree planting and regeneration, but not as instruments of village politics and power (without full commitment to tree planting and associated programmes).
- Encourage private sector involvement in establishing and maintaining plantations, giving priority to planting of deforested lands not suited for annual crops.
- Reassess wood prices and wood distribution networks and evaluate the potential for increasing "farmgate" prices of wood.
- Increase local involvement in protecting and managing forests and woodlands and organize community control over access and use of these resources, by using techniques that conserve

soil moisture and enhance natural vegetation.

- Strengthen forestry extension parallel to agricultural and rural extension services by training more agents and developing audio-visual materials that clearly demonstrate the relationship between managed use and sustained productivity of water, soil, pastures and forests.

STRATEGY II

REDUCE CONSUMPTION OF FUELWOOD AND CUTTING OF FORESTS

Fuelwood Conservation

In the Himalayan region, fuelwood is required not only for cooking but also for heating during the cold winters. Due to the poor access to commercial fuel (LPG, kerosene) an overwhelmingly large proportion of the population of the region is dependent upon fuelwood. The traditional hearths are not efficient and a large amount of the fuelwood is wasted. A major project has therefore to be undertaken for improving woodstoves. Simultaneously, use of alternative renewable energy should be promoted in a big way. Large-scale bio-gas adoption is the need of the hour, for better fuel, fertilizer and environment. There is need for diversifying bio-gas input from cattle dung to rural waste, urban waste and human waste. Prejudices against the use of human waste should be steadily removed through concerted action as part of a sanitation and pollution control drive. Bio-gas techniques also need to be adopted to suit the cold climatic conditions of the Himalayas. The use of solar cookers, solar and wind devices for crop drying and other allied usage, where applicable, should be encouraged. The Uttarakhand region holds promise for the development of wind energy parks. The khals and dhars have a sustained and adequately strong flow of wind. This however requires extensive wind mapping in the region. Other recommended actions in this context are:

- Briquetting techniques need to be promoted in the region in a big way. All logging wastes and other farm and crop wastes should be collected and utilized as fuel through briquetting techniques. This has the potential of giving employment to large number of people besides providing a viable alternative energy source.

- An overwhelmingly large part of Uttarakhand is unelectrified and the power supply in the remote regions that are electrified is miserably uncertain. Rural and urban electrification through mini / micro hydropower plants needs serious thought and action.
- Commercial fuels such as LPG and kerosene should be provided at subsidised rates and the use of pressure cookers for efficient use of fuel should be popularised besides supporting outreach programmes to increase efficiency of fuelwood use.
- Changes in wood cutting licence fees and current methods of collection need to be considered. These would give rural communities greater control over tree harvesting and eliminate "free" wood.

Substitution of Fruit Packing Cases

There is need for developing cheaper and durable substitutes for fruit packaging to minimize damage during transit, storage and marketing. Pine needle hard-board packaging boxes appear to hold good promise and should be given a fair trial. Corrugated fibre-board cartons offer advantages of lighter weight, lesser bruising of fruits, controlled ventilation, pilferage-proof nature, easier handling and possibilities of recycling. Rationalization of packaging of fruits and vegetables can also be achieved by introducing 36 litres and 18 litres plastic returnable crates with collapsible modular sides. Further research is required on different aspects such as optimum ventilation, cushioning material and resistance to rough handling. Many of the above recommendations have been adapted especially in Himachal Pradesh. Other improvements include :

- Standardization of techniques for bulk storage and transit of fruit juices/concentrates based on cheaper conservation methods such as solar dehydration, pickling and chemical treatment for use in homes and on farms (using techniques which process wastes into value-added by-products (e.g. animal/poultry feeds).

- Development of mobile fruit processing centres in the region. These would be economically viable as they can be regularly shifted from season to season and would reduce the wastage to the minimum. Besides the villagers would be able to get a good price for their produce.
- Organisation of demonstration and training (using audio-visual aids and simple slide material) on basic principles of fruit and vegetable management to groups of field workers and village communities.
- The produce of the region should be marketed in an organised and aggressive manner, and a unique brand consciousness should be developed based on the pure and pristine environment of the Himalayas.
- Food Processing should be given special attention including institution of marketing on the lines of milk cooperatives.

Promotion of Renewable Energy

Use of bio-gas, solar cookers, wind-mills, improved chulhas and implementing of other renewable energy programmes need to be aggressively promoted in the Himalayan Districts.

The Himalayan terrain has a large potential for hydropower. This energy has to be tapped in an eco-friendly manner through a series of mini and micro-hydel schemes, rather than constructing large dams. Energy tapped locally can be utilised for powering local cottage industries besides lighting the villages. Experience has shown that transmission losses to remote areas are extremely high and micro/mini-hydel projects are the only cost effective alternative in this terrain. The hilly terrain does have a battery of watermills that can be utilised to generate energy for local use in a cost effective manner. Subsidies, technical know-how and other incentives should be made available to the local entrepreneurs for establishing these.

STRATEGY III

SEVERELY DAMAGED AREAS WARRANT SPECIAL AND IMMEDIATE ATTENTION

Critical Micro and Mini Watersheds

These are the areas where man-made damage has been extensive through deforestation, clearance, overgrazing and environmental degradation as a whole. Destructive landuse on watersheds is found on a vast scale throughout the Himalayas. The degradation of upland watersheds due to road construction and other unplanned and inconsiderate human activities has resulted in massive soil erosion and sedimentation of rivers, dams and reservoirs. The consequences in the lowlands include increased severity of floods leading to losses of crops, land, buildings and even human life. The Alaknanda landslides and floods in 1977, Belakuchi landslide of 1980, Guwahati landslide in 1983, Okhimath and Malpa landslides of 1998, and many such landslides in the upper Brahmaputra are examples of watershed degradation. The consequences of such degradation may be complicated, because the devastation can in fact occur far away from the source of damage and often across political boundaries. Other major causes of watershed degradation are:

- High rainfall in the upland areas, which has caused watershed degradation mostly in the northeast and partly in the Central Himalayas in deforested and unprotected areas. Rapid population growth and search for food, fuel and fodder have caused virtual invasion and destruction of upland forests. Subsequent misuse of exposed slopes through intensive overgazing by livestock and unprotected cultivation is causing further degradation of soil and water resources.
- Medium to low rainfall in the uplands, which has affected water sources mostly in Himachal Pradesh and Jammu & Kashmir. Increasing human and livestock populations are reducing these areas to unproductive wastelands on a vast scale, primarily due to extensive fuelwood gathering, uncontrolled overgrazing and depletion of soil fertility through continuous cropping.

Success Stories

Although not in the Himalayas, the success story of the Damodar valley in soil conservation in the upper catchment is worth mentioning. Here reforestation and soil conservation have successfully stabilized the watersheds above the major dams. As a result, the floods in the Damodar valley have been moderate, the rate of sedimentation has reduced, more water is now available for human and livestock use, and crop yields have increased in the last 30 years. Another success story is from the Shiwaliks where the eroded catchment of the Sukhna lake in Chandigarh, in the foothills of the Himalayas, was severely overgrazed, contributing large quantities of silt to the watershed, so much so that the water supply for the city of Chandigarh was threatened. The people of Sukhomajiri village, where the major catchment lies, decided to build small ponds to supplement their irrigation. The result: they have increased crop and fodder production, and are able to stall-feed the cattle through increased grass production (and have enough surplus to sell, which flows back into development of the village). The villagers resorted to social as well as some bio-fencing, which has now fully controlled erosion, so that no sediment flows into the Sukhna lake. It is a wonderful example of people's action. It is important here to mention that this was totally a people's programme and the people refused aid from the government except technical assistance of committed people, like Shri Mishra and Shri Bansal, who won the confidence of the villagers after hard work.

TFL/HIMCON is undertaking watershed management work in the remote villages of Tehri Garhwal. IGSSS New Delhi financially assists this work and the people of the watershed are participating in these programmes very enthusiastically. Under this programme a massive afforestation drive is being undertaken in the watershed together with the introduction of seed banks to promote high yielding varieties. Water management is being given special emphasis and a detailed study has been undertaken of the hydrological regime. To enhance the recharge of groundwater *khaals* have been erected together with various water harvesting structures. A series of rainwater harvesting structures have also been erected in the watershed and a spring has been rejuvenated. People of the watershed are supporting the work of the organisation and this testifies to the fact that they are benefiting from these works.

Proposals for Action

In most parts of the Himalayan region, there is a need to change land-use practices to establish and rehabilitate degraded upland watersheds. Technically proven and economically sound methods are available for different social and ecological conditions. Experience has shown that proper landuse can sustain and improve the productivity of both forests and agricultural lands. Solutions vary with local conditions, and pilot projects are still needed in some watersheds. The recommended programme focuses on three main activities:

- Establishing tree and grass cover to stabilize upland areas and to ensure adequate supplies of fuelwood, fodder and building material.
- Controlling livestock grazing to the extent of total stall-feeding.
- Developing and promoting sustainable and integrated farming systems.

To apply this strategy, important policy issues need to be considered. Some of these are:

- Government policy must be based on the inter-dependence of upland and lowland communities.
- Government (central, state or local) must provide more support for the upland communities to deal with problems of poverty and remoteness from technical help, both of which cause land misuse. Change in land-use practices requires incentives and full participation and support of local communities. The most practical incentives are short-term daily wages for soil conservation and tree and fodder plantation. This is being practiced in many parts of the Himalayas. The problem lies in the fact that when the short-term programmes stop, the degradation sets in. The self-interest of the locals has to be inbuilt in any such incentive programme. Provision of seeds and fertilizers at subsidized rates could be another incentive.

Multi-disciplinary Approach

Since expertise from several disciplines is needed to rehabilitate and manage degraded watersheds, effective actions cannot be taken by just foresters or agriculturists or water-resource engineers or administrators alone; they must join hands and act harmoniously which is what integrated watershed management is.

Framework for Action

In view of the scarce resources, the focus should be, at least for the coming five or ten years, on "most severely degraded areas which are also the most populated." A survey is being conducted (using remote-sensing imagery and aerial photographs) to identify the specific villages and the lands around them that need to be conserved and developed. Areas affected by landslides need to be urgently stabilized preferable by the *in situ* plantation technique developed at Roorkee University (Mahinder Pant, University of Roorkee). This Mist Propagation or Controlled Environment Regeneration System is a continuous plant generation technique with many times the yield of conventional nurseries in equivalent space. These techniques are to be the foundation for the Himalayan Technology Hardware Development Programme, especially for stabilizing landslide and other critically damaged areas.

Implementation of the Himalayan Technology Hardware Development Programme

- In each of the eight sectors of the Indian Himalayas, a Himalayan Resources and Technology Development Centre (HRTDC) should be established, preferably as part of an already existing technical University / Engineering College / Technology R&D Institute. The avowed objective of such envisaged centres would be to evolve, standardize and extend a range of Technology Hardware Units / Products / Systems / complexes, appropriate for Himalayan needs, aspirations and conditions. Such a network of HRTDCs should have a single apex body to coordinate and monitor the policy, functions and programmes of each of the envisaged centres.

- Pending the establishment of HRTDCs, a series of long-term Technology Hardware R&D and Extension Projects/Programmes should be initiated in select areas of relevance in the Himalayan context in our IITs/engineering universities / colleges / technology R&D institutes / Centres. Such projects / programmes should be funded both by conventional R&D funding organization / agencies such as DST, DRDO, CSIR, Department of Electronics and others; as also by the major users / concerned departments / agencies such as the National Wasteland Development Board (NWDB), Department of Environment and Forests, Department of Non-conventional Energy resources, Department of Tourism, to name a few. Such projects / programmes would foster the creation and growth of distinct R&D groups within the country working exclusively on Himalayan resources and allied technologies.
- In each of the significant altitude zones of each of the eight major sectors of the Indian Himalayas, Technology Demonstration and Training (D&T) Centres should be established for purposes of field testing, demonstration and training in respect of those specific technology hardware packages that are found to be appropriate for large-scale extension in the Himalayas. Such centres should be developed as permanent facilities accessible to technologists, scientists, extension cadres, voluntary activists and others involved in Himalayan development and allied programmes.
- Special incentives should be given to attract outstanding field researchers, technology hardware specialists / innovators, skilled technicians, and extension workers. Such incentives should include provision of special leave ranging from three to ten years and special emoluments for field oriented Himalayan R&D and extension personnel.
- A panel of consultants in Himalayan resources and allied technologies should be formed at the level of Department of Science & Technology, Government of India. This panel should identify specific technologies to be developed on a priority basis exclusively for Himalayan needs, aspirations

and conditions.

- The area of Himalayan plant culture technology should be accorded the status of a full fledged technology mission as has been done in the case of rural drinking water supply, oil seed production and a few others by the Government of India.
- Engineering and technical universities / colleges / institutes of technology as are coming up or may come up in the major sectors of the Indian Himalayas should offer a new range of interdisciplinary degree / diploma / continuing education courses relevant from the stand point of Himalayan resources, needs, conditions and aspirations. As far as possible such institutes should desist from offering conventional courses that are divorced from the existing realities of the Himalayan regions.
- A series of international conferences should be hosted in the country on those specialized subjects / technologies which have immediate applications in the Himalayas.

In keeping with the above theme of technology hardware development exclusively for Himalayan needs, aspirations and conditions the present efforts seek to focus attention on the hardware requrements in three distinct areas of Himalayan endeavours, namely,

- Intensive off-season vegetable production under controlled phyto-environmental (CPEN) conditions.
- Eco-Stabilization of Himalayan Landslides—both roadside landslides and hamlet threatening landslides.
- Demonstration and Training (D&T) facilities for Himalayan eco-awareness and cadre field training purposes.

The work and recommendations of the Appropriate Eco-Technology Development Group (AEDG) of the University of Roorkee are worth quoting. The note prepared by the Coordinator, Shri Mahinder Pant, says: "People's involvement" in eco-development / wasteland development will carry conviction only when the local people take up one or more forms of Himalayan Plant Culture as a full-time professional vocation. This, in turn, would be the most effective long-term guarantee for the restoration-cum-rejuvenation of Himalayan eco-resources. To transform Himalayan Plant Culture from its present largely rudimentary and primitive state to a highly developed and professional discipline capable of giving the crucial economic returns, the basic needs are:

(a) Himalayan Plant Culture being highly specialized and involved would require development of skills and expertise in specific areas. Development of demonstration and training centres throughout the Himalayan region is therefore an urgent and imperative need.
(b) In view of the highly specialized nature of Himalayan plant culture and Himalayan eco-field operations, virtually at every step, appropriate grades of technology hardware/equipment are required which presently simply do not exist. There is, therefore, an imperative need to develop and standardize the entire range of technology hardware packages as are required for updating/modernizing different forms of Himalayan plant culture.
(c) Based on the above technology hardware packages a range of plant culture practices, techniques and field operations need to be standardized and extended on the required scale.
(d) An intensive programme of training the Himalayan people in various facets of Himalayan plant culture practices, techniques and methodologies through initiation of "earn while you learn" schemes need to be launched on a large scale.

Recommendations

1. There is an immediate need to scientifically catalogue the entire range of what could be appropriately termed as the High Potential Himalayan Local Species for various high priority needs such as fodder, fuel, eco-stabilization of landslide hit slopes, soil fertility restoration, etc.
2. A high priority programme for developing Himalayan eco-technologies should be launched forthwith based on both intermediate and high-end technologies.
3. There is an urgent need to re-orient Himalayan eco-development programmes towards field operations, field

investigations and field missions. The emphasis must be on prolonged field operations in the Himalayas.

4. Himalayan eco-development programmes must be highly selective and specific. Some priority areas which deserve immediate field action are as under:

   (a) Restoration-cum-rejuvenation of the prized Himalayan oaks.
   (b) Natural regeneration enhancement in the Himalayas on altitudinal / zonal basis.
   (c) Restoration of important high-altitude species like juniper, birch, fir, rhododendron, etc.
   (d) Soil fertility restoration of Himalayan watersheds.

Projects and Programmes Initiated by AEDG

The Upper Bhagirathi Valley Himalayan Eco-Culture (UBV/HEC) Mission : As part of this field operations mission it is envisaged that a total of five Controlled Phyto-environment (CPEN) Complexes would be established as under:

(1) The Ranichauri open field Operations Complex at the Ranichauri Hill Campus of Pantnagar University (Distt. Tehri Garhwal).
(2) The Uttarkashi Open Eco-Adventure Complex at the Nehru Institute of Mountaineering, Uttarkashi (In progress).
(3) The Harsil Open Eco-Enterprises Complex at Harsil (8,500 ft) in Uttarkashi.
(4) The Nagini Open Floriculture Complex at Nagini (2,500 ft.)
(5) The Roorkee Open Eco-Technology Complex (already established).

STRATEGY IV

JUDICIOUS WATER CONSERVATION AND HARVESTING: AN URGENT NECESSITY

Revive / Regenerate Springs

The Problem

Water is equally important as food. Man needs it to drink and also to grow food to eat. Human habitations always have wells or streams, rivers or springs to meet this need. Due to increasing deforestation, the flow from springs has been diminishing and even drying up in the past few decades in many parts of the Himalayas. Only a minute fraction of the water available in streams and rivers is used for irrigation in the hills owing to difficulties in conveying water to the fields. The same rivers are a major source of irrigation in the downstream areas. Water harvesting specially during the monsoons has not been given enough attention in the mountains. Much of the people's need for power and water in the hills can be met by springs, ponds, mini/micro-hydel or even major hydro-electric projects, but these resources still remain predominantly untapped in the Himalayas.

Success Stories

Himachal Pradesh has been paying serious attention to mini / micro-hydel projects and there are at present several successfully operating units in Palampur, Chamba, Shimla, Solan and Bilaspur districts. These projects are providing the much needed energy to the rural people, besides meeting their water needs. Water harvesting in the foothills and associated areas of the Shiwaliks (Sukhomajri) has done wonders for the people—transforming their lives through irrigation, multiple cropping and good drinking water supply. Mini-hydels have also made a good beginning in Arunachal Pradesh and need to be extended to other parts of the North-Eastern Himalayas.Water storage tanks provide full irrigation to vegetables on the Kasauni Farm (District Almora) of Radha Bhatt, located on a steep hillside. The farm is also being used for training young girls in village industries.

Rainwater if harvested in a judicious manner has the potential of fulfilling a major proportion of the needs of the masses. TFL/HIMCON has therefore erected a series of ferro-cement and LDPE tanks to harvest rainwater from roofs. The water harvested in these tanks is being used for drinking and for cattle for households and for small-scale irrigation of vegetable or nursery plants. TFL/HIMCON has long been propagating judicious use of spring water in the Himalayan terrain: Shankar Sarod constructed near Ranichauri under the spring water rejuvenation scheme still fulfils the water related needs of a number of people of the region. This strategy is now being replicated in other areas.

Some recommendations related to water conservation, water storage, spring rejuvenation and water management developed in the last decade are given below:

1. *Drinking Water*: Springs in protected catchments are generally potable; elsewhere, they may well be carriers of disease, worms being the commonest in the hills. Intensive study and action are needed to provide potable water in the catchments. All catchment springs should be protected to ensure purity of water and should have a suitable number of off-take points to provide potable water to the people
2. *Irrigation*: The strategy for agriculture should be replacement of extensive by intensive agriculture. Crops (cereals, vegetables, etc.) should be grown only in irrigated terraced fields. Unirrigated hill sides should be devoted to tree crops (fruits, nuts, commercial crops). Irrigation in the hills increases yields three or four times and water requirement is often less than in the plains.
3. *Medium Irrigation*: Studies should be undertaken where not done as yet, stream by stream, with the objective of providing maximum irrigation from streams and rivers in the area selected for intensive agriculture. These should be treated as public works for which funds should be set apart in state/district plans.
4. *Minor Irrigation*: The proposed Catchment Development Boards should provide funds for minor irrigation and existing subsidies should be liberally given. Piping of water preferably through strong plastic pipes can be a solution

for both small-scale cultivation, as well as for development of plant nurseries.

5. *Storage Tanks*: Tanks for rainwater for houses can be provided above the stream level. These should preferably be cement tanks lined with coal-tar or plastic to reduce losses. Special units for manufacture of plastic storage tanks should be set up at convenient places and purchase should be subsidized. People do use rainwater for drinking but such storage tanks can also help in irrigation of small vegetable or nursery plots to increase their yields manifold. Roof rainwater harvesting in cement, ferro-cement or plastic lined tanks need to be adopted in most areas.
6. *Water harvesting in Ponds/Tanks*: These need special sites which can be dammed or where some big dugout can be made. Each village should have at least one or several ponds of much larger size than the individual water storage tanks for each household. Such ponds can be used for fish culture or for fish culture and beautification/ recreation with trees planted all around. Farmers and villagers should be given subsidy, if required, for maintaining such water storage works. Hydrams can be used for lifting water wherever feasible for increasing crop production.
7. *Mini/Micro-hydels*: The inexhaustible renewable resource available in the form of water flow should be utilized in developing micro-projects for each catchment. This should be supplemented by a subsidised issue of cooking / heating equipment. In addition, clusters of villages should be provided with electric light and power connections for development of cottage industries. Hydropower resource potential is immense in the Himalayas, and only eight per cent has currently been harnessed. This potential should be steadily utilized, first for the benefit of the hill people.
8. *Aquifer Recharge*: Specific areas should be reforested to forestall possible drying up of available aquifers and springs.
9. *Water Management*: It is the combined anti-erosion and water use plan for each catchment which constitutes the

water management plan. Such plans must be prepared for all the priority catchments.

10. *Multi-purpose Projects*: Dams built in the hills are almost exclusively meant for multi-purpose projects whose benefits are derived by consumers in the plains. Recent studies have created doubt about the advisability of such projects especially when they dislocate large numbers of hill people. Financing of such large projects has to he critically reviewed and, where possible, curtailed.

Spring Rejuvenation Programme, Chamba-Narendra Nagar stretch, Tehri Garhwal District (U.P)

A quick survey was made of all the springs which have their outlet on the Chamba-Narendra Nagar Route in Tehri Garhwal District. For a stretch of about 46 kms the survey indicated the number of springs, the names of the villages closest to them, the number of sub-springs in this complex, the distance of the springs from Chamba, the size of the spring, (whether big, medium or small) and the quantity of water in the spring at the time of survey (to find out whether it is a permanent or non-permanent spring and any suggestions about the more efficient utilization of the spring water). The observations pertain to 24 springs.

A very clear observation was that a substantial proportion of the water of these springs ranging from 30 to 80 per cent was going waste. It was felt that a proper measurement of the quantity of water be made again in December / January / February, and once again in May - June, the low discharge time. After that a master plan could be prepared for rejuvenation of these springs. *Water is the life-blood of agriculture and horticulture in this area.* But more than this, these springs are the sources of life-giving drinking water for quite a number of villages and, therefore, their linkage with the Drinking Water Mission should be established. Further, water in this part of the Himalayas has multi-purpose use—for irrigation for the paddy crop when the rain is not timely, supplemental irrigation for wheat in winter and spring, irrigation for orchards, and for aquaculture and fresh water fisheries. Thus the spring waters have multiple use which make them extremely important.

STRATEGY V

INTEGRATED LAND AND WATER USE

Integrated land and water use will include various aspects of crops, livestock, horticulture, forests, fisheries, etc., in a well knitted programme that will ultimately benefit the people of the area, while preserving the eco-system. Improved land and water use will be according to the capability of the area. This multi-disciplinary programme has to be developed in further detail, keeping the specific needs of the people and of the Himalayan environment in view. The objective of the programme is to get the optimum use of each square metre of land and each cubic metre of water. Plans need to be made at the level of the individual farms to promote an Integrated Farming System in the hill areas.

The greatest handicap in this connection is the land holding size and there is urgent need for consolidation of such holdings into rational ones. Land reforms have to be carried out on a priority basis in all the areas where land consolidation has not been done, for example, in the Uttarakhand region. Case studies made in the hill areas of Uttar Pradesh reveal that on an average holding may be distributed in five or six localities, broken up into as many as 25 pieces. This severely constrains the level of productivity as the poor farmer is not able to generate enough income to invest in irrigation, fertilizers, etc. This vicious circle of poverty can be broken only if there is land consolidation and each farmer is allotted an economically viable piece of land.

STRATEGY VI

A CALL TO THE PEOPLE

This is a call to the hill people who are fast shifting from their traditional "hard" life to one of slumber, lethargy, lack of self-reliance and indifference. "I will abandon the fields, go to the plains and work there", says one of the songs, to be replaced by a Kumaoni folk song, "Return to the hills, your home and hearth". This call is particularly directed to the youth "Don't run away. Take up the Challenge. You alone can save the Himalayas". Gainful employment and activities other than farming to augment the income of the family are thus becoming urgent, especially for the educated and school-leaving youth.

Success Stories of People's Action in the Himalayas

There are many: Chamoli Gram Swarajya Mandal in the Garhwal Himalayas is one such example. Tuper in Almora is the second. Berinag Gram Swarajya Mandal in Pithoragarh district is yet another example. CHIRAG (Central Himalaya Rural Action Group) at Sitla (Nainital) and TFL/HIMCON (Ranichauri) are some other success stories of people's action in the Himalayas.

Proposal for Action

Population control and family planning have become an imperative necessity in the hills. All educational and practical measures should be geared up for this purpose. The people must produce less children to safeguard their future.*People's Action Groups* like local conservation societies and District Forest Associations are essential in the work for environmental conservation. But these institutions should not be politicized. *Ex-Servicemen* of whom there are more than 65,000 in Almora district alone and probably over a million in the whole of the Himalayas, have a great role to play. Even if 10 per cent of them devote 50 per cent of their time to the common good (with some return for their efforts) a lot can be done. They can contribute their mite through activities such as nursery establishment, planting and safeguarding of trees, water harvesting, construction of tanks, mini-hydels for irrigation and so on. *Students* should acquire their work experience from working for the Himalayan eco-systems and their teachers must help them towards this end. An immense potential of university and college and school-leaving students is to be harnessed both as part of the curriculum, practical experience, even as an essential pre-requisite and work experience, for the degree. Vocationalization of environment careers should be given high priority in the Himalayan region. Income-generating activities such as sericulture, apiculture, mushroom culture, horticulture and floriculture need to be promoted.

NGO's and Voluntary Groups should adopt a critical catchment and concentrate all their resources and expertise on restoring it to health.

Leadership initiated through *People's Participation* is a must for regenerating the decaying eco-system of the Himalayan region. The age old practices of resource management that have been neglected for decades need revitalisation.

STRATEGY VII

A CALL TO THE GOVERNMENT

The various programmes indicated earlier cannot be fully implemented without adequate and committed governmental involvement and support. Indeed, the government is already acting on many of these strategies. However, it is incumbent on the part of the government at the centre, state, district and local levels to work in the Himalayas with speed and compassion, so as not to create more problems than they solve. The central and state governments' role includes overall guidance, research and development, and allocation of necessary funds and resources. The government should especially assist those below the poverty line through free services, subsidies and technical support. The priority areas are enumerated below :

- Integrated farming by small farmers on plots of land available with them. Experiences in China have shown that smallness of a plot up to a certain limit is no bar on practicing integrated farming. This system based on crop, livestock, agro-forestry, fisheries, etc. gives the best returns to the farmer while promoting conservation and development of the eco-system.
- Employment generation, through non-polluting eco-development programmes such as people's nurseries and cottage industries like silk, honey, mushroom and other subsidiary activities.
- Assistance to those of the poor who are ready to help themselves.
- Utilization of available expertise and resources of NGOs / Voluntary Agencies, ex-servicemen, military and para-military personnel in implementing the environmental conservation and tree-planting programmes in the Himalayas.
- Decentralization of the decision making process to promote

action at or near the site and involvement of the local Catchment Development Boards, District Forest Associations, Village Van Panchayats, etc., in these tasks.

- Support to the G.B. Pant Institute for Himalayan Environment and Development as well as a people and NGOs "Centre for Himalayan Rejuvenation" charged with the responsibility of: (a) Conducting training programmes for all categories of people together with provision of training material and aids; (b) Formulating general strategy and policy issues on Himalayan conservation and development; (c) Operating an Information Centre on all aspects of eco-development in the Himalayas; and (d) Coordinating the activities of various Action Groups—Government, Non-government or Voluntary, working in the Himalayas.
- Set up one Krishi and Van Vigyan Kendra (KVK) for each Himalayan district on the lines of KVK at Ranichanri Hill Campus of Pantnagar Agriculture University.
- Establish at least one "Energy Village" Urjagram in each Himalayan district initially supported by Department of Non-Conventional Energy.
- Participate but not control the operation of the Himalayan Conservation Fund.

True Knowledge
Enables a Man to Realize
That he is
The Soul with a Body
Now, in his Ignorance, he
Thinks
That he is
A Body with a Soul.

18
Case Study - HIMCON's Pilot Projects in Tehri Garhwal, Uttarakhand, UP

Himalayan Consortium for Himalayan Conservation (HIMCON)

Himalayan Consortium for Himalayan Conservation (HIMCON) has been active in the Himalayan region for about 10 years and has been working on different problems that the people of this region face at grass-roots level. It is through its long and close association with the region and the people inhabiting it, together with the understanding of the ground realities that it has been able to promote people's participation for its programmes. Its programmes have been people's own programmes with their participation as the prime motive.

With the vision and direction provided by the experience of its Chairman Dr. M.L. Dewan who is amongst the pioneers of Watershed Management, HIMCON has come to identify scarcity of basic resources; water, energy, fodder, as one of the major and serious problems of the hilly terrain. HIMCON a partner of TFL and other NGO's is enlarging the scope and activities in the Central and Western Himalayan is following the strategy given below :

- Establishment of nurseries, transplanting and protection of trees of all types especially Fruits, Fuel Fodder and various types of fencing including Bio-fencing;
- Imparting special corrective treatment to severely damaged areas as well those affected by landslides.
- Regeneration of springs, water use and Watershed Management;
- Promotion of income generation activities of the Himalayan

Communities through mass propogation of medicinal and aromatic plants and other measures

- Stimulating participation of the Himalayan communities for promotion of their self reliance and promoting People's movement for Himalayan Rejuvenation

Studies, awareness building and working for the Himalayan Communities are all important but the real importance is in "Project and Programme". This chapter is a Case Study of what can be done by Himalayan Communities in partnership with the NGO—HIMCON—which is proud to serve these communities.

II. Participatory Watershed Management in Lawadhar and Paturi Villages in Chamba Block of Tehri Garhwal : An Executive Summary

TFL/HIMCON has undertaken regenerative work in the Himalayan region through a series of projects, the latest in the list being the Watershed Management project at Lawadhar and Paturi villages of Chamba Block of Tehri Garhwal with the support of Indo-German Social Service Society (IGSSS), New Delhi. This project works upon various aspects that have been taken care of in a cost effective and time bound manner; mass mobilization, people's participation, mobilization of technical inputs, managerial skills and the capacity of the grassroots level cadre.

During the course of interventions spanning two years the two watersheds have witnessed the following through the catalytic efforts of TFL/HIMCON.

Organization of Mahila Mandal Dals
Organisation of Watershed Committees
Organisation of Self Help Groups
Awareness and literacy campaigns
Establishment of Seed Banks
Establishment of Health Banks
Construction of a series of water harvesting structures (LDPE & ferrocement Tanks)
Construction of recharge pits and other water harvesting structures
Afforestation drive

Vegetative bunding of agricultural fields
Grafting drive for fruit plants
Promotion of horticulture
Promotion of cash crops

Work has also been carried out in animal husbandry, health awareness, sanitation, and income generation.

III. Government Inter College Nagini (School Nursery Programme, TFL/HIMCON)

Report of the TFL sponsored citrus plantation programme in Government Inter College, Nagini undertaken in monsoon 1999.

1. Preparation of the plot :	Shrubs on around 20 nali (unit of land) barren about 4000 sq. metres land were cleared for undertaking plantation. This exercise is necessary to improve the survival rates of the saplings.
2. Stone wall for fencing :	A 315 metres long and 1.5 metres high dry stone wall was constructed around the land selected for plantation. This acts as a fence and enhances the survival rates of the plantation.
3. Water availability :	A 200 metres long pipeline was setup to bring water to school, tapping water from the nearby perennial springs.
4. Ferrocement tank :	A 3,000 litres capacity ferrocement tank was constructed for irrigation and allied purposes. The water diverted from the spring through the above mentioned pipeline feeds this tank.
5. Preparation of the pits:	With the labour contribution (Shramdan) of the students 300 plantation pits were prepared and the same were manured.

6. Plantation : With the involvement of the school children 100 lemon, 100 kinu and 100 orange plants were planted in the pits so prepared.

7. Chowkidar : HIMCON has arranged for Chowkidar (watchman) for a period of one year for ensuring high survival rates of the plants. After one year the plants are expected to be sturdy enough to sustain on their own.

8. Survival : All the plants so planted are surviving.

These TFL sponsored initiatives of HIMCON has made the school children environmentally conscious and they feel encouraged to take up similar activities around their villages.

IV. Trees for Prasad

Experience of Trees for Life in the Allahabad Kumbh Mela has shown that when fruit seeds like guava when distributed after getting the blessings of Ganga and Vedic Mantras, people in lakhs are enthused to plant these seeds and the seedlings are considered sacred and thus it is possible to spread such fruit plants by the rural people who visit such Kumbh Melas. These trees are considered as Prasad blessed by the gods and goddesses. The people thus take care of such trees and acquire a source of nutrition for the family.

V. Mahila Shakti I

The goal of HIMCON and its partner CHIRAG is to improve the quality of life of the villagers of the region (especially the women and the poorer sections) and make them more self-reliant. People here live at a subsistence level in small villages and hamlets. Their livelihood and survival depends on the fuelwood, fodder and water they collect from the forests in their vicinity. As the forests are being degraded, these resources are becoming more scarce. The management of these natural resources in a sustainable and equitable manner is of primary importance. Consequently, social forestry has been one of the major activities of HIMCON and CHIRAG. In the last ten years about 3000 hectares of degraded community forests have been reafforested by planting over 4.5 million saplings by CHIRAG and about one quarter of these by TFL/ HIMCON. Production of grass from these community forests has also increased significantly as a result of controlling the free grazing of cattle. Apart from increasing the availability of biomass resources, CHIRAG and HIMCON recognised that pressure on these shrinking resources must also be reduced through alternative approaches and appropriate technological interventions. The two activities should go hand-in-hand, the common objective being the restoration of the depleted natural resource base.

The sustainable energy project was the outcome of this approach.

Project Components

The project started in April 1993 and comprise two phases—the first one for three years and the second one for two years and nine months. The physical components of the project are :

Biogas Plants

This is the main component of the propeat aining at providing easy access to energy and putting forth an alternative for fuelwood. It is a simple, low-cost technology which helps in eco-restoration, utilises renewable resources (dung) and, above all, has been implemented by training local villagers. It not only provides biogas for cooking but excellent biofertiliser in the form of slurry. As anticipated, roughly 40% of the plants were built of 1 cu.m. capacity requiring about 15-20 kg. of dung per day and the balance were of 2 cu.m. capacity requiring double the amount of dung.

Solar Cooker

A useful fuel saving device using the sun's rays for cooking, it involves only a one-time cost and almost no running costs.

Smokeless 'Chulha' (Open Cooking Stove)

Apart from providing a smokeless kitchen, it uses about 30% less fuelwood than the open 'Chulha' traditionally in use. The sheet metal chimney heats the room and an improved version with water jacket round the chimney provides hot water.

Pressure Cooker

Experiments have shown that at altitudes of 2000 m this simple device reduces cooking time for staple diet items such as pulses and potato by more than 50%. CHIRAG's and HIMCON's role was simply that of buying this item in bulk directly from the manufactures (at about 65-70% of market price) and making it available to the villagers at purchase price, a classic example of a facilitator's role.

Water Tank

Build of ferrocement/brick masonry in sizes varying from 1000-5000 litres capacity for storing water for domestic consumption from roof run-off and other sources. These tanks built near the house have proved very popular and useful.

Solar/improved kerosene Lantern

These energy-saving items were added in the last twelve months to assist villagers to get the benefit of government subsidies.

VI. Mahila Shakti II

The Himalayan eco-system is under stress due to a multitude of reasons and so is its indigenous population. The burden of routine work of the females of this region is on the rise and despite modernisation their drudgery is mounting. The Himalayan region where this project is to be taken up is facing severe crisis of basic resources, water, fuel, fodder. Outmigration rates in the region are high amongst males and this adds to the routine work of the females. Except for ploughing she is incharge of all the agricultural activities, she has to take care of the animals and fetch fuel, fodder and water besides taking care of the other routine household chores. There is thus no surprise that the awareness levels of these females are very low. Despite lack of awareness the females of the region are very sensitive towards environmental conservation and have in the past taken active part in many social movements; viz. Chipko, Sharab-bandi. This project aims at : bringing about an awareness amongst the females regarding their rights, various welfare schemes, other income enhancing activities, agriculture, horticulture etc. To bring about an awareness amongst the females regarding the various alternative energy devices that can free them from the routine work of firewood collection besides adding to the greenery in their surroundings. To demonstrate the efficacy of these alternate energy devices and to bring about a change in the energy consumption pattern of the masses. To bring about awareness amongst the masses regarding the depleting water resources of the region and thus to stress the need of conserving the same. To introduce various water harvesting practices in the villages and to demonstrate their efficacy. Though written at the last the foremost objective of the project is to strengthen women's movement in this region and to bring about a change in their perception. Survey of 2 sample villages has shown :

Energy source	Number of families
Only fuelwood	90
Fuel wood + kerosene oil	30
Fuel wood + kerosene oil + LPG	10

Collection of fuelwood is generally the burden of the females and children (especially girls) aid in this task. The following table shows that the share of menfolk in the two watersheds is a mere five per cent.

Group	Contribution in fuelwood collection (in %)
Men	5
Children	25
Females	70

Surveyed villages resort to fuel collection on a weekly basis. On an average seven kilograms of fuelwood is consumed by one household daily.

VII. TFL/HIMCON Awareness Generation and Training for use and Cultivation of Medicinal Plants & Herbals for Family Health & Welfare

Seventy per cent of the Indian population is living in villages where very few modern medical facilities are available. Nestled in the lap of nature, these villages are surrounded by innumerable medicinal plants or herbs. Due to lack of information and low skill most people however run to the hospitals in town and cities. Therefore in this situation, it has become necessary to give them essential knowledge about medicinal plants or herbs which can be helpful in day to day requirements of family health care and to improve their health and living standard through self use and sale of these plants, either in their raw form, or partially or fully processed.

With increasing cost of treatment through allopathic medicine and in some cases adverse effects of synthetic drugs, people are increasingly looking towards traditional medicines for relief. In any case all systems of medicine, including allopathic, depend either directly or indirectly on medicinal plants.

In the past, when we had rich virgin mixed forests, important medicinal plants or herbs were easily available in plenty. But now due to change in landuse pattern, over expliotation and various kinds of biotic pressure a number of medicinal plants are facing varying degrees of threat of extinction.

Considering the increasing demand for medicinal plants or herbs in national and international markets, it was considered necessary, to take up intensive cultivation, collection, identification, storage and distribution of medicinal plants using modern agrotechnologies and active people's participation. The present project being supported by DST is promoting awareness regarding the use of medicinal plants and conducting training programmes aimed at promoting cultivation of medicinal plants and herbs for family health and welfare. Two major nurseries have been established and three Women-Mahila Mandals nurseries are in process out of ten already selected. Short training sessions have been held for the women of the area and over 50 women have been exposed to this training programme. Twelve medicinal plants adapted to the Himalayan environment are being promoted through this programme. These are:

1. Atis 2. Meetha Telia/Bachnag 3. Safed Musali 4. Mamira Mishmi-Bitter 5. Salam Panja/Salep 6. Jatamansi 7. Goazamban 8. Kutki 9. Sarpagandha 10. Chobchini Gulabi 11. Chiraiyita 12. Bnafsha

VIII. Plan of Operation of International Humanitarian Project 9777 jointly by Rotary Club of Delhi South, Metropolitan Rotary Club of Surbiton, England and the Rotary Foundation of Rotary International : The Project Description

Rotary Club of Delhi South Metropolitan (RCDSM) has been active for last 10 years in the field of community development, training, tree planting, vocational training etc. RCDSM has now set up a "Rotary Vocational & Environmental Centre" in Tehri Garhwal, India in collaboration with Rotary Club of Surbiton and TFL/HIMCON, Tehri Garhwal.

The main aim of this programme is to initiate a Pilot Project for Sustainable Development in five selected villages in Tehri Garhwal district of Uttar Pradesh in the Central Himalayas with four specific objectives:

1. Initiating integrated agriculture, horticulture and forestry activity within the framework of watershed management concept including
   a. Land, soil and water management;
   b. Water harvesting and optimum utilization of water resources;
   c. Propagation of selected species of trees which can play dual role of improving the environment and becoming a source of sustainable income;
   d. Promoting horticulture and medicinal and aromatic plants;
   e. Scientific training;
   f. Establishing nurseries and seed farms;
   g. Value added processing so that the people get good value for what they produce;
2. Promoting and strengthening people's organizations and networking with them through non-government organizations, Government Institutions and programmes, specially in literacy family planning, renewable energy,

promotion of women's organizations and strengthening of mother and child centres.
3. Strengthening and establishing self help groups; savings, thrift and credit management institutions for institutional finance and training Mahila and Yuvak Mandals
4. Promoting active involvement of local Rotary Clubs in the area

IX. Sri Dorabji Tata Trust Project — Himalayan Rejuvenation I

Supported by Sri Dorabji Tata Trust Bombay this ambitious project aims at systematic and scientific investigation of mass wastage in the Himalayas. Through the use of state of art GIS and remote sensing techniques, supplemented by detailed fieldwork landslide hazard zonation is to be carried out and risk factor to which the people are exposed is to be ascertained. Armed with this mitigative strategy, the project is to be implemented with full co-operation of the masses.

This project thus aims at minimising human sufferings associated with landslides, besides rejuvenating digraded tracts through a restoration drive.

X. People's Health in People's Hands — A Social Marketing Approach to Participatory Health Awareness in Tehri Garhwal (in pipeline)

High altitude socio-economic problems such as poverty, illiteracy, lack of communication, reduced forest cover, water scarcity, inadequate health infrastructure.

The health problems of the area :

- Lack of hygiene and sanitation
- Malnutrition
- Inadequate anti-natal and post-natal care
- Concept of child care inadequate
- Respiratory diseases
- Aches and Pains
- STD and HIV/AIDS

The need statement

- To bring an improvement (Positive Change) in the Existing Health indicators
- Create an environment for women's empowerment
- Restore ecological balance through commercial farming of medicinal plants, useful for family health and specially under threat of extinction

The Intervention

- Create an enabling environment utilising social marketing techniques which empower the people to manage their own health & hygiene needs.

Campaign Components :

- Situation Study
- Development of Communication Packages
- Mobile Health Clinic
- People's participation
- Communication Campaign
- Concurrent Evaluation
- Impact Evaluation

XI. Nurses Training at Kasturba Gram

Since the last six years, HIMCON and earlier TFL/HIMCON have been sending interested girls who have done well in their intermediate/college and want to work in their rural areas, to Kasturbagram Nurses Training College at Indore's for 2 years training as Rural Health worker, we have trained seven such girls and some of them are working in Mother & Child Centres. This aspect of the health programme has been helpful to the rural areas. Recently we have received some funds through "Will" to make this a sustainable programme whereby these funds have been deposited at Kasturbagram. The interest on this fund can support two or three girls from Uttarakhand at one time for such a training programme.

XII. Walnut Programme

Nut crops are very important tree crops of the temperate region.

They are rich sources of vitamins, fats, proteins and minerals. The Uttarakhand region and north-west Himalayas offer a great opportunity for the growers and promoters of this activity. Also being non-perishable in nature, nut fruits can be a high income source as against other perishable crops.

TFL with the cooperation of Hill Campus of G.B. Pant University of Agriculture and Technology, some NGOs and Mahila Mandals have made certain valuable efforts in promoting plantation activity in Uttarakhand region. Walnut seeds, collected from Banihal Pass of J&K, were planted here and subsequently skills pertinent to raising of nurseries for walnut, almond and chestnut etc., were imparted by organizing training programmes. Also superior genotypes of walnut and almonds were imported from California for establishing mother orchards of these crops at few selected sites and more recently grafted walnuts were brought from Kashmir from an FAO assisted project on walnut grafting.

Efforts are also underway to form a consortium of nut fruits growers in this region. The objective of this consortium will be to share the experience and skills, plant material, information etc. The consortium will also stimulate its collaboration with nut-growers in J&K and Himachal Pradesh. "Nut Fruits in the Himalayas" a book published by TFL is circulated in the Himalayan Institutes, NGO & Himalayan Communities. TFL/HIMCON is making efforts not only in promoting these activities in the region but also in importing high quality planting stock.

A Horticulture Guide for Uttarakhand has been published. This guide gives information regarding climate, type of soil, topography etc., of the Himalayan region as well as also about the type of horticulture plants that can be grown in the area. The guide is helping to improve the management of fruit trees, processing, training and other cultural practices for optimum and suitable production. The guide will also be brought out in Hindi later. The guide is prepared by Dr. Harbans Singh, Ex-Horticulture Commissioner, Dr. M.L. Dewan and Mr. V.K. Suri, Member, Indian Economic Service.

XIII. Entrepreneur Training and Income Generation

An effort was made for an entrepreneur training in small scale rural industries such as a pisciculture, sericulture, mushroom culture and cultivation of medicinal plants. It is in the early stages and a great boost is required in this direction.

XIV. Consortium of NGOs for Medicinal Plants (in pipeline)

HIMCON — Himalaya Consortium for Himalaya Conservation is holding a workshop on "Consortium of NGOs for Medicinal Plants in Uttarakhand (Garhwal & Kumaon)" from April 10 to 12, 2000 at Swasthya Vatika 1, Ranichauri - 249199, Tehri Garhwal Dist. U.P.

The objectives of the Workshop are :

i. To appraise one another about the work being done by each NGO and Organization in the field of medicinal plants, nursery, production, training, semi processing or processing, quality control, use in home remedies marketing and associated practices.

ii. To work towards medicinal plant promotion which should include
   - nursery, production and processing as well as
   - Ayurved preparations for home remedies for health and welfare for Himalayan communities
   - Marketing of medicinal plants preparations for increased income generation
   - Increasing use of medicinal plants for family health and welfare as well as co-operative marketing aspects of medicinal plants (Model and Vision : White Revolution for Milk).

iii. Hopefully work towards projects whereby NGOs of both Garhwal and Kumaon will get assistance from Donor agencies towards promotion of such efforts. About 10 NGOs are expected to join and about 5-8 Resource Persons. An Action Plan and a Project proposal for donor funding are expected to result from this 3-day workshop.

XV. Eco-System Development and Watershed Management with Himalayan Communities

Associated Agencies	Partner Agencies of HIMCON
M.S. Swaminathan Research Foundation	Central Himalaya Rural Action Group (CHIRAG)
Service Civil International	
Indian Institute of Ecology and Environment	Energy and Environment Group (EEG)
Hill Campus of Pant Nagar Agriculture University, Ranichauri	Parvateeya Jan Kalyan Samiti (PJKS)
Sericulture Centre, Dehra Dun	Uttarakhand Jan Jagrati Sansthan (UJJS)
Ranichauri, Yuvak Mandal	Sabli Mahila Mandal
Eco Monitoring Society	Academy for Mountain Environics
Rotary Clubs in Dist. 3010	Vishwa Vriksha Paryavaran Foundation
Centre for Inducing Enterprises to Rural Areas (CFIETRA)	
University of Horticulture & Forestry (UHF) Solan, H.P.	Inter Colleges Ranichauri, Gaja, Kafel Pani, Pujargaon
Indian Voluntary Action Network (IVAN) Hamilton, Ontario, Canada.	Bal Vikas Bharti - Boodha Kedar
Foundation for International Training (FIT) Toronto, Canada	Sudershan Welfare Trust

XVI. Books Published by HIMCON and TFL/HIMCON

- People's Participation in Himalayan Eco System Development by M.L. Dewan, Concept Publishers, Discover Himalayan Series No. 1, 1990
- Nut Fruits in the Himalayas by M.L. Dewan, M.C. Nautiyal and V.K. Sah, Concept Publishers, Discover Himalayan Series No. 2, 1992.
- Vedic Philosophy & Himalayan Eco System Development by M.L. Dewan & B.D. Joshi, Concept Publishers, Discover Himalayas Series No. 3, 1993.
- Horticulture Guide for Uttrakhand by Harbans Singh, M.L. Dewan & V.R. Suri, Concept Publishers, Discover Himalayas Series No. 4, 1997
- Himalayan Meditations and Hymns by M.L. Dewan & Henryk Skolimowski 1997
- Human Values - A Task for all by M.R. Chilana & M.L. Dewan, Concept Publishers, 1998
- Water Resources in the Himalayas, 2000
- People's Participation and Movement for Himalayan Rejuvenation

XVII. Presented Papers by M.L. Dewan

	Title	Where Presented	Date
1.	Water harvesting schemes planning and design	Water and Power Consultancy Services India, Ltd.	Dec. 85
2.	Empowerment of People for a Sustainable Society in the Himalayas	Sustainable Reconstruction of Highland and Headwater Regions	
3.	National Land Use and Conservation Board	Soil Conservation Society of India	1985
4.	State of Himalayas A Call for Action.	J. Soil & Water, Conser. India	1986
5.	An open letter to all citizens of Himalayan States and of India from a Citizen Who is deeply concerned about the health of Himalayas	Environmental Awareness Vol. 9	November 1, 1986

No.	Title	Published in	Date
6.	Horticulture : Vital Role in Himalayan Ecosystem Development		Nov. 1986
7.	An Autobiography of a Water-drop in Beas River	SCSI News	May 5, 1987
8.	Themes of Development, I, II & III		1989
9.	Himalayan Eco-system Naked and Bleeding		Aug. 1989
10.	The Manipur Experiment	A Programe for People's Participation in Providing Alternative to Jhum cultivation	
11.	Women in the Hills: Need for Alleviating Distress		Jul-Aug. 1990
12.	Vocationalisation of Environmental Careers	IIEE	1990
13.	Food for the Future	FAO	Oct. 1990
14.	Human Values for Sustainable Society		
15.	Value System in Development		
16.	The Trees for Life Perspective	Voice of the 21st Century	
17.	Ancient Vedic Philosophy and Himalayan Eco-system Development		Jan. 1990
18.	Watershed Management and Development		1992
19.	People's Participation in Himalayan Eco-system Development		1990
20.	An Educational Campaign for Children in Rural India		
21.	Human Systems, Environment, Ethnicity and Culture of the Himalayas	The Himalayan Heritage and Environment	1991
22.	Uttarkashi Tehri Garhwal to Latur-Earthquake	Lessons to be Learnt	Oct. 1991
23.	Role of Appropriate Technology in Himalayan Eco-System Development	Introducing Himalayan Eco-system Development	1991
24.	Fruit Revolution in India		March, 1992
25.	A Million Trees, a Million Fruits		1992
26.	Farm Forestry as a Tool of Socio-economic uplift of Hill People		1992
27.	Resource Mapping and Action Priorities	The Action Research Unit for Development	Oct. 1992
28.	Progress Report on Watershed Management in Himalayan Communities		April 92-Nov. 92
29.	One Earth-One Family	World Environment Day	June 5, 1994

30.	Soil and Water Conservation Challenge & Opportunities	Eighth ISCO Conference	Dec. 4-8, 1994
31.	Vedic Philosophy for Eco-System Development		Feb. 1994
32.	Towards a Sustainable Society, Perceptions	Book release at M.S. Swaminathan Foundation	Feb. 1995
33.	Role of Education in Eco-Development	Himalayan Region Study and Research Institute	June 10, 1995
34.	National Seminar on Community, Forestry Bio-diversity of Forest Species	Indian Society of Tree Scientistis	April 11, 1995
35.	Panchayat Raj—Key to National Food Security and Nutrition	FAO Sponsored	July 2-3, 1996
36.	Multi Dimensional Nature of Our Indian Society		November, 1996
37.	Possible Project Funding for Medicinal and Aromatic Plants Promotion	International Conference	Nov. 4-6, 1996 at UHF, Nauni
38.	Council for Development of Rural Areas	Exhibitions & Seminar On Phyto-medicines medicinal plants	Fab. 21-22, 1997
39.	Medicinal & Herbal Plant Production Pogramme in Uttarakhand	Polypathy Conference Indian Institute of Ecology & Environment	Jan- 21-25, 1997
40.	101 True Stories of a Life Experience		March 2000

You are Successful
and
Creative only When
You see
An Opportunity
In
Every Difficulty

APPENDIX - I

HIMALAYAN CONSERVATION FUND

Objectives

1. To assist conservation volunteers, farmers, planters, schools, etc. in:
   a) running nurseries;
   b) planting trees;
   c) setting up social/bio-fencing;
   d) regenerative forestry;
   e) water harvesting;
   f) rejuvenation of springs and streams;
   g) horticulture; and
   h) training programmes
2. To institute and operate a fund to promote directly or indirectly projects working towards self-reliance of the Himalayan communities.

II. Conditions of Support

The Himalayan Conservation Fund (HCF) will support projects which are

a) for a maximum of two years duration;
b) action oriented and involve people's participation; and
c) directly aimed at building up local self-reliance.

The amounts of funding would depend on the implementing capacity of the NGOs.

III. Operation

1. The HCF shall be operated by a specially created autonomous organization with over 50 percent participation of voluntary organizations. It may be an annexe of the G.B. Pant Institute of Himalayan

Environment and Development, Almora, UP, or CHR (Centre for Himalayan Rejuvenation).

2. The disbursement policy of the HCF shall depend on its own system of identification of genuine needs of action groups, preferably by a travel group of two/three persons moving through the Himalayan districts or by any other suitable mechanism of identifying groups, communities or individuals working for Himalayan conservation.

IV. Constitution

The HCF shall be formed as a society which may be called Himalayan Conservation Society or Society for Himalayan Conservation or simply Himalayan Conservation Fund Society, or Centre for Himalayan Society and shall be registered under the Societies Registration Act, 1860.

V. Sources of Funding

1. The HCF shall be set up with initial corpus from:

(a) Environmental action groups, both national and international;
(b) Contributions from Business/Industrial houses located both in the Himalayas and in the plains and from individuals and groups both from the Himalayas and outside the Himalayas but essentially from people of Himalayan origin;
(c) Government of India and the concerned States; and
(d) UN Agencies (FAO, WHO, UNICEF, UNDP, UNEP, WB etc.)

2. The fund may be augmented from:

(a) Public contributions;
(b) Himalayan Tourist Cess (of, say, Rs. 5 per tourist) for Himalayan conservation; and
(c) Self-generated incomes from some special projects/ programmes (e.g. cooperative marketing, special tree/ grass/legume nurseries, consultancy in eco-development conservation, medicinal and aromatic plants etc)

This is only a bare outline of the proposal in the form of a suggestion. Details of the constitution, mode of collection of funds and operation on non-bureaucratic lines need to be worked out in further detail, and may possibly involve attachment to an already existing non-government organization registered, working in and known throughout the Himalayas. Linkage with NABARD also needs to be considered actively.

VI A Summary of South Asian Fund Raising Group Workshops and their impact on HCF

(Kathmandu September 13-16, 1998)

Six workshops were held led by committed and experienced resource persons who discussed their experience in Fund raising by different methods applicable in India and in the Himalayas.

Raising Money from Corporate Bodies or Companies

It is important to remember that a business person never, never, never donates. He/she always invests. Therefore providing him/her with that opportunity constitutes the starting point of corporate fund raising.

In the Fund raising context however, the corporate needs to be looked under three heads:

(a) Establishment
(b) the Disposable Funds
(c) the Charity Policy

The officials of some relevance to the fund raiser in the corporate establishment would be:

(i) the decision maker (Chairman/M.D.)
(ii) Director Marketing
(iii) Director Finance
(iv) Executive Incharge PR/Communications
(v) Company Secretary/Officer Incharge of Charitable Trust

The eight golden steps to reach out for corporate money to support a cause could be as follows:

(i) Identification of 'target' corporates
(ii) Information acquisition
(iii) Opportunity analysis
(iv) Formulation of the proposal
(v) Gaining access
(vi) Presentation of the case
(vii) Management of the relationship
(viii) Spin-offs

Traditional Community Fund Raising

On the traditional fund raising methods and practices, a "Captive Institutionalized Community" is used to present a case study.

The captive community is for example a church or a temple unit or a community, the methods are institutionalized over a period and have become a tradition themselves. These institutionalized traditional methods of fund raising are used from time immemorial. New approaches and strategies are added and in due course they also become traditional. The institution and its activities religious, social and developmental are run from the income of traditional fund raising, making the institution self-reliant. These practices can be suitably adapted for practice by NGOs or other institutions.

Some norms/principles involved are :

Identity — The fund giving community is organized and linked to a cultural-social-religious identity.

Sharing for others — The concept of sharing is inculcated right from a young age and giving for others is nurtured as a tradition.

Paying for Institutional Services — Individuals and groups are prompted to pay for services rendered by the institutions.

The traditional fund raising methods are grouped into those related to

(1) Occasions
(2) Purpose,
(3) Sacrifice,
(4) Institutional support/Identity,

(5) Festivals, and
(6) Special projects.

Donation Boxes

There could be many different ways to maximize contributions through donation boxes depending on the circumstances and the general environment. Each set of circumstances will warrant a somewhat modified standard operating procedure (SOP) for optimal results.

We must however remember that the Donation Box is an inanimate, inconspicuous entity which neither asks for donations nor gives a reason for it. Hence, it is lowest in the list of methods of fund raising with ranking (Lower to higher order) which is perhaps something like this:

a. Donation Boxes
b. Press appeals
c. Direct Mail
d. Tele Marketing
e. Video Film
f. Personal Presentation
g. *In situ* demonstration-cum-personal presentation with video support.

Then why are we talking about donation boxes?

The answer is that if we were to neutralize all the disadvantages of a donation box while retaining the advantages which it offers, we would have a solid fund raiser in our hands.

For this purpose, it is important to recognize the disadvantages and advantages of fund raising through donation boxes before we develop a strategy to eliminate the weaknesses and reinforce strengths of this technique.

These are as follows:

(a) Disadvantages:
- (i) Does not invite attention
- (ii) No use is made of human 'senses'
- (iii) Does not explain the cause of the case
- (iv) Lacks projection of emotion

(v) Does not define the quantity of donation
(vi) Is incapable of persisting in inviting donations
(vii) It does not offer any incentives
(viii) It does not give back change
(ix) There is no donor identification; hence no donor nursing for future spin-offs
(x) Cannot express gratitude
(xi) In the event of a substantial donation there is no Income - Tax exemption.

(b) Advantages:
(i) Offers scope for spontaneous response
(ii) No receipts involved
(iii) Results in savings in infrastructure
(iv) Minimizes documentation
(v) Does not involve cheques/draft payments etc.
(vi) Nominal monies can also be contributed by a donor

While the disadvantages outweigh the advantages, a good fund raiser very well knows that donation boxes utilized imaginatively can still be, perhaps, one of the most cost effective methods of fund raising.

Special Events

To organize an Event is to create an occasion for the general public/select audience to participate and in turn enjoy some benefit or be entertained. An event becomes special and memorable when it is related to a special cause. Events have to happen in a certain time frame and are organized for various purposes by commercial organizations, industries, Government and NGOs.

The main objectives are to-

* Raise money
* Public relations
* Entertain guests/volunteers
* Make work better known amongst influential audience/groups

Types of events:

Events can be classified into Micro- or Mega-levels depending on various factors such as opportunity, the organization's need for funds, administrative set-up, donor involvement, contacts and the expertise of the fund raiser.

(i) Micro-level Events — where funds between rupees three lakh to rupees five lakh are raised, for example Ghazal nights, charity film shows, Christmas parties, sponsored events with ladies clubs, theatre shows etc.

(ii) Mega-level Events — through which funds exceeding Rs. 5 lakh are raised, for example, musical extravaganzas, film stars, cricket matches, auctions of paintings/garments, celebrity dinners, etc.

Internet

Today a quarter of all Americans use the Internet, and the total number is estimated to be 62 million. No longer can fund raisers afford to ignore this 'Electronic Revolution'. But unfortunately the Internet remains veiled in computer jargon and mysticism, often discouraging the fund raiser from taking full advantage of this medium. But just as one does not need to know how to make a car in order to drive it, a fund raiser can tame the Internet without getting lost in its technical complexities. A fund raiser must understand the Internet as one more medium to add to an already powerful arsenal of media-television, radio, print, mail, telephone and direct contact. The real challenge however, lies in adapting and applying the fund raising experience effectively to this new medium. For the Internet though powerful is not yet proven.

The Internet is the largest network of computers on the earth. Thousands of powerful computers across the globe, are permanently interconnected by high speed communication lines. This global network has not slept for the last 30 years. People across the globe use computers and phone lines to temporarily connect to the Internet. Once connected they access and use various services and tools. The computers that temporarily connect are called 'Clients'. The Servers provide services to the clients. The services available on the Internet are World Wide Web, E-mail, Internet Relay Chat, File Transfers, Gopher Directories, etc.

People on the 'Client' computer use these services to communicate, coordinate, collaborate, sell, buy, advertise, entertain, bank, work and play. The Internet today is redefining life. And rapidly so, experts say by the year 2001, sales on the Internet will cross US $1 trillion. The advantages of this medium include its immense global reach, and the fact that it is cheap, it provides a level playing field, it is fast, personal and interactive and is available 24 hours a day, 7 days a week, and last but not the least it is eco-friendly.

Conclusion

The basic concept of fund raising is simple. There are a number of organisations working for all kinds of social causes, and they regularly need funds to carry on the good work. In India, NGOs normally access Government sources and foreign donor agencies for funds. In Nepal, on the other hand, almost all the funds come from foreign donors. Funds from all these sources, however, come with strings attached and also lead to dangers of dependence on a few large organizations driven by their own agendas. Fund raising is an alternative to these sources. It involves raising money locally by the use of various techniques which have been presented above.

THE GENESIS OF CLOUDS*

I am at present staying in Hakone region, 600 m from Lake Ashi in Mount Fuji area of Japan, completely surrounded by dense pine and mixed forests which are a part of the Fuji Hakone National Park area. I am here mainly to complete the Report on the State of Himalayans 1986—A Call for Action, after having just spent one month in Sichaun, China, as FAO/UNDP Training Coordinator for the Fifth International Biogas Training Course held at the Biogas Training and Research Centre of the Chinese Ministry of Agriculture, Fisheries and Livestock.

There is light outside (dawn). I am up since 4 a.m. And walking near the window; I can observe a lot. I can see how the sunrise and the sudden sunshine on these forested slopes illuminates the patches of moisture rising above the dense forest cover. Travelling upwards, these patches of moisture are soon joined by other mini-clouds coming from the lake. The wind takes them upward to join larger clouds. These clouds gather volume and soon the hills across the lake are full of clouds. Later in the day these very clouds may give a drizzle—a mist like rain which, even under a very light breeze, falls at an angle decided by the wind direction and velocity.

I wish I could capture the scenery on a video tape. But my mind is as clear as a video, and having previously observed clouds in dense, medium and light forests as well as in arid/semi-arid desert areas, I am convinced that both dense forests and lakes and other water bodies do influence the amount and intensity of rain received by the region.

Although there are a number of phenomena between the genesis of clouds and the precipitation of rain from them, the relationship between the density of forests and cloud formation and subsequent rainfall is positive.

I would therefore like to make this plea :

- Plant More Trees

---

* This piece is the narrative experience of the senior author (MLD)

- Cut Less Trees
- Harvest More Water
- Build More Ponds and Mini Lakes

Through these actions you will help in even distribution of rain. If there is little or no forest, the rain is likely to come as thunder-showers, which may cause floods. In case of high density forests, even when high intensity rains fall on steep slopes, the tree cover is ready to retard the impact on the soil; so there is less soil erosion, reduced loss of water for the region, and a lesser number of damaging floods.

CENTRE FOR HIMALAYAN REJUVENATION (CHR) : A PROPOSAL BY HIMALAYAN MOUNTAIN SCHOLARS, REVOLUTIONARIES AND LOCAL RESIDENTS

The Himalayas are one of the most crucial ecosystems on Earth. The Himalayan mountains are regarded as the water towers for mankind. They are inhabited by diverse cultures but the mountain people are among the poorest in the world. Mountains send happiness to the plains (happiness in terms of favourable climate, monsoons, rich top soil, streams and numerous raw materials) and yet the Himalayan mountains remain on the periphery of mainstream thinking and just a hinterland for the plains.

Global thinking about mountains is now changing. They are gradually occupying a central place in development intervention. The well-being of the mountains is necessary for the well-being of the plains. The importance of the mountain ecosystems is reflected in the first ever Mountain Agenda that came into being in 1992. Now the year 2002 has been declared as the International Year of the Mountains.

Since the sustainability of the mountain ecosystems is a must for the sustainability of the whole globe, the need for a Regional and/or national centre to assist in the rejuvenation of the fast deteriorating Himalayas is being felt by mountain scholars, revolutionaries and local residents. Therefore, a national/regional centre, outlines of which are being presented below is being proposed. ICIMOD is working wonderfully as an International Centre based in Kathmandu and CHR will work closly with ICIMOD.

Centre for Himalayan Rejuvenation (CHR)

The Centre for Action and Development of Himalayan People and Watersheds would work in collaboration with the Almora-based Himalayan Institute for Environment and Development and other Government agencies and NGOs connected with the Himalayan Environment.

The main spheres of specialisation of the Centre would be :

i. Watershed Management — Trees for Life (TFL) Himalayan Consortium for Himalayan Conservation (HIMCON)
ii. Education, Vedic & Eco - Philosophy, Eco-Dharma, Human Values, Revival of Dying wisdom.
iii. Health banks for rural Himalayas, mother and child, geriatric and handicapped centres.
iv. Sustainable society, sustainable development and sustainable farming system centre, ecology and resource management.
v. Self reliance of Himalayan communities including rural industrialization.
vi Medicinal and aromatic plants.
vii. Eco-tourism including conservation and promotion of culture art, music, dances, handicrafts and sports.
viii. Computer centre and training, management, administration and finance.

1. Watershed Management

Trees for Life/Himalayan Consortium for Himalayan Conservation of Land Water and Bio-resources (HIMCON)

Watershed Management

A Watershed is a geographical area drained by a stream or a system of connecting streams in which all the surface run off originating due to atmospheric precipitation leaves the geographical limits in a concentrated flow through a single outlet.

A Watershed like a block, village or district, pertains to geographical limits of an area but unlike these it is defined by nature and cannot be altered to suit administrative convenience. Regardless of their dimensions, watersheds have some common characteristics:

(i) A watershed area contains a single water outlet,
(ii) No area is shared by two similar order watersheds.

On the basis of past experience relating to development, particularly in the hills, it has been felt that the integration of various developomental programmes is a must for yielding optimum benefits and multiplying the effects. The need in the Himalayas is to shift towards regeneration oriented development. It is difficult to regenerate resources without conserving them. The process of conservation begins with better management of primary resources, namely soil,water and bio-resources and influences the quality of life.

All the processes within the limits of a watershed influence one another. The sustainability of any process thus depends upon the understanding these linkages and working in harmony with nature. Watershed development is therefore a conscious effort to optimise and maintain the productivity of the land through integrated and optimal utilization of resources, appropriate land use practices, causing least environmental damage. The Watershed approach also endeavours to identify traditional and indigenous wisdom of the local people and to utilise it as the driving force in related activities. Historically, resource use has subconsciously developed on the lines of watershed. The present landuse, particularly in the hills, is one such example where the interaction between land, water, vegetation and livestock dictates the status of quality of life.

Trees for Life

Trees for Life is designed to help and encourage people in the rural Himalayan areas to grow trees for fruit, fuel and fodder to improve and maintain the health of their families as well as to help uplift their socio-economic levels. Each tree protects the environment and provides a low cost, self renewing source of food for large numbers of people. The Trees for Life movement empowers people to solve problems for themselves.

By providing people with the motivation and training to plant and care for their own trees, TFL programmes create a sense of dignity, self sufficiency and pride in themselves. Not only this, the trees also play an important and integral role in maintaining the ecological balance of the environment.

The whole life of trees is to serve. With their leaves, flowers, fruits, branches, roots, shade, fragrance, sap, bark, wood and finally their ashes and coal, they exist for others.

Bio-resources

The Himalayas are endorsed as a treasure of bio-resources. The local people have conserved them for generations. There is a serious threat to local germplasm and traditional knowledge due to the achievement of new technologies including varieties and races. The centre will address these aspects and will aim at collection, documentation and conservation of these valuable resources.

HIMCON focuses on the allied activities of soil, water and bio-resource conservation and watershed management. It is designed with alternative development approaches to bring about a qualitative change in the lives of the communities through their own active involvement and participation. HIMCON, enlarging the scope and activities of TFL in the Central and Western Himalayan, is designed to follow the strategy given below :

- Establishment of nurseries, transplanting and protection of trees of all types especially fruits, fuel, fodder and various types of fencing including Bio-fencing as well as promotion of grasses and legumes and bushes.
- Reduction of the dependence on fuel wood through promotion of renewable energy and other associated measures such as briquetting from biomass; biogas, solar cookers, solar water heaters, mini/micro hydels, etc.
- Imparting special corrective treatment to severely damaged areas, wastelands, as well those affected by landslides.
- Regeneration of springs, water harvesting, efficient water use and watershed management.
- Integration of land and water use, soil and water conservation into the lives of people, their needs, food security etc.
- Collection, evaluation and conservation of local bio-resources and documentation of traditional knowledge relating to them.

2. Ecological Dharma - Eco-philosophy, Human and Environment values, Revival of Dying Wisdom

India has been doing well, and steadily improving. There is a building boom all over the country. And the economy has been in a good shape. However the Himalayas and rural India as one integral and holistic entity has not been doing so well partly because of environmental pollution, environmental carelessness, and environmental blindness.

Before the last election no political party of importance had anything to say in their manifestoes about environmental protection. And the problem of the environment is a huge one. Hundreds of thousands of people are dying every year as a result of environmental pollution. Millions are affected, their health undermined in one way or another. This is a terrible loss to the country — economic, psychological and health-wise.

The problem of pollution is not only of cleaning our streets of plastic bags and of building more processing plants. The problem is much more important and much deeper. It is a problem of right *Dharma,* it is a moral problem, it is a spiritual problem. We cannot chant Vedas and talk of the beauty of the universe while we are fouling the world. The environmental and the spiritual are aspects of each other. This is why ecological Dharma is second to none now a days. This is why it is a concern of every Indian who cares for his or her life. This is why we need to work on our consciousness and heart and purify them.

Ecological Dharma is the vehicle that can accomodate all and can inspire all. The fruits of Ecological Dharma are going to benefit all—as the general health improves, as the conditions of life become more and more tolerable for all, as the meaning of life deepens to remind us again of the great legacy of ancient *rishis*. This is not a pipe dream but a palpable programme.

To make this programme a reality, political parties and everybody must first re-educate themselves in the ABC of ecological thinking, ecological consciousness and ecological Dharma. Second, they must start large scale educational initiatives, from the level of villages and the level of the capitals, whereby the meaning of Eco-Dharma will be probed, explained and implemented.

We must clean the environment not because the Western countries are doing so and we want to imitate them, but because it is our Dharma to do so, because it is our moral responsibility to do so, because it is a part of our inner purification. We must purify and clean our own land. Ecological Dharma is second to none!

The great environmental-cum-spiritual renewal cannot be accomplished by specialized isolated institutions or by increasing the number of existing cleaners. It must be a national action, almost a crusade, for which a billion Indians are responsible. The awareness must reach our consciousness and hearts that we are taking care of ourselves, of our beautiful and fabulous Himalayas and Country while we are cleaning our environment. This cleaning must not be superficial — by sweeping the dust from the front yard and pushing it to some hidden corner. It is not only the visible dust (which eats our lungs) that must be eliminated. The invisible chemicals which slowly poison and diminish our bodies must also be eliminated. Moreover, it is also this invisible moral pollution which must be eliminated — the political and industrial corruption and all these practices which cheapen, undermine and diminish our lives. The great Himalayas that India is proud of, the great spiritual traditions and sustaining life-styles which follow from these traditions, have been undermined, polluted and distorted. In the process of the great environmental cleaning and renewal we must create a Eco-Dharma Corps within which young inspired but unemployed people can find an outlet for their dreams and energies to guide and fuel the new process of tansformation.

This can be done if there is enough will and insight to appreciate the importance and far reaching consequences of the task. The third Millennium is here. Let us welcome it with right visions and programmes for which our children will be grateful to us.

Eco-philosophy is dedicated to the promotion of ideas that contribute to the integrity of the planet, that enhance the symbiosis between human beings and the rest of creation, that help to create justice and equity among people, that help us gain knowledge about the environment and the universe. Eco-philosophy aims to heal the world in order to heal ourselves, and to guide us meaningfully in the present complex world. Additionally we have to promote environmental ethics with the following principles:

1. We need to develop a concept of sufficiency or "enoughness"
2. We must recognize the inherent rights of nature and natural systems to survive.
3. We must limit human members to the true carrying capacity of the earth, country, region or any geographical unit.
4. We must develop an economic system based on equality of exchange, not just profit.
5. We must develop an industrial process that maximizes

recycling and minimizes throughput of materials.

6. We must develop an economic system that favours life sustaining processes.
7. We must live consciously so as to be aware of the results of our collective needs.

In addition to the promotion of Eco-Dharma, Eco-Philosophy and Eco-Ethics, CHR would need to promote what is described in "The Human Values — A Task for all:

These human values will make us all realize that trees are holy, forest are sanctuaries, Himalayas are sacred, as also the Mother Earth, and all these must be conserved and developed.

All these are linked with proper education of the Himalayan communities. The scope of education is to form the character of pupils, that is to say to cultivate in them infinite potentialities of mind nourished on the real values of human life. *Moral behaviour (the Right Action, Dharma) Peace, Love and Non Violence* signifies the laying of the foundations for the construction of human personality in its various aspects: Physical, Intellectual, Emotional, Psychic and Spiritual.

We nourish the hope that the best and the most illuminated energies of the country and the Himalayan region will rally around this educational methodology and strategy, apart from conventional educational methods being used in order to enable the educational process to itself become an instrument of true, moral and civil progress.

3. Health Banks For Rural Himalayas — Mother and Child, Geriatric and Handicapped Care Centres

Despite various Government and Non-Government programmes embodying "Health for all", the people of the Himalayan region suffer from various ailments (as surveyed in schools and rural areas by various doctors and agencies) such as malnutrition, TB and many other diseases. Revival of Health facilities is possible through "Barefoot Nurses" and "Barefoot Doctors" as is being promoted recently. Establishment of health banks needs to be encouraged where people participate by paying for medicines, whether ayurvedic, homeopathic or allopathic, and Mother and Child Centres should be established together with Panchayati Raj establishments. In the first instance, such 'Health bank' experiences are being developed in Uttarakhand and need to be further studied and promoted on the following lines:

(i) The ancient Indian system, which is making a comeback is as much concerned with promoting health and preventing diseases as it is with curing ailments.
(ii) India remains the world's largest repository of alternative medicine which heals more people than allopathy does.
(iii) Ayurveda is again becoming the first choice therapy for many in India.
(iv) True progress lies in being able to see the play of inter-connectedness around us and connecting deeply with our Body, Mind and Soul, with other people and with nature and includes the practice of Yoga.

The average age is also increasing in the Himalayas as in the rest of India. Hence a greater number of Senior Citizens need geriatric care and so also handicapped persons need special care. The Health Bank must include all aspects of care of the people.

4. Sustainable Society, Sustainable Development and Sustainable Farming System Centre

While there still are people who deny a purpose behind the creation of the world and the evolutionary progress of life, a many splendoured design of existence can be read on the visage of nature. It sustains millions of species of flora and fauna in a close knit web of inter-dependent life.

In the earlier phase the automatisms of nature, the tropisms of plants and the instincts of animals, conserved this design. But when man conceived his self as a self-in-opposition, it was threatened and today it stands in real danger of being totally wrecked, thus wrecking, in turn, the fate of love in mankind too.

The world out there cannot be redeemed if here man does not redeem his integrity. This has implications in many aspects and spheres of human behaviour. A sense of the sacred has to be regained. The realisation has to dawn that survival economy coincides with nature's economy while the market economy pushed indiscriminately leads to the waste of the life supporting resources of the planet. What is urgently required is a holistic approach to the subject of sustainable development and the need to view development as a part of ensuing society.

The Department will cover elements of sustainable development especially sustainable agriculture (sustainable farming system based on recycling of inputs) horticulture and forestry, all leading to development of a society that lasts. In this task, renewable forms of energy, such as solar energy, wind energy, mini-micro hydel and biomass, are of utmost importance. In addition, social and economic aspects of Himalayan societies will also be covered.

5. Department of Self Reliance of Himalayan Communities including Rural Industrialization and Handicrafts

The Himalayan region, especially the central Himalayas and Uttarakhand (hill area of UP) are highly vulnerable to the natural processes of weathering and erosion. Nature's regulatory mechanism to control the rate of erosion is vegetation. Rapid destruction of this vegetation is leading to degradation of vast fragile lands, steep upper slopes, sensitive middle slopes and the Shivalik range. This has resulted in increasing subsidence, land slides, exhausted soil, heavy siltation, frequent floods and droughts in the region and the adjoining Indo-Gangetic Plains. Poverty of land and consequently of the people resulting in migration of people from several pockets where the soil does not yield enough crops, is a matter of great concern. The people migrate into cities also because there are no income generating activities in the hills thus leading to growing urban slums where quality of life and human dignity are almost absent.

The time is overdue to analyse various aspects of rural industrialization-linkages between agriculture, rural industrialization and rural development for breaking the levels of poverty through efficient resource utilization and sustainable development including financing, marketing and entrepreneurship training programmes leading to income generation and increasing prosperity.

The present effort is a determined and collaborative one between various NGOs and Himalayan communities, especially women and youth, for self-employment. Handicrafts, for which there is great potential and resources are easily available, have a great potential for providing people with opportunities for income generation, and also contribute to preservation of local culture.

6. Medicinal and Aromatic Plants

The cold climate in the Kumaon and Garhwal region of Uttar Pradesh and parts of Himachal Pradesh make the region ideal for the growth of medicinal plants. The region is richly endowed with herbs and plants ideally suited for medicinal formulations. However, lack of (i) identification of medicinal plants; (ii) their characterization; and (iii) technology for higher production and processing has deprived the local communities of an opportunity to earn through harvesting their own local and natural resources. Such communities have remained poor and are looking forward to higher and better income generation and employment generation opportunities.

The 5000 medical firms in India, involved in production of formulations of medicines under Indian System of Medicine and Health need to be supported so that their increasing demands of raw materials are fully met. As the prices of allopathic drugs increase, the demand for medicinal plants will also increase and margins for their marketing will make their production financially attractive and more effective. Recent reports on the use of allopathic formulations have indicated a number of adverse side effects. On the other hand herbal medicines are proving important in life saving drugs and for serious diseases like cancer. New formulations based on herbs are being developed and therefore the demand for herbs and medicinal plants is on the increase.

This is a great potential for production and processing of medicinal and aromatic plants in the Himalayan region and they could become an important means and income generation for the local farmers. Geranium is already proving such a resource in the Ranichauri area of Tehri Garhwal District.

7. Eco-Tourism, including Promotion of Culture, Arts, Music and Dances

While the role of tourism in regional and national development has received considerable attention from the Government and others, there are a number of issues involved in the field of tourism development which need to be clearly understood and articulated. One such issue is the carrying capacity of the environment. Another concern is how to adequately involve the local communities in the planning process and ensure their fair share in the benefits.

Eco-tourism is defined as "Purposeful travel to natural areas to understand the culture and natural history of the environment taking care not to alter the integrity of the eco-system while producing economic activities that make the conservation of natural resources beneficial to local people."

The Uttarakhand, Himachal and J & k regions and so also the N.E states are rich in natural beauty, and biodiversity as well as cultural, historical and religious diversity. In the past they have attracted pilgrims, sadhus, people seeking recreation and sight seeing, naturalists and explorers.

In recent years, mountaineers, trekkers and cultural tourists have also been attracted to this region. The already well developed pilgrim tourism in this region can serve as a fertile ground for launching an Eco-tourism drive.

In addition, if properly planned and implemented, Eco-tourism can be a catalyst for economic and social development bringing about many positive impacts while eliminating or minimising the negative impacts. This can only happen through an integrated approach and effective partnership with all concerned including the local people.

Conservation of the culture, art, music and dances of the region and their promotion could be one of the direct impacts of the promotion of Eco-tourism.

8. Computer Centre and Training, Management, Administration and Finance

This Department is essential for a Centre for Himalayan Rejuvenation. The aim is to train local people, especially youth who should not migrate* to the plains but help in the sustainable development of the hilly region.

---

* A Positive Trend is emerging, retired army personnel are returning to Garhwal, Kumaon and Himachal Himalayas and are playing an active role in Himalayan rejuvenation.

APPENDIX - IV

STRATEGY FOR A GREENER TOMORROW — HORTICULTURE GUIDE

Tree plantations and other forms of vegetation can help in reversing the trend of erosion in Uttarakhand. Horticulture crops contribute effectively in improving environment, ecology and landscape. The World Resources Institute has evaluated the benefits from trees in a 50-year life-cycle. It is estimated that a tree generates 50 tonnes of oxygen during this period. Other benefits are shelter to birds, squirrels and insects and recycling of water. The total benefits from tropical forests of one hectare are estimated to be Rs 50 lakhs each year. Horticulture crop production is eminently suited to the agroclimatic conditions prevailing in the Himalayan region. Efforts have been made to develop horticulture in this region. However, there is a wide gap between the technology available and actually applied in the field. The Horticulture Guide for Uttarakhand aims at bridging this gap effectively. It provides easy to understand guidelines for growers, extension workers and students of horticulture science.

The physical systems of the Himalayas, being relatively young, are highly vulnerable to the natural processes of weathering and erosion. Nature's regulatory mechanism to control the rate of erosion is the vegetation cover. The rate of change brought about by these processes is altered by human use and misuse of the system.

Earlier, people have lived here on a sustainable basis and occupied the least vulnerable land, namely the flat valleys and the lower slopes. The people of the region still depend at least partially, if not wholly, on the region itself for their basic needs (emanating from the mountainous character) and produce daily necessities like wheat, rice, timber, fruits, vegetables and livestock. The region further sustains a vast tourist industry, partly due to the presence of places of pilgrimage such as Haridwar, Rishikesh, Yamnotri, Gangotri, Kedarnath, Badrinath and Hemkund.

Trees for Life (TFL)

Trees for Life was founded as a World Organization by Balbir Mathur, with a Trust registered at Allahabad. The Himalayan Operations are directed by Dr. M.L. Dewan, Adviser, TFL, and Founder Chairman of HIMCON (Himalayan Consortium for Himalayan Conservation).

Trees for Life provides management and know-how to people to plant and care for food-bearing trees to fight hunger and malnutrition. Trees for life is a non-profit organization

TFL was started with the following objectives:

(i) To provide techniques and materials required to plant, cultivate and harvest food-bearing and other trees as well as to undertake plantation and/or assist others in plantation of such trees.
(ii) To organise programmes and talks at public places, schools and service clubs etc. to provide education, training, infusion of appropriate technology and awareness amongst people for plantation of trees to fight malnourishment, hunger and for improvement of ecosystems.
(iii) To develop and make available a series of clear, concise and candid materials for all such public organisations and societies who are genuinely concerned with the problem of fighting hunger and malnourishment, so as to enable them to convey the message and necessity of planting more food bearing and other trees in the most correct manner.

Himalayan Consortium for Himalayan Conservation (HIMCON)

Focusing on the fragile eco-system of the Central Himalayas, HIMCON, in conjunction with TFL, and other voluntary and people's organisations is attempting to find alternative development approaches to bring about a qualitative change in the lives of the simple communities through their own active involvement and participation. Thus HIMCON as a partner of TFL in the Himalayas is enlarging the scope and activities of TFL in the Central and Western Himalayas, by following the strategy well established for horticulture growth and development of the region.

Horticulture Guide for Uttarakhand

One of the activities of TFL/HIMCON is to bring out a Horticulture Guide for Uttarakhand under the able leadership of Dr. Harbans Singh a well known horticulturist who has worked as Horticulture Commissioner, Government of India and has been the person behind the horticulture revolution in Himachal Pradesh. He has been ably assisted by Mr. V.R. Suri, a long-term associate.

The Guide will be of help to many people including NGOs, people's organizations and even Government officials in Uttarakhand and other Himalayan states.

The importance of organic farming needs no emphasis now. Global research work has established a significant link between diet, health and old age. A diet rich in fruits and vegetables is associated with lower incidence of diseases, and it is recognised that vegetarians live longer as they are healthier and less prone to high blood pressure, heart attack and cancer. The importance and value of the fruits and vegetables is regularly being emphasised in a large number of publications including newspapers for public awareness and use.

The main objectives of training and pruning of fruit trees abstracted from the Horticulture Guide are:

(i) To give the tree a proper shape and form,
(ii) To increase the strength of the tree so that it is capable of bearing heavy crop loads without damage or breakage,
(iii) Regulate the bearing habit of the tree,
(iv) To improve health, vigour, yield and quality of fruit, and
(v) To make orchard operations like pruning, picking, control of pests and diseases easier.

Training and pruning is necessary in the case of all trees. Some need more and others less pruning. It should, however, cause minimum interference with the natural growth habit of the tree and its fruiting.

Training and pruning itself is very vast and complex. Training is generally done to develop a strong and well balanced framework of the tree so that it can bear optimum load of crop without breaking. This is called pruning for form and is done during the first few formative years of the tree. Pruning in subsequent years is done keeping in view the growth and bearing habit of the tree.

For the purpose of this guide, training and pruning of apples and peaches which are two typical examples of heavy fruit on old wood (spurs) and last season's growth (peach) are presented as broad guidelines.

The role of nuts and dry fruits in human diet, nutrition and their therapeutic value needs no emphasis at the present stage of scientific development and health consciousness. These fruits have special significance for the Himalayan region where climate is eminently suitable (in selected zones) and communication and transport system are inadequately developed. Moreover, the entire produce has to be transported over a long distance in the absence of markets and appreciable consumption locally. In fact the production of high value, low volume durable products as against perishables like fruits and vegetables would be a priority for agro-climatic conditions of this area. Nuts (like walnut, almond, peanut, hazelnuts) and dry fruits (like apricot, prune and raisin grapes) fit in this category.

Several sub-regions of the Himalayan region are very well suited for their cultivation for example, some areas of Jammu & Kashmir, Himachal Pradesh and Uttar Pradesh in the North West Himalayan region. Walnut, almonds, and dry apricots are grown on commercial scale in competition with other fruits in Jammu & Kashmir. Similarly almonds, walnut, raisin grapes, dry apricots and prunes (dried plum) have been found to flourish in Kinnaur, and Lahaul and Spiti districts of H.P. Unfortunately these have not been tried on an appreciable scale in Uttranchal region and therefore, deserve special focus.

One of the basic requirements for the commercial production of nuts and dry fruits is a dry climate or humidity free atmosphere during ripening stage. Wet season (or high humidity condition) is a major impediment. However, walnut is more tolerant and is growing as scattered trees in medium to high hill zones. Some of these yield over a 100 kilograms of nuts (in shell). Many growers are getting over Rs. 1000 per tree. Such success stories need to be replicated in surrounding areas with high quality planting material raised from outstanding trees. It is high time we earmark trees of outstanding merit in our own areas. Attempts can also be made to market almonds as a green crop.

Even at this stage the fruit is not easily perishable, is not bulky like apples, pear or peach and can be packed in gunny bags and transported to distant markets. The kernels are delicious at this stage. Almonds are harvested when the kernel is fully developed but the fruit is not infected by gummosis (as yet). Gummosis is the main hurdle in commercial production of dry almonds in monsoon areas.

Whereas the dry regions of this state(s) can be specially focussed to the production of nuts, dry fruits, walnuts, and almonds (green) to some extent peanuts can be promoted in other areas also. It may be ensured that hard shell varieties of almond be grown in areas with high humidity during ripening time.

Medicinal Plants

India lives in her villages. Hence, a large proportion of its population lives in rural areas where adequate medical facilities are not available. Since time immemorial people have been using herbs in their surroundings and spices in their kitchen to cure day-to-day ailments. A majority of these medicinal plants are also used by established indigenous medical systems. More than 250 species of such medicinal plants are being used commonly by Ayurvedic physicians, local practitioners and by the pharmaceutical industry.

With the increasing cost of treatment through allopathic science and the adverse effects of synthetic drugs, people all over the world are looking towards medicinal plants for their health needs.

The poor socio-economic status of rural population prompts us to explore this wealth of medicinal plants which is available in the Himalayas and is cost effective. The use of medicinal plants in common ailments does not often require resources and technology beyond the villages.

So far medicinal plants have been exploited mostly from their natural habitat. But this has been under severe strain due to deforestation, indiscriminate commercial exploitation and export. The traditional pattern of collection and utilisation by Vaidyas is slowly vanishing. Hence there is an immediate need for conservation and propagation of medicinal plants to meet the needs of individuals and market demands. It is also necessary to design simple technologies to convert these medicinal plants into palatable forms to cater to the rural communities.

The agricultural and horticultural universities should become centres of training for various non-governmental agencies regarding the propagation and collection aspects of medicinal plants. They should also impart knowledge on seed banks and nurseries.

The task of the forest research institutes should be the survey of local medicinal flora with the help of ethnobotanists and conservation of endangered species.

It is a matter of great concern that though our country and specially the Himalayan region is a huge potential source of a large number of medicinal and herbal plants very little work has been done on their agro-technology. Keeping in mind the locally available medicinal plant species we need to work further on their propagation methods and simple conversion techniques and where necessary a potential market. There should be a systematic and regular study on market research so that growers are informed about the changing demand patterns.

APPENDIX - V

HIMALAYAN MEDITATIONS AND HYMNS

By
M.L. Dewan
Henryk Skolimowski

To discover the Himalayas, we need to have them. We need to have them, not destroyed but shining in their pristine beauty. To save the Himalayas—now seriously threatened—is a high priority requirement of our times.

To save the Himalayas will require more than human physical effort and expertise in forestry and mountain agriculture and horticulture. What will be required, above all, is motivation and inspiration, guided by an altruistic philosophy based on spiritual values. The force of living spirituality is second to none. Society seems to have lost this force today.

We offer to the reader this small collection of meditations and hymns that they may become an inspiration, which will then ignite the Will to Act. We do not offer here technical knowledge on how to save the Himalayas but something more important—a vision, which is intangible in itself and yet may lead to very tangible results, if and when it inspires human imagination to act.

Since time immemorial, great social deeds have been accomplished when the right vision inspired the people. Even seemingly impossible deeds have been achieved. We need such a vision and such an inspiration to save the Himalayas. The hymns presented here are the result of a series of inspirations and have been put together to inspire such a vision. If our reflections would contribute even to a small degree in making such a vision a reality, our mission would be accomplished.

My Conversation with the Gods about the Himalayas

I have come here from far away to be in the heart of the Himalayas. I am at present halfway through between Rishikesh and Badrinath—two holy places of the Hindus. Being close to the abode of Gods, I try to listen intently to their whispers, to their voices, to their wills. They do not speak in Sanskrit to me now-a-days. They do not sing the sweet melodies of the Vedic hymns. They are angry because their abode, the tops of the peaks, have been defiled by pollution coming on the wings of the wind. They are angry because the rivers which they have given birth to have been polluted beyond belief. They are angry because the forests they have nurtured have been brutally decimated. They are angry because the earth and soil they have nursed have been denuded, polluted, fouled. This is why the Gods in the snow-clad abode of the Himalayas are angry.

I now hear a new message from the abode. The Gods tell me that meditation is good. But planting trees is better; anyway, planting trees is meditation in action. The Gods tell me that reciting mantras is wonderful, but they tell me at the same time that the most important mantra of our times is a cooperative effort to unite together—to save the earth, to reclaim the beauty of the Himalayas, to purify the abode of Gods. They tell me that common participation to make all the hills of the Himalayas green and all the rivers free of pollution is the most important prayer of our times. They tell me that participation is our strength, our empowerment, our road to a meaningful and sustainable future.

Ode to the Himalayas 1990

October 2, the day the country celebrates
Is also a day of monitoring
Lessons taught by the great teacher
Are they being followed or just forgotten?

On this day normally mid Himalayas
Review the work of the year
In your service O Mighty Himalayas
To green, protect, conserve you, to bow to you
And speak to you without restraint and fear.

I share today with you, O revered one
A handful nay, brainful of my dreams
Dreams in clear practical terms
Not vague, void or empty dreams

A green army of million youth
girls even more than boys
Women more than men
March and pledge to save you
To green you and protect each
Plant of fuel, fodder, fruit trees.

Streams and springs muddy and gushing in monsoons
Quiet and serene in other months
Becoming clear and crystal all or
Most of the time

Women and men, girls and boys
Labouring, working self-reliant
Proud of you, O Himalayas
Chanting pledging we will green you
Stay with you, serve you
We are proud of you.

These are the dreams but talk

Of progress, achievement, O mortals
Resorts the mighty wounded Himalayas
You talk a lot, conferences, seminars
Meetings, symposia and what not
All to hide your inaction
Wanting to look like action.

Achievements, Plantings not enough,
Must venture to give two examples
Ranichauri, Sitla
At Ranichauri and around
A thousand youth marched from schools
To nursery sites to planting sites
Singing pledging we will protect our
Sacred Himalayas

Eighty-one thousand oaks, bhimal
Kharag, danken, apricots, even walnuts
Planted with care and love
Reviewed, monitored in one small part
Of Tehri Garhwal, through
Parvateeya Jan Kalyan Samiti, Sabli Mahila
Mandal, Uttarakhand Jan Jagriti Sansthan
Ranichauri and Khadi Jajal Inter Colleges
Pantnagar Hill campus and
Himalaya Sanrakshan Ashram with support from
Trees for Life and Tata Tea

Examples of collaborative work of
People's voluntary agencies and industry
Same and more in Sitla district, Nainital
Through people's voluntary agency called Chirag
Spreading Light among people.
Heartening the disheartened
Through farmers, nurseries, water harvesting
Medicare and scores of other activities.

Other voluntary agencies will striving hard
Mention of work in Pithoragarh district where
Berinag Gram Swarajya Mandal helps
Green Himalayas

Carry on, say Himalayas, talk of small
Temple of learning, of service glad you call it
Himalaya Sanrakshan Ashram born 7 April, 1990
With considerable birth pangs but ready to serve
Communities and people around, schools,
Mahila mandals, and others

The hill campus with Krishi Vigyan Kendra
Re-dedicating to serve, train and promote
Local communities.

Himalaya Institute, Almora, Kosi
Determined with new leadership
To help, serve and promote your conservation

A plan of action called "People's Participation
In Himalayan Ecosystem Development" released
By Minister of State for Environment being promoted
All these and many more activities in the offing

More projects financed by World Bank, EEC
Hill development of U.P., also Himachal Pradesh
J & K, North-East Himalayas in progress or in making
Himalayan horticulture project by
World Bank and a Himalayan nut project
In progress by Trees for Life and Tata Tea
Involving volags and advisers, promoters.

All these significant, some successful
Others not so much but contributing to greening.
However, many questions, problems still remain
Big dams vs small dams
Lots of hydro power potential underutilised
Water harvesting, spring rejuvenation
Tasks of today and tomorrow
Small-scale non-polluting industries
Sericulture, apiculture, mushroom culture
Fruit nut culture, medicinal plants
Plant and protect and produce
Working on common and wastelands.
Local people to keep attracted
Encouraged not discouraged, inspired
Not migrating
Voluntary agencies to become partners
Through consortia such as Himcon in making.

Let me repeat and pledge
On this sacred morning
Let us all together work
With healthy bodies and clear minds
People, voluntary agencies and
Government not slumber or shirk

Let people awake for common good
For your majestic glory which
We see from Himalaya Sanrakshan Ashram
and hundred other sites
With "Surya Namaskar" today and everyday
to Bapu and to rising sun of glorious Himalayas

APPENDIX - VI

INTERNATIONAL YEAR OF THE MOUNTAINS 2002

On the 10th of November 1998 at the 53rd session of the UN General Assembly, the year 2002 was declared the International Year of the Mountains. This decision was the result of the initiative of A. Akaev, President of the Kyrgyz Republic. His initiative was an extension of the 1996 International Conference for Problems of Sustainable Development, which was held in Bishkek, Kyrgyz Republic. At this conference over 300 scientists from around the world agreed on the importance of bringing to public attention the problems of the mountain regions and their people as rates of development, exploitation of resources, economic assimilation and cultural exposure increase.

The mountains are the planet's largest ecosystem. They occupy one-fifth of the dry land and are home to over 10 percent of the earth's population. More than half of the planet's human population relies on the resources of the mountain regions. Because the upper reaches of the largest rivers in the world are situated in the mountains, the well-being of their ecosystems is a prerequisite to the continued supply of fresh water to the earth's inhabitants. It is the judgement of the UN Commission for Sustainable Development that in the future the pace and quality of human development on the whole will depend on the mountains.

The UN resolution for 2002 offers opportunities for ideas and activities which support the mountain regions to achieve public recognition. In service of this goal, the President of the Kyrgyz Republic has issued an Edict creating the National Foundation for preparing and holding the International Year of the Mountains. A key task of the Republic's programme for 2002 is the building of a model mountain settlement. This project, called "Too ayil" ("Mountain Village") will incorporate contemporary technologies in the production of agricultural products, and it will also utilise ecologically clean systems and mechanisms for natural fuel exploitation. In the framework of this project a number of related activities have also been proposed. These include conferences, symposiums, folk festivals, mountain sports competitions, exhibitions and more.

The National Foundation for preparing and conducting the IYM in the Kyrgyz Republic is grateful for assistance and involvement, financial or otherwise, in preparing and conducting projects for IYM 2002.

Their address is:
256, Room 223, Chui St,
Bishkek, 720071, the Kyrgyz Republic
email : mount@iuk.kg

ICIMOD — Poster Exhibition

The International Centre for Integrated Mountain Development (ICIMOD) has prepared a set of ten posters in order to create awareness about mountain issues and to raise them higher on the national, regional and global agenda.

The posters are titled:

1. International year of the mountains 2002.
2. The Hindu Kush-Himalayas : A landscape of diversity.
3. Mountains and People : The challenges of living in the Hindu Kush-Himalayas.
4. The Strengths of Mountain People : Collective effort and traditional knowledge.
5. The Wealth of the Future : Land, water, forests and rangelands.
6. Crops, Jobs and Markets : Diversifying economies for mountain households.
7. Heroines of the Hindu Kush-Himalayas : The role of mountain women in development.
8. Mountain Communities : Custodians and beneficiaries of resources.
9. Mountains of Hope : Better options for better livelihoods.
10. Partnership in Mountain Development : ICIMOD promotes collaboration.

Orders for these posters (priced at US$ 30 for individuals/ institutions based in the Hindu Kush - Himalayan Region and US$ 50 for individuals/institutions based outside the region) can be placed through :

The Distribution Officer
ICIMOD
distri@icimod.org.np

The posters can also be viewed and ordered online at http://www.icimod.org.sg/publications/posters.htm.

APPENDIX - VIA

MOUNTAIN FORUM

Mountain People, Forests and Trees : Strategies for Balancing Local Management and Outside Interests

Every week on E-mail we receive summary of the Week's inputs from members of the Mountain Forum throughout the world. Very useful points come out of this Forum of which HIMCON and M.L. Dewan are members

Email Address of Mountain Forum is "Mertin Price <mprice@nts1.tsu.ox.ac.uk>

APPENDIX - VII

PEOPLE'S PARTICIPATION IN FOREST MANAGEMENT

Samar Singh*

Introduction

Global concern for environmental sustainability culminated in the United Nations Conference on Environment and Development (UNCED) held at Rio in June 1992. The Rio Declaration states that 'human beings are at the centre of concerns for sustainable development' and indigenous people and their communities have a vital role in environmental management and development because of their knowledge and traditional practices. States should recognize and duly support their identity, culture and interests and enable their effective participation in the achievement of sustainable development.

Agenda 21, the main action programme agreed upon at the Rio Conference, also voices similar sentiments, while emphasizing the need for recognizing and strengthening the role of indigenous people and local communities in general (Chapter 26), and combating deforestation in particular (Chapter II). Likewise, the Forestry Principles enunciated for a global consensus on the management, conservation and sustainable development of all types of forests emphasize that national forest policies should recognize and duly support the identity, culture and rights of the indigenous people, communities and forest dwellers.

Appropriate conditions should be promoted for these groups to enable them to have an economic stake in forest use, perform economic activities and achieve and maintain cultural identity and social organization as well as adequate levels of livelihood and well-being through, *inter alia,* those land tenure arrangements which serve as incentives for the sustainable management of forests.

International agreements by their very nature reflect the relative bargaining strength of various participating nations and their

---

* *Source* : Samar Singh, Secretary General, *World Environment Foundation,* pp. 9-12.

interests. In this game-plan, people's participation in the management of natural resources can hardly become the main agenda. Yet, if people's participation figures as one of the recurring themes in the various agreements reached at Rio, it is a late through only partial recognition of ground reality.

Situation in Developing Countries

A number of developing countries had already realized the importance of the above mentioned principles, having gone through a hard historical experience. A distinguishing feature of these countries is extreme poverty and dependence of the rural population on natural resources. Most of these economies are characterized by low per capita income, inequity and more than 50 per cent of population directly surviving on land-based activities. Colonialism and other forms of totalitarian regimes governed these countries in the eighteenth and nineteenth centuries. By the mid-nineteenth century the state forest agencies began to emerge as the operational mechanism through which the governments could assert control over forest lands. A century later during the post-war developments, the governments concerned allocated vast tracts of forest lands for commercial logging, plantations, resettlement, and infrastructure development projects, with little consideration for the future of the forests and the people dependent on them for subsistence.

The net effect of centralized control over forest resources was (i) diminishing access to forest lands and products thereof for the resident communities, with serious consequences for their lifestyles and livelihood security; and (ii) virtual extinction of the traditional practices and institutional mechanisms which regulate forest usage through a set of self abnegation rules. To meet the challenge the communities evolved coping mechanisms, which have been little understood and usually misinterpreted. Thus, the poor have been blamed for the destruction of forests.

The historic reality is that the centralized forest agencies, which emerged as the operational mechanism for the control of forest lands under the colonial regimes, have not been able to prevent forest degradation. Eventually, the realization has come that without the willing and active participation of the communities living in and around the forests, no programme for the sustainable management of forests can succeed. This recognition has generated varying responses in different countries.

Responses

The responses are at various stages of development, since each nation is at a different stage of historical evolution and the forest departments operate under a complex political environment which differs from country to country. The term 'people's participation' itself has been interpreted in a variety of ways, as would be discernible from the different country programmes, e.g. the integrated Social Forestry Programme in the Philippines with its reliance on certificates of stewardship, the Forest Village Programme of Thailand involving resettlement of groups on forest lands, the Community Fuelwood Plantations in Korea, Community Forestry through User Groups in Nepal and Participatory Forest Management in India. The tenurial, institutional and sharing mechanisms in each experience also vary according to the local milieu.

Tenurial Issue

In terms of legal arrangements, the Philippines programme provides land tenure for 25 years (renewable for another 25 years) but, in essence, it is 'tree tenure forestry', which seeks to adopt a farming systems approach to make the best of a situation arising out of large scale unauthorized occupation of forest lands. While the resettlement programme in Thailand is in terms of groups (not more than 150 families per village) the land tenure (2.4 hectares of farm land) is given to individual families, which is inheritable but not negotiable for sale or transfer. In a totally different situation in Korea where 73 per cent of the forest area is privately owned, small forest owners pooled their lands to establish community fuelwood plantations, as a result of the strong support provided by the government under the Saemaul Undong, the national campaign to develop self-reliance, diligence and cooperation among the rural people. In Nepal and India, the land ownership of forest lands continues to be vested with the forest departments but security of usufructuary rights is guaranteed along with protection and management responsibility to the community groups or organization.

These examples point to a trend of transition from control of forest lands by the centralized agencies to granting of individual or collective tenures to the local communities with some degree of security. Overall, in the present stage of development, two approaches are noticeable

- beneficiary approach
- participatory approach

In most of the countries, the forestry programmes are still conceived and assessed in terms of achievement of physical targets and, therefore, the beneficiary approach in the form of individual tenure is preferred, as the goal is mostly measurable. This, in a sense, privatizes the common property. However, grant of individual tenure on common property has rarely empowered the communities to protect or manage their lands. On the other hand, the participatory approach involves initiating a process of change which enables the communities to manage their lands sustainably and equitably. In a situation where the land-man ratio is continuously declining, the issue of equity is indeed crucial. The conventional assessment procedures of the forest departments are not really equipped to deal with the participatory approach.

Institutional Issues

There are two principal ways of organizing and sustaining community participation:

- employing agents of change; and
- building institutions at the grassroots/local level.

Individual tenure requires outside intervention, which may come from the NGOs or the forest departments. They act as the agents of change to help the local people to protect and develop the forests. Wherever collective tenure is envisaged, establishment of local institutions as the operational mechanism for providing the space and opportunity to the people to participate in the management of forest lands becomes essential. The User Groups in Nepal and the Forest Protection Committees (FPCs) in India are some known examples.

Conceptually, most of these institutions have been envisaged as management units and as an interface between the forest department and the local people. A major task performed by them is ensuring the implementation of mutual obligations. Recognition of a community's right to forests is conditional on fulfilment of certain obligations mostly relating to protection including preventing of fires, thefts, etc. and responsibility for regeneration. In return, the community is assured a share in the forest produce, which may range from 10 per cent of the harvest to the forest owners in Korea to 100 per cent share to the user groups in Nepal.

Changing Role of Forest Agencies

The new management systems are now changing the role of the forest agencies from the conventional custodial and timber production managers to one which responds to community interests and initiatives. In Thailand, the forest department has taken a significant turn. Initially, their role was to protect the forest by policing. The Forest Village Programme envisages forest rehabilitation as an integrated rural development programme, which enjoins several functions hitherto unfamiliar to the forest department. In Korea, Nepal and India, the new programme envisages organizing the village people into cooperatives, user groups or forest protection committees. The fixed models of timber production are giving way to site specific plans through micro-planning and multi-product production systems. These are new roles involving functions hitherto not envisaged and performed by the government agencies. These are hopeful signs of the foresters adapting to their new role, though the pace varies from country to country and agency to agency.

Some interesting and more hopeful examples of meaningful community participation in forest management are emerging in India.

The Indian Experience

The National Forest Policy of 1998 provides the foundation for the new initiative in facilitating people's participation in the management of forests. It states that the holders of customary rights and concessions in forest areas should be motivated to identify themselves with the protection and development of forests from which they derive benefits. The rights and concessions from forests should primarily be for the bona fide use of the communities living within and around the forest areas, especially the tribals. The policy further stipulates that the life of tribals and the other poor living within and near forests revolves around forests. The rights and concessions enjoyed by them should be fully protected, their domestic requirements of fuelwood, fodder, minor forest produce and construction timber should be the first charge on the forest produce.

In pursuance of this policy, the Government of India (GOI) issued in June 1990 a circular to all the states setting out the framework for the involvement of village communities and voluntary agencies in the regeneration of degraded forest lands. On the basis of this circular, so far 21 State Governments have issued facilitating orders for its implementation in their areas. These three sets of documents, namely the Forest Policy of 1988, the GOI circular of June 1990, and the relevant orders of the concerned State Governments, form the overall legal and policy framework facilitating people's participation in the management of forests. The basic features are:

i) it provides a basis for access to the local communities to forest lands in their neighbourhood;
ii) it enjoins the local communities to protect the forest areas, to check free grazing of animals and to assist in stopping illegal activities by outsiders, etc.; and
iii) it assures the local communities a certain part of the produce coming from the forest lands protected by them.

However, it is necessary to mention that neither the Forest Policy of 1988 nor the Government of India circular of June 1990 nor the relevant orders of the State Governments are legal enactments and, to that extent, are not enforceable in a court of law. These do, however, represent appreciation of the ground realities and are thus more in the nature of serious political commitment in the direction that has been taken. A great deal will depend on the honesty of purpose of the forest department and of the facilitating institutions to give this basic framework, meaningful content in the future.

Extent and Impact

From the rather modest and experimental beginnings in West Bengal in the late seventies and the first positive governmental action in 1990, the new concept has expanded fairly rapidly, partly as a result of enthusiastic work done by the foresters and largely because of the spontaneous community response in the various states. By mid-1998, about six million hectares of forest lands were being protected and managed by the village communities through more than 28,000 forest protection committees in various states of the country. Compared to the total forest area, these efforts are no doubt very modest. Various studies, however, show that wherever the participatory approach has been adopted the impact and the results are visible. For example, the availability of fuelwood in the Harda range (Hosangabad district in Madhya Pradesh) has increased by four times; fodder production from the protected forest land in Richaria village (in the same area) provided a surplus worth about Rs. 20,000; the mean annual income from non-timber forest produce to the tribal households has increased to about Rs. 2,523 per household, constituting 22 per cent of the total household income in South West Bengal. Using a sample of 42 Forest protection Committees (FPCs), a study undertaken in West Bengal, found that:

— Seventy four per cent of the FPCs were functioning reasonably well.

— There was considerable heterogeneity of ethnic composition, number of villages, and proportion of participating households among the FPCs.

— The smaller the number of villages participating, the greater the FPC effectiveness.

— The greater the proportion of tribal composition in the FPC, the greater the effectiveness.

— The greater the proportion of households in each participating village included as FPC members, the better its overall performance.

Rights and Obligations

Considering the fact that the forest departments in India are more than 100 years old, the process of change from controlling the people to facilitating their participation in management of the forests shows a great variation across the country. This is reflected in the enunciation of rights and responsibilities in the various orders of the State Governments. An analysis of the relevant provisions shows that while there is clarity about the rights of the village people in some orders, others are quite vague in this respect, especially on the issues of investment and community share of the produce. The same is true in the case of state trading in minor forest produce, which had been a source of substantial revenue to the states. It is hoped that these difficulties will get sorted out with greater experience.

Institutional Aspects

A unique feature of the participatory approach in India is the creation of a village level body called the forest protection committee, which is the main instrument for implementing the new arrangements. Depending on the working methods and self-regulatory mechanisms, this provides inherently the most potent expression of people's control over local forest resources. Case studies on some forest protection committees set up in West Bengal, Madhya Pradesh, Haryana, Gujarat, Orissa and Andhra Pradesh show that these institutions have started playing a useful role in implementation, improved upon their own methods of working and have even helped in sorting out the sharing arrangements with the user industries. The initial signs are hopeful. But there is a long way to go before these institutions get well-established on democratic lines, giving expression to all sections of village society in controlling and managing the local forest resources. The functional arm of the forest protection committee is its executive committee. A number of them at the moment reflect a power structure which does not seem to do justice to the poorer segments of the rural populace. The same applies to the question of representation of women in the executive committees.

Besides, the distribution of power between the forest department and the forest protection committees is somewhat unequal and may prove to be an impediment in developing a truly participatory mode of management. Some forest departments continue to retain the right to cancel the committees and to punish offenders. This will also have to change before participatory forest management becomes a functional reality.

There are undoubtedly several problems that need to be resolved. The silver lining is the sincerity of purpose displayed by some forest departments, the non-government organizations, academicians and researchers. But the move from centralized forest bureaucracies to people-managed forest systems is still at a nascent stage. It is already noted that a very small area of forests in the country is covered under the new arrangements. During the transitional period, long-term policies, especially for providing security of tenure, will have to be developed, the departmental attitudes will have to change and even 'silviculture' responding to community needs will have to evolve. Undoubtedly, this represents a tremendous social change.

Role of Donors

Meanwhile, the emerging participatory modes of management have attracted the attention of donors and a substantial amount of resources are being committed to facilitate this programme. There is however a real danger of 'he who pays the piper calls the tune' and people-oriented processes getting only cursory attention. This can easily divert the programme towards target chasing and time-frames only. Similarly, there is a difference between the emergence of new policies as a response to ground realities and those adopted as donor conditionalities.

Lesson for Future

The experiences in various countries so far provide indications of conditions under which people's participation becomes feasible. The emergence of a large framework for such participation in the management of forests requires fulfilment of certain preconditions:

1. Without a serious political commitment, it is virtually impossible to have meaningful participation of the people in managing and restoring the degraded forests. In the ultimate analysis, it means devolution of power to the people, which can only come from a strong political faith in their capability.

2. The implementing agencies require clear-cut policy guidelines to play the facilitating role. They need clarity especially in relation to the objectives of management and their own role. Unambiguous legislation and working rules can certainly facilitate this.
3. Realistic institutional arrangements need to be made for project management. Wherever collective tenure is envisaged for the community's participation, local institutional arrangements become crucial for providing a forum for collective assertion of rights, resolution of internal conflicts and implementation of self-abnegation rules. The more democratic and transparent these institutions become the greater the probability of success.
4. Land tenure issues and access rights of the intended beneficiaries need specific attention and resolution. Uncertain tenure and insecurity relating to usage rights dilute commitment on the part of the people.
5. The adversarial relationship between the forest departments and the people, reflecting the historical realities of past centuries, calls for reorientation and attitudinal changes not only in the forest departments but also in the communities.

In a nutshell, people's participation is a process-oriented activity. A great deal of experimentation, research and, above all, patience is needed for the process to evolve. If the programme is undertaken in the same way as any other government programme with pre-set targets to be achieved in a given time-frame, this will hinder the process of involving the people meaningfully and is not likely to work eventually. People-based management systems call for area-specific planning and implementation. The plans will vary according to each site and the requirements of the local community with the scale of operation being within manageable limits. There are also questions relating to project design relevance and adequacy of finance, and the need for integration and coordination among the participating organizations of institutions.

Ultimately, people's participation has to be viewed as a movement towards greater humanization and democratization in the post-colonial developing world, with the aim of attaining equity and sustainability. This is particularly relevant in the management and sustainable development of forests. The process in this direction has begun with promise in recent years, even if belatedly. The time to nurture it with care and to build on it is now. The opportunity must not be lost in the interest of forests, the people who depend on them and the human race as a whole.

APPENDIX-VIII

NATIONAL POLICY FOR INTEGRATED DEVELOPMENT IN THE HIMALAYAS : REPORT OF THE EXPERT GROUP

Planning Commission had constituted an Expert Group to formulate a National Policy for integrated development in the Himalayas in March, 1992. The terms of reference included (1) to make recommendations towards development of a national policy on the Himalayas for integrated mountain development with a view to ensure that the region is used to the best advantage of our country; (2) to make an assessment of the scientific, environmental and material resources of the region; (3) to identify specific areas of activity which fit into the ecology of the Himalayan region and are consistent with the socio-economic character of the region; (4) to estimate the carrying capacity of environmentally sensitive areas within the Himalayan region; and (5) to suggest suitable organisational mechanisms to implement the proposed policy.

The report was submitted in October, 1993 and stressed the necessity for creating an administrative mechanism which would aim at harmonious integration of the twin aims of environmental preservation and sound socio-economic development. The group has recommended setting up of a High Power Himalayan Development Authority and the creation of a Himalayan Environment and Development Fund to support the innovative actions, programmes and studies emerging from the recommendations. These recommendations are reproduced below:

RECOMMENDATION - 1

Constitution of Himalayan Development Authority (HDA)

The Group would recommend the creation of an Apex Body at the national level. Such an apex body called the Himalayan Development Authority (HDA) should be headed by the Prime Minister with Deputy Chairman, Planning Commission, the Ministers of the concerned Central Ministries/Departments and the Chief Ministers of the Himalayan States, as a Policy Planning Authority. This could be assisted by a Steering Group headed by the Member in-charge of Environment in Planning Commission and associating Secretaries of the concerned Central Ministries/ Departments and Chief Secretaries of the concerned states. If, however, because of the preoccupations of the Prime Minister, he is unable to chair the Authority, then it should be chaired by the Deputy Chairman. The Secretariat of the Authority should be the Planning Commission.

RECOMMENDATION - 2

Creation of National Himalayan Environment and Development Fund (NHEDF)

The Group recommends that a National Himalayan Environment and Development Fund (NHEDF) would be necessary to accelerate the implementation of the National Policy for integrated Development in the Himalayas. The Fund should start with a reasonable allocation and once its effectiveness and role gets established, the allocation should be enhanced suitably.

RECOMMENDATION - 3

Enlarged Role of the Ministry of Environment and Forests (MOEF)

The Ministry of Environment and Forests must strengthen its role in the Himalayan region. It should have a separate Division dealing with the problems of the Himalayas in an integrated fashion. This Division must have competent staff members dealing with administration, management and scientific inputs leading to better quality of life of the people of the Himalayan regions. The G.B. Pant Institute of Himalayan Environment & Development under the MOEF should be used as a nodal agency to identify the problems to be effectively tackled by the Ministry. Similarly the Botanical Survey of India and the Zoological Survey of India should continuously monitor the biodiversity and the fate of endangered species of plants and animals. The Group will recommend that, if there is a need, the MOEF should be provided with additional statutory responsibility and authority to deal with the implementation of the National Policy. There is also a need for considerable improvement in the management of National Parks,

Sanctuaries and Biosphere Reserves spread in different parts of the Himalayan Region. These require, not only policing and vigilance but the enforcement of a proper scheme for the management of wild life. If the MOEF feels considerable difficulty in the management, a decentralised approach of making the states fully responsible for their protection may be considered.

RECOMMENDATION - 4

Linkages and Cooperation of Scientific Institutions

There are a host of institutions working in the country where work undertaken would be relevant to both development process and environmental conservation. The Government of India has established the G.B. Pant Himalayan Institute of Environment and Development (GBPHIED) as the Nodal Agency. It is, therefore, necessary that under the leadership role of the GBPHIED, an effective networking with the various other scientific institutions is systematically established.

It may not be easy to bring on one platform different scientific institutions working in different fields. There may be a vast diversity in the orientation of these institutions — educational, basic scientific research, applied sciences and technology generation etc. While some of the institutions are managed by the Central Government, some are run by the State Governments, others by autonomous bodies.

Nevertheless, in view of the critical importance of the Himalayan Region in several ways, it is necessary to create a mechanism where different scientific institutions can interact with each other. They may deal with any one aspect or several others of relevance to the development and preservation of the environment of the Himalayas. The Group recommends that the GBPHIED should organise get-togethers of the scientific institutions annually. The task before the scientific community is large enough to warrant pooling of resources be that manpower, infrastructure, etc. to undertake studies/research of immediate relevance. The possibility of creating a separate all India Association on the pattern of Agriculture Sciences and others called the Himalayan Region Scientific Association with its Headquarters in GBPHIED may be explored. It should meet annually at some selected place in the region.

RECOMMENDATION - 5

Interaction of Natural Sciences with Social Sciences

Many social factors have influence both on development and the manner in which the society looks at the environmental issues as also effective communication to bring about awareness on the sustainability of the development paths being followed. It would be very useful if the Social Sciences are also dovetailed with the Natural Science and Technology inputs in bringing about environmental friendly development process of the Hiimalayan Region.

The Group feels that the country's socio-economic development should be seen as one comprehensive whole. Any integrated policy of the Himalayan region will be just a segment of the country's socio-economic development process. Islands of exclusiveness in the development of one region or the other may be socio-politically unsustainable. Any attempt at "we and they syndrome" would result in sub-optimality of the planning for development as also from the conservation angle.

The entire Himalayan region from the conservation angle must be broadly seen as comprising of three sub regions namely, hills, the middle hills and the higher reaches. These have significant variations in terms of flora and fauna and the kind of development measures required to be taken up. The Group, therefore recommends a proper interaction between Natural Scientists and Social Scientists in the Annual Session noted earlier.

RECOMMENDATION - 6

Preparation of Guidelines for Development Projects in States

By and large the states action in attempting an environmentally friendly development process may be seen to lie in two broad fields. The first relates to regulation process with a view to preserve ecology and environment. The second looks at programmes which seek to reduce the adverse impact of development projects on environment as well as those measures aiming at qualitative upgradation. The Himalayan Region has been considered as an ecologically fragile area. In this light the Group recommends that the Ministry of Environment and Forests must frame detailed guidelines on various considerations which need to be kept in view while providing environemtnal clearances for development projects under the Environment Protection Act, be that by the central or state Governments. It is necessary to make these guidelines transparent and enforced in a fair manner free from arbitrariness.

RECOMMENDATION - 7

Preservation of Biodiversity and Genetic Resources

The vast genetic diversity that exists in the Himalayan region, both of flora and fauna, needs to be preserved for posterity. *In situ* conservation of the genetic diversity and resources in many stituations may be inescapable. However, declaration of any area as a biosphere reserve and closing down the area from human interference can have substantial impacts on those living within or in adjoining areas.

The Group recommends a time bound programme for inventorisation of genetic resources in the Himalayan region under the aegis of the Botanical Survey of India and Zoological Survey of India. In this, the traditional universities and other academic institutions or agencies, must also be associated to complete this process in a well-definied time framework.

A fuller understanding of the flora and fauna and their propagation can assist in *ex situ* conservation of endangered species, wherever such measures are essential or desirable and feasuble. A systematic attempt at the conservation of germ plasm and genetic resources must be attempted for which a detailed master plan must be evolved.

RECOMMENDATION - 8

Maintenance of Forest Cover

Maintenance of the forest cover and its upgradation through forestry programmes is a matter of urgent importance. Under the Forest Preservation Act, diversion of forest to non-forest uses has been highly regulated. The Government of India has also laid down a policy of compulsory afforestation wherever diversion to non-forest purposes cannot be avoided. The Group recommends that it needs to be examined whether afforestation of degraded areas in the Himalayan region could be accelerated under this policy even by the deployment of resources to be provided by projects being taken up not essentially within the same states. Part of the funds to be provided by the project authorities for compulosry afforestation could be deployed in the Himalayan region, even if such projects are being established in a state outside the Himalayan region.

RECOMMENDATION - 9

Management of Forests

In some of the states green felling has been prohibited. The Group suggests that green felling should be uniformly and totally prohibited in all the states of the Himalayan region. However, the requirements of the local people of fuel wood to be drawn from lopings, branches and fodder should be met and the existing rights of the local communities safeguarded. Commercial-scale exploitation of the forests should be comprehensively banned.

Forest management as traditionally practised in the area needs to be reviewed. The Group accepts the need for species diversity in the forest area. However, to create employment opportuinities and improving the economic well-being, the present policy of afforestation in degraded areas needs to be reviewed. In a multiple tree cropping, as part of the social forestry programme, inclusion of some types of horticultural crops especially the nut bearing trees may contribute both to bringing degraded areas under vegetative cover as well as creation of employment opportunities and increased income flow to the local communities.

The country can gain a great deal from the experiences gained in forestry management in several other countries. A systematic attempt at collection of malayan region, needs to be undertaken.

RECOMMENDATION - 10

Agriculture and Allied Activities

Agricultural development in the Himalayan region is characterised by extremely small land holdings and very low land : man rations.

Due to migration of the menfolk from the region seeking employment in the plains, in several areas, agriculture is predominantly in the hands of women. The issue in agricultural development process is critical. Efforts that agriculture technlogy reaches the women folk and the financial credit to women need special focussing.

Given the topography of the area, the rainfall, particularly in the mid hills and higher reaches, agriculture development, defined in a comprehensive way, may have to be quite distinct. Raising of the seasonal crops without proper terracing, an expensive proposition in any event, makes agriculture operations prone to large scale top soil erosion and unregulated surface run-off leading to degradation of land. Agriculture development may essentially centre round raising perennial vegetation in the form of horticultural crops, fuel and fodder trees, pastures to support animal husbandry programmes etc.

Further agro-forestry and sericulture could also be promoted both from the point of view of increasing the income through high value generating enterprises as well as maintenance/upgradation of ecological balance.

A systematic attempt at the development of perennials should be fully backed by research in terms of tree cropping systems, species to be grown and should be worked out in detail. A master plan for the development of horticulture, sericulture and other tree based farming system, should be prepared in a time bound manner.

It would also be necessary for the concerned State Governments to be associated with the Union administrative Ministries dealing with the subjects to establish all backward linkages in the form of nurseries to raise sufficienmt planting material to give operational context to the master plan.

RECOMMENDATION - 11

Packing and Marketing of Horticulture Products

Another critical need is to establish adequate and effective marketing arrangements, particularly when the agricultural commodities produced are perishable in nature such as apples, peaches, strawberries, plums, lichies etc.

The Group would recommend that even in the choice of horticulture programmes it may be worthwhile to pay attention to low volume high value crops which are not highly perishable such as the various types of nuts. Marketing of horticulture products to ensure remunerative returns to the growers will largely influence the success of the horticulture programmes.

Growers, organisations should be actively encouraged by the States to collect fruits, vegetables to bring these to central points and thereafter market in different parts of the country.

Often the requirement of packing materials has had unhealthy influence on the maintenace of tree cover in the region due to the over-emphasis on using wooden crates. There are several agences which have designed polymer-based packing materials which could be re-cycled. Specific programmes need to be launched for weaning away the producers, traders etc. from using the wooden crates and promoting the use of plastic materials to reduce the dependence on wood.

An attempt had been made to establish processing units to process fruits, particularly culls and those not fit for table purposes. The Group understands that some of these processing units are languishing. A detailed analysis and review of the functioning of the processing units must be undertaken and corrective measures taken. Establishments for ensuring value addition, higher returns to producers which will also create employment opportunities in these regions are recommended.

RECOMMENDATION - 12

Marketing of Horticultural Products to Nighbouring Countries

Another aspect of marketing of agricultural products in the Himalayan region is that the poducts were being earlier marketed traditionally to China or to Bangladesh. The Group recognises that the Government of India had initiated measures through the Ministry of External Affairs to improve border trade. This aspect is critical for the marketing of agricultural products and needs to be substantially stepped up. This could greatly assist in the producers getting marketing outlets for their products and probably getting a better price.

RECOMMENDATION -13

Jhuming Cultivation

The slash and burn system of agriculture operations called jhooming is widely prevalent in many of the States of Noth Eastern Region. Increase of population pressure has reduced the slash and burn cycle from 20-30 years to 5 years or even less. The impact of this on the forest cover and soil erosion has been extensive. Agriculture practices need to be substantially stepped up through minimal terracing arrangement and by the provision of appropriate implements and machinery, minimal irrigation facilities to enable farmers to improve productivity in properly cultivated settled plots. The existing jhooming cultivation has disastrous impact especially in steep slopes. Promotion of horticulture, agro-forestry, and sericulture may be intensively carried out under appropriate schemes for the rehabilitation of cultivators practising jhooming.

Success of the programme will be contingent on meeting the requirements of foodgrains and other essentials to the population in the region. The Group cannot over-emphasise on an effective public distribution system to reach the basic essentials to the population if a dent on the jhuming is to be made.

RECOMMENDATION - 14

Irrigation

Provision of irrigation in the hilly terrain is not simple. Presently a system of diversi9n of water for irrigation of crops in the slopes is being resorted to. Technologies for irrigation practices should be systematically studied and extended under appropriate programmes to the farmers. Installation of improved irrigation devices such as sprinklers and drip irrigation in these regions, especially for the orchards, should be actively promoted.

RECOMMENDATION - 15

Energy

The Himalayan region is rich in resources for production of

commercial energy, especially the hydel power. The basic conundrum has, however, been that except in one or two states, the extension of electrification in the region has been tardy. If the benefits of generation of hydel power do not reach the local inhabitants, this is bound to create difficulties in the exploitation of the available natural resources. The Group recommends that in all programmes for tapping of energy sources, meeting the requirements of the people living in the area should merit the highest priority even if the cost of the extension of electricity grid is likely to be relativly more expensive than in the plains. The energy needs of those living in the Himalayas arise for cooking, lighting and warming. A larger network of electricity distribution would reduce the dependence on firewood and hence will protect the forestry resources.

The Himalayan region is rich with sites for generation of micro-hydel power, based on perennial streams. Recently emphasis has been laid on tapping of the micro-hydel generation potential. To the extent that the local community is involved in the operation and maintenanc of the micro-hydel generation units through proper build up of skills and distribution is completely entrusted to the local people, this could facilitate realisation of the potential.

In the region, sparsely populated villages in remote areas are a common feature. Non-conventional sources of energy, such as photo-voltaic cells, use of organic materials for gassification (biogas) and wind turbines can enable meeting the needs of lighting and pumping devices in such villages. The Group recommends that a systematic study of the demand and measures for the supply of energy needs should be attempted and concrete programmes drawn up to be implemented in a time bound manner. For this, a proper mix of the supply through both conventional and non-conventional sources of energy should be attempted.

RECOMMENDATION - 16

Given the fragility of the Himalayan ecosystem, a large scale industrialisation following the pattern in the plains would be totally unsound environmentally. Some attempts have been made to develop service engineering, especially in terms of extension of the use of electronics in the Hill regions. The choice of industry including the services, which could be extended in the region would need to be carefully worked out.

Apart from the agro-based industries which are highly recommended, it is necessary to explore other industries based upon usufructs of forests which could be established in the region. This can augment the economic activities, and should generate higher incomes and provide employment opportunities. Mushroom cultivation and bee-keeping have proved to be most remunerative activities leading to prosperity and must be encouraged to devlop their full potential.

RECOMMENDATION - 17

Health, Nutrition and Family Welfare

The Himalayan States have major health problems as prevalent in other parts of the country as also some which are more intensively seen in the Region such as Goitre, Malaria, Respiratory Disorders, STD, AIDS etc. Generally, the contributory factors are under-nutrition, special geo-physical, geo-climatic, socio-economic and other variables present in the Region.

The Group, therefore, recommends that the Ministry of Health & Family Welfare should provide more funds on priority basis for strengthening of National Malaria Eradication Programme, National Tuberculosis Control Programme, Child Survival and Safe Motherhood propramme, National Iodine Deficiency Disorder Control Programme and National AIDS Control Programme in these areas.

The Group also recommends that the access to health services should be significantly improved in the area particularly in relation to establishment of the Sub-centres and Primary Health and Family Welfare Services. The backlog of establishment of Sub-Centres, particularly in the tribal and difficult areas should be removed as early as early as possible.

The Sub-Centres, Primary health Centres, Community Health Centres and other health institutions should be fully operationalized by providing physical facilities including buldings and residential quarters, filling up of all vacant posts and ensuring supply of essential drugs, dressings and other consummables. Resources of Rural Development schemes like JRY, special area projects and adoption of cheaper technology for building construction should be used for removing the backlog in physical facilities. Because of the acute shortage of medical facilities in these areas the use of indigenous systems of Medicine should be promoted and integrated in general health services.

Pilot studies should be undertaken in a few districts in each Himalayan State to generate district level date base for assessing the prevalence and causes of morbidity and mortality in the Region. National level institutions viz. ICMR, NIHFW, selected Medical Colleges (including colleges of Indian Systems of Medicine) may be entrusted the above responsibility.

RECOMMENDATION - 18

Preparedness for living in Earthquake - prone areas

Some regions of the Himalayas are very vulnerable to earthquakes as they form a part of the Alpine seismic belt. More than a dozen earthquakes, equal to or exceeding the magnitude 7.5 have occurred in these areas during the last 100 years including the Uttarkashi Earthquake of October 20, 1991. Since it is difficult to make accurate predictions of the earthquakes, the Group recommends the following measures:

1) Adoption of a building code for earthquake-prone zones. There are inexpensive methods adopted by Japan and other countries which should be strictly followed while designing the buildings and houses in the seismic zone. The Central Building Research Institute, Roorkee has developed some inexpensive designs.

2) Standards for earthquake resistant structures should be developed for the Indian conditions.

3) To reduce future danger in the event of earthquakes, the very pattern of living of the people must be modified and adapted in a suitable manner. Precautions like not keeping heavy objects above the head level, not leaving heavy objects loose on the ground, keeping first aid kit and emergency supplies of food ready at all times should be followed. There are many guidelines for preparedness. It is very desirable to discuss these amongst the family and community so that some organised efforts could be made at the time of any eventuality. People are just not aware of them.

RECOMMENDATION - 19

Roads and Communication

Improving the access to the inhabitants of the region, on one hand, and the adverse effect of the construction of large network of roads do produce a dilemma. Adverse effects of the construction of roads, without safeguards, have posed serious problems of land slides. This not only affects the movement of men and material, leading to heavy siltation, but also destroys agricultural lands and forests. Special studies ought to be conducted on the construction methodology of roads in the hills as would minimise the adverse effects and all safeguards, even if these increase the costs, should be taken so that the construction of roads is not environmentally damaging and will not lead to ecological disturbances, land degradation and soil erosion, disruption in drainage pattern, loss of forestry, vegetation and asthetic degradation. The Group recommends that the Central Road Research Institute of the Council of Scientific and Industrial Research (CSIR) must be consulted for the design and construction of roads under specialised conditions such as the Himalayan Region.

It is also necessary that the road network should be so planned that no attempt is made to reach each and every habitation. Alternative construction of bridle paths, trollies, and ropeways to move materials from hamlets and orchards to central collection points on the main roads, would need to be explored. All villages or groups of villages with a population of 500 or above should be connected with all-weather roads.

RECOMMENDATION - 20

Tourism

One of the major activities in the Himalayas is tourism both in the form of pilgrim tourism and for pleasure and adventure. While infrastructural facilities would need to be created to enable tourism to develop fully in the Himalayan region and become a major economic activity, it is necessary that the impact of the creation of luxury hotels and eating places at the cost of local ecology must be studied in depth.

Home/cottage tourism, especially for the pilgrim and middle class tourists, would need to be promoted actively. Liberal credit should be available to the local inhabitants to construct paying guest accommodation. This will provide both income and employment to the local population, while simultaneously creating infrastructure for the middle-class tourist coming from outside.

RECOMMENDATION - 21

Development of Tribal Population

Most of the tribal population lives in isolated rural areas. They are directly or indirectly dependent on agriculture and agro-realated activites. Food security is an important component not only for their survival but also for their well-being. Other element of their overall development is related to employment of their fight to work. The Group, therefore, feels that highest priority should also form components of developmental plan. Promotion of the role and status of women in the tribal society must receive major consideration to make human development holistic. The ultimate objective of our planning should be that all basic needs should become within the reach of the tribal population of the Himalayan region. The concerned state governments must develop action plans to bring in prosperity to the tribals.

RECOMMENDATION - 22

Institutional Arrangements in States

In the states, which fall entirely in the Himalayan region, one could expect that in every aspect of its administration, the special features of the Himalayan region, particularly the fragile ecological system, would be kept uppermost in mind. In Uttar Pradesh, a separate Hill Development Department has been created to address itself to the principal issues peculiar to the region. In the case of West Bengal, a separate Darjeeling Gorkha Hill Council has been established. The District Councils in the North-Eastern region play an extremely important role in guiding the affairs of the local areas. Nevertheless, the Group feels that in many ways the administrative pattern seems to be more or less parallel and on the model, carried out elsewhere. The Group cannot over-emphasise the fact that in every aspect of the administration of the affairs of the people living in the hills, special considerations which require to be bestowed on various aspects of socio-economic development must be integrally incorporated. Preservation of environment and maintenance of ecological balance must merit maximum attention.

RECOMMENDATION - 23

Involvement of NGOs, Voluntary Organisations etc.

In several regions of the Himalayan States, the local people have adopted technologies as have enabled them to meet their needs without serious adverse implications on environmental preservation and ensuring the local ecology does not get impaired. The Group suggests that in the process of generation of technologies for development, adequate attention needs to be paid for integrating indigenous technologies which have stood the test of time and this must be consciously looked at and promoted.

There is an increasing recognition that sound socio-economic development would only be possible through active people's involvement and participation in the formulation and implementation of plans, especially in terms of harmonising the environmental concerns and economic growth. The Group recommends a fuller understanding of the felt-needs of the local people, their wisdom can be expected to contribute towards this. Several NGOs have been actively involved in the upliftment of the local communities and have been able to articulate the perceptions of the local community. The developmental programmes must associate NGOs which could improve their efficacy. The Group also feels that the association of the International Centre for Integrated Development of Mountains (ICIMOD) would be extremely beneficial for further guidelines and advice in the removal of poverty.

RECOMMENDATION - 24

Source of Funding

Projects, schemes, new studies of investigations emerging from the recommendations noted above will require financial inputs. For this very reason the creation of National Himalayan Environmental and Development Fund (NHEDF) has been suggested. This fund, initially would not be large enough to cover all what might be needed, but depending upon the success in the implementation and the response that this report receives, the quantum of allocation could be enlarged suitably.

The Group has not suggested the establishment of any new institutions or research centres but has stressed upon the need for creating linkages and cooperation between the existing institutions, agencies, voluntary organisations and the States dealing with the Himalayan Region. It has identified one institute as a nodal point and has suggested the creation of a platform for holding annual meetings and the formation of an Association in which all the existing institutions and agencies would be clubbed to work together to bring in prosperity and sustainable development in the Himalayas. All legitimate expenditure in implementing such a programme should be met by the NHEDF.

APPENDIX-IX

PAST SCRIPT ON INAUGURATION OF UTTRANCHAL

ODE TO HIMALAYAS-2000

Dear Revreed Himalayas,
New Year and Beginning of Millenium Special
First New State of Uttranchal gets
inaugurated on November 1st 2000.
Four highlights from prospect of a small
NGO-Himcon-Himalaya
Consortium for Himalaya
Conservation and a
Humble devotee and
Supporter of Himalayan
Conservation and Rejuvenation Requesting

Uttranchal Proposed Priorities of Development
Peoples Movement Towards Sacred Uttaranchal
A plan for Greening Himalaya and Rejuvenation
NGO Forum for ISM and Medicinal Plants
Watershed Management through People Participation
Need to be implemented with
Small scale industries for Self Help Group and for all

The Principles of Rejuvenation are—

Consciousness
Concern
Commitment
Competence

Let us pray and work together with sustainable
effort on Himalayan Greening and Rejuvenation
to all present pledge on this Second Day of October
in your presence in heart of Himalayas at Ranichauri
at Himalaya Sanrakshan Ashram with FAO, Rotarians
and local residents and university and other Development
workers of Himalayas.

Thoughts and prayers of the
morning of the sacred Day, of October
Bowing to the peaks and all Himalyas
We are lucky that a benevolent and understanding
FAO Rep. is amongst us who believes in small projects
for the rural people and jointly with Rotary and
NGOs approve Telefood project of which he is keen and
determined to promote.

Nabard and its chief declares that it is ready to promote
Self Help Groups all over Tehri and Garhwal.
Rural leaders both Men and Women have pledged
to go forward in Himalayan
Communities for programs of watershed management
tree plantings, nut fruit revolution.

> The Hill Campus and its committed Dean and others
> believe in and implementing
> Action programmes born out of their research and experience.
> small NGOs like HIMCON and many others ready to and
> already spearheading worthwhile programmes
> An Action Plan for Ecological Security and greening of
> Himalayas
> through Aerial seeding and People cooperation is readied
> by a man of Immense experience, a stalwart amongst men.

Born are following spearhead programmes and priorities of
Development
Ganges/Tributaries/Yamuna Tributaries Full of Silt
And we must reduce such silt content? through
— Soil and Water Conservation
— Watershed Management
— Water Harvesting
— Tree Planting
— Fuel Fodder Fruit Planting
— Other Associated Projects

Uttranchal Residents should not nor need not migrate
To cities in the plains to a miserable polluted
Environment of Delhi/Mumbai/Lucknow etc. leaving the

Inspiring clean environment of Garhwal/Kumaon.
Enterpreunership promotion through small scale environment friendly
Resource management developmenmt and income generation
Training centre, List of industries starting with medicinal plants,
Sericulture, Apiculture, Horticulture, production preservation Nut Fruit
Revolution, Floriculture, Off season vegetables, special fruits,
Bamboo/Rengal industries, paper, briquetting from Biomass
Renewable Energy Industries

Tourism

Uttranchal has great potential for;
Eco-tourism, religious tourism with presence of
Yamnotri, Gangotri, Kedarnath, Badrinath, Hemkund sahib,
Also Haridwar / Rishikesh
— Sport Tourism, General Tourism - seasonal
looking at the expension of tourism in last 1-2 decades in
— Singapore, Bangkok, Jakarta, Bali

I can confidentally say that if properly organized, managed by trained people, the tourism can expand many times and bring in lots of income variety and talent to the region.
A word of caution about environmentaly unfriendly tourism.

Medicinal plants

The Himalayan region especially Garhwal and Kumaon has a large number of Medicinal Plants and herbs distributed over a large area of different habitats. However, their identification and subsequent collection on a massive scale has deprived the local people of the utilization of these plants for health care and supplementing their income. These local people, especially the women, who are the backbone of the hill economy, have remained poor due to unsustainable exploitation of local natural resources.

The demand for traditional medicinal or herbal plants is steadily Increasing, as the allopathic medicines become costlier and have negative side-effects. It is estimated that 50-70 per cent of the population of India still relies on traditional medicine rather than modern synthetic drugs.

With huge potenital and market for medicinal plants,
Uttranchal can earn much more income from medicinal
aromatic and herbal plants in addition
to take care of health needs of local communities

Horticulture :
Nut Fruit Revolution and production of
Temperatre fruits
Off seasons vegetable, flowers
All under Horticulture promotion can if
Systamatically organized and managed, preserved
Plus marketed can promote
Employment, income, nutrition and health of local people
More emphasis is needed by the Himalayan Communities.

Health Educaiton and family resource management
Emphaisis on these aspect will add to the
level and efficiency of local communities and hence
improvement in their quality of life.

Renewable energy
Mini/micro hydel, briquetting from biomass
solar technology specially photo voltaic, solar lanterns etc
have great potential for energy in Uttranchal
wind energy.
Interstate relations and centre-state relations and mutuality of inerest
Uttranchal and H.P.
Uttranchal and J & K
Uttranchal and UP
Uttranchal and other Himalayan States
Centre - Uttranchal relations
learning from one another
technical co-operation among development regions
nut fruits, marketing network for temperate fruits,
vegetables, their processing flower production and marketing
Himalayan States Co-operatives

On this Sacred Day, we gathered concerned
and planned following projects
Tele food project for aquaculture fisheries
in Henwal river by Rotary through Uttrakhand Jan Jagiriti Sansthan
A citrus revolution through well known local horticulturist
and spearhead also through tele food and other means.
Chals, more chals for traditional water harvesting by
Rotarians, Interactors also through NGO like one in Lamgaon
Walnuts as promoted in already approved Telefood
projects especially in coming planting winter season -
let us give a lead by planting some today.
A dynamic project through Dynamic women of Mahila Samakhya
through its leader a dynamic lady ready to promote
Rotary Motto Service Above Self.

A young enterpreuner leader new generation social worker
leader determined to promote Self Reliance like done
through Angora Rabbit program
Men and women boys and girls, Rotarians and Interactors
who are taking a pledge today and putting Service above Self.
model rotary village from present 6 to future 60 through
Rotary International 3H Program

Let us close this ODE, this Prayer through Forty Commitment under
Peoples Movement Towards Sacred Uttranchal
Our Sacred land to make it an ideal
Efficient peaceful state
Let us work hard, let us be honest efficient and kind
Let us not fight with one another, let us aim to equity
Let us not be polluted by money
Let us practice human values
Our land of milk and honey, let us work
For milk health cattle and good fodder land of trees fruits
Tourism - healthy - eco friendy religious

Local culture-use of our own resources local foods
Self pride - not self pity
We, the people must rejuvenate
Profile of Uttranchal must permeate the masses
Mini micro hydel, anti poverty, alternate education
Let balanced development predominate
Bhagirathi Development Authority
Be given priority master plan for watershed management
Work ethics must improve dignity of labour must be promoted
Stories of work ethics of Garhwal and Kumaon
Be propagated,
Gandhian education has to be promoted
Linkage between education, work ethics and dignity of labour
Computerization must develop and let us make it a
Modern computer and internat region and promote software technology

Interactors and Rotary system a movement for
Service Above Self start Swamiram Tirath Centre for Spiritual Values
Also develop and promote sound
Land use policy, Water Policy, Forest policy, Small scale industry policy
Watershed management policy collective responsibility and net-working
Forsoruum of NGO for Himalayan Conservation and Rejuvenation

Mini micro hydel and our power policy
Watershed development key to prosperity
Of Uttranchal, Dorabji Tata Trust
And other Trusts and Donors
Please help our People Movement of Healthy
Efficient Modern Sacred Uttranchal
Under a charter of policy framework,

We pledge present
Over 100 people of—three Generations
Ourselves with you Sacred Himalayas and
And on this *Bapu Birthday of New Millenium*
Work Towards an Efficient State of Uttranchal

Bibliography

Agarwal, A. & S. Narain (1997) *Dying Wisdom: Rise, Fall and Potential of India's Traditional Water Harvesting Systems*, Centre for Science and Environment, New Delhi.

Alford, D. (1985) Mountain hydrologic systems, *Mountain Research and Development*, 5, 349-363.

Alford, D. (1992) *Hydrological Aspects of the Himalayan Region*, ICIMOD Occasional Paper, 18, 68p.

APHA, (1989) Standard methods for the examination of water and waste water, 17th Edition, *American Public Health Association*, Washington DC.

Baker, F. (1944) Mountain climates of western United States, *Ecological Monographs*, 14, 223-254.

Bandhopadhyay, J. (1987) Political ecology of drought and water scarcity — Need for an ecological water resource policy, *Environmental Protection Works*, XXII (980), 2159-2169.

Banerjee, J.M. (1967) *History of Feroz Shah Tuglaq*, Delhi.

Barry, R. (1981) *Mountain Weather and Climate*, Methuen & Co. Ltd. London.

Bartarya, S.K. (1995) Hydrology and water resources of intermontane Doon valley, *Journal of Himalayan Geology*, 6, 1995, 17-28.

Bosch, J.M. & J.D. Hewlett (1982) A review of catchment experiments to determine the effect of vegetation changes on water yield and evaporation, *Journal of Hydrology*, 55, 3-23.

Bowonder, B. (1982) Deforestation in India, *International Journal of Environmental Studies*, 18, 223-236.

Central Water Commission (1991) *Water and Related Statistics*.

Chhabra, B. & Gai, G.S. (1981) Inscriptions of the early Gupta kings, In: *Corpus Inscriptionum Indicarum*, Archeological Survey of India, New Delhi, 3, 296-305.

Chilana, M.R. & M.L. Dewan (1998) *The Human Values : A Task For*

All, Concept Publishing Co.

Dewan, M.L. (1990) *People's Prticipation in Eco-system Development*, Concept Publishing Co., New Delhi, 274 p.

Dewan, M.L. (1986) *People's Participation in Himalayan Eco-system Development.*

Dewan, M.L. & Henryk Skolimowski (1997) *Himalayan Meditations and Hymns*, Tara Art Printers.

Dewan, M.L. (1995) *Towards a Sustainable Society, Perceptions*, Clarion Books.

Dewan, M.L. & B.D. Joshi (1993) *Vedic Philosophy for Himalayan Eco-System Development*, Concept Publishing Co.

Dewan, M.L., Harbans Singh & V.R. Suri (1997) *Horticulture Guide for Uttrakhand Trees For Life.*

Dewan, M.L., M.C. Nautiyal, V.K. Sah (1992) *Nut Fruits for the Himalayas*; Concept Publishing Co.

Dhyani, B.L., Ram Babu, Sewa Ram, V.S. Katiyar, Y.K. Arora, G.P. Juyal, & M.K. Vishwanatham, (1993) Economic analysis of watershed management programme in Outer Himalayas — A case study of ORP Fakot, *Indian Journal of Agriculture and Economy*, 48, 237-245.

Dowson. J., (1953) *Tarikh-e-Feroz Shah of Shams-i-Siraj Afif, The History of India told by its own Historians*, Calcutta.

Drever, J.I. (1982) *The Geochemistry of Natural Waters*, Prentice Hall Inc, London.

Dunne, T. & L. Leopold, (1978) *Water in Environmental Planning*, W.H. Freeman & Co., New York.

Flohn, H. (1974) Contributions to the comparative meteorology of mountain areas, In: *Arctic and Alpine Environments*, J. Ives & R. Barry (eds.), Methuen, London.

Geiger, R. (1966) *The Climate Near the Ground*, Harvard University Press, Massachusetts Cambridge.

Gilmour, D.A. (1977) Effect of logging and clearing on water quality in a high rainfall zone of northeast Queensland, In: *Hydrology of Australia*, Institution of Engineers, Australia, National Conference Publication, 77.

Goel, P.K. (1980) Impacts of sewage, *International Journal of Economics and Environmental Sciences*, 6, 86-96.

Goel, S.L. & R.K. Jain, (1987) Administration of environmental health, In: *Environmental Pollution and Health Hazards in India*, Kumar, R. (ed.), Ashish Publishing House, New Delhi, 29-52.

Gupta, R.K. & V.S. Katiyar, (1982) Rain water cistern systems for the Himalayan region, Proceedings International Conference on Rainwater Cistern Systems, Honolulu, Hawaii, USA.

Habib, I. (1969) Potentialities of capitalistic development in the economy of Mughal India, *The Journal of Economic History*, 29.

Hagen, T. (1980) *Nepal*, Oxford and IBH Publishing Co. New Delhi.

Haigh, M. (1989) Deforestation and disaster in northern India, In: *Studies in Himalayan Ecology*, T.V. Singh & J. Kaur (eds.), Himalayan Books, New Delhi, 67-80.

Hamilton, L.S., (1983) *Forest and Watershed Development and Conservation in Asia and the Pacific*, Westview Press, Boulder Colorado.

Hamilton, L.S. (1987) What are the impacts of Himalayan deforestation on the Ganga - Brahmaputra lowlands and the delta? Assumptions and facts, *Mountain Research and Development*, 7, 256-263.

Hengeveld, H. & C. De Vocht (1982) *Role of Water in Urban Ecology*, Elsevier Scientific Publishing Company, Amsterdam.

Hussenappa, V., G. Sastry, & A.K. Khullar, (1980) Rainfall analysis for water harvesting in Doon valley, National Symposium on Soil Conservation and Watershed Management, CSWCRTI Dehradun.

ISI, (1993) Indian standard specification for drinking water, IS: 10500-1993, Indian Standards Institute, New Delhi, 6-11.

Ives, J.D. & B. Meserli (1989) *The Himalayan Dilemma*, Routledge London & New York, 295p.

Jana, B.B., (1973) Seasonal periodicity of plankton in fresh water pond in West Bengal, *Indian Inst. Rev. Ges. Hydrobiol.*, 58, 127-143.

Jha, Pt. A., (1988) *Varhat Samhita (550 AD) by Varahamihira*, Chow Khamba Vidyabhawan, Varanasi.

Juyal, G.P. & Gupta, R.K. (1985) Construction of LDPE lined tanks in hills — A case study, *Indian Journal of Soil Conservation*, 13, 10-13.

Juyal, G.P. & V.S. Katiyar (1991) Water resource development and management in small hilly watersheds, *Journal Indian Water Resources Society*, 11, 14-17.

Kangle, R.P. (1963) *The Kautilya Arthasastra*, University of Mumbai, Part I & II.

Krishnamurthi, B.V. & U.R.S. Schoettli, (19) Environment in India's religious and cultural heritage, In: *India's Environment: Crisis and Responses*, Bandhopadhyay, J., Jayal, N.D.; Schoettli, U & Singh C., (eds.), Natraj Publishers Dehradun, 159-171.

Kumar, K. & D.S. Rawat (1996) *Water Management in Himalayan Ecosystem: A Study of Natural Springs of Almora*, Indus Publishing Company, New Delhi.

Kumarappa, J.C. (1930) *Public Finance and Our Poverty*, Navajivan Publishing House, Ahmedabad.

Lambert, L. & B. Chitrakar, (1987) Variation of potential evapotranspiration with elevation in Nepal, *Mountain Research and Development*, 9, 145-152.

Leopold, L., M. Holman & J. Miller (1964) *Fluvial Processes in Geomorphology*, W.H. Freeman, San Francisco.

Metcalf & Eddy, (1979) *Wastewater Engineering; Treatment, Disposal, Reuse*, Tata McGraw Hill, New Delhi.

Myers, N., (1983) Tropical moist forests: over exploited and under utilised? *Forest Ecology and Management*, 6, 59-79.

Naudou, J., (1971) An example of engineering in Medieval India, In: *Prof. K.. Nilakanta Sastri Felicitation Volume*, Madras, 224-230.

Nehru, J.L., (1946) *Discovery of India*, Reprint 1989, Oxford University Press, New Delhi.

Pande, R.K.; Y.C. Pande & G. Gangola, (1992) Quality of urban water supply in Central Himalaya, *Conserving Wildlife in India*, 89-101.

Pant, N., (1989) Farmer managed irrigation systems in India, FMIS Network, *International Workshop on Design Issues in Farmer Managed Irrigation Systems*, Chiang Mai, Thailand.

Pant, P.C. (1995) *Parvatiya Jal Strot* (in Hindi), Shree Almora Book Depot, Almora,

Petts, G. & I. Foster, (1985) *Rivers and Landscape*, Edward Arnold Publishers Ltd., London.

Possehl, G.L., & M.H. Raval, (1989) *Harappan Civilization and Rejdi*, Oxford IBH, New Delhi.

Rao, E.G.K. & P.O. Kotekar, (1971) Exploration of underground water springs according to the ancient Hindus, *Indian Journal of History of Science*, 6, 139-146.

Rawat Rukoa (1997) *Return Migration and Rural Development*, R.S. Prints, Sidhi Publishers & Distributors, Tehri Garhwal.

Ratnagar, S. (1986) An aspect of Harappan agricultural production, *Studies in History*, 2, 137-153.

Rautela, Meeta, (1996) Ecobiology of a snow trout *Oreinus richardsonii* (Gray) from Sarju river, Kumaun Himalaya, Unpublished Ph.D. thesis, Kumaun University, Nainital.

Roy, A.K. (1995) Water resources in Doon valley: Development and constraints related to hydrological environment, *Journal of Himalayan Geology*, 6, 123-125.

Sawyer, C.N. (1960) *Chemistry for Sanitary Engineers*, McGraw Hill, New York.

Sharma, J.S., V.N. Sharda & A.K. Sikka (1996) *Water Harvesting and Recycling: Indian Experiences*, Central Soil & Water Conservation Research & Training Institute, Dehradun, 248p.

Sharma, Y.D. (1974) *Delhi and its Neighbourhood*, New Delhi.

Shiva, V., H.C. Sharatchandra & J. Bandyopadhyay (1981) Social, economic and ecological impact of social forestry in Kolar, Indian Institute of Management, Bangalore, India (mimeo).

Singh, R.B.P. & S.K. Choudhary (1996) Trace metal in surface and ground water in Simlong coal mining area, Rajmahal, Bihar, *Proc. Nat. Sym. on Plant Diversification and Human Welfare*, 5 & 6 April 1995, Bhagalpur University.

Singh, R.B.P. (1997) Impact of coal mining on water, soil and vegetation of Simlong area, Unpubl. Ph.D. thesis, Bhagalpur University.

Spears, J. (1982) Rehabilitating watersheds, *Finance & Development*, 19, 30-33.

Srinivasan, T.M. (1970) A brief account of the ancient irrigation engineering systems prevalent in South India, *Indian Journal of History of Science*, 5, 314-325.

Thandhani, P.K. *Chronicles of the Doon Valley: An Environmental Expose*, Indus Publishing Company, New Delhi.

Thomas, C.P. & S. Backford (1982) Tracing well water pollution in a limestone aquifer, *Journal of American Water Works Association*, 74, 182-187.

Thornthwaite, C.W., (1953) Topoclimatology, Symposium on Microclimatology & Micrometeorology, Toronto Meteorological Conference, Toronto, Canada.

Tiwari, R.S. & P.K. Garg (1995) Landform and landuse of Doon valley and their role in resource development, *Journal of Himalayan Geology*, 6, 9-15.

Welch, P.S. (1948). *Limonological Methods*, McGraw Hill, New York.

WHO, (1985). Guidelines for drinking water quality, *Recommendations, WHO,* Geneva.

World Resources Institute (1985). *Tropical Forests: A Call for Action*, WRI, Washington D.C.

Index